Praise for Along the Amber Route

*Shortlisted for the Stanford Dolman
Travel Book of the Year 2021*

Longlisted for the 2021 Wingate Prize

*Shortlisted for the Bookmark Book Festival's
Book of the Year Award 2020*

'Full of incident and anecdote and the oddest facts imaginable. Pure pleasure.'

IAN THOMSON

'Artfully woven into this poetic memoir ... are beautifully painted portraits of the people and places he visits, some of which prove to have strong personal resonances.'

RACHEL LICHTENSTEIN

'Deserves to join the great literature of Mitteleuropa.'
Irish Examiner

'An excellent book, and perfect holiday reading. Deeply moving.'

EDWARD BIDDULPH, Oxford Archaeology

C.J. Schüler is the author of three illustrated histories of cartography: *Mapping the World, Mapping the City* and *Mapping the Sea and Stars* (Éditions Place des Victoires/ Frechmann), and *Writers, Lovers, Soldiers, Spies*, a history of the Authors' Club of London, of which he was chairman from 2008 to 2015.

He has written on literature, travel and the arts for *The Independent*, the *Independent on Sunday*, *The Tablet* and the *Financial Times*. A former staff member with *The Independent* and the Rough Guides, he was elected a Fellow of the Royal Geographical Society in 2011.

www.cjschuler.com

BY THE SAME AUTHOR

Mapping the World

Mapping the City

Mapping the Sea and Stars

Writers, Lovers, Soldiers, Spies: A History of the Authors' Club of London, 1891–2016

The Wood that Built London: A human history of the Great North Wood

ALONG THE AMBER ROUTE

St PETERSBURG to VENICE

C. J. SCHÜLER

SANDSTONE PRESS

First published in Great Britain in 2020 by
Sandstone Press Ltd
PO Box 41
Muir of Ord
IV6 7YX
Scotland

www.sandstonepress.com

This edition 2022

Copyright © C. J. Schüler
Editor: Robert Davidson

ISBN: 978-1-913207-99-1
ISBNe: 978-1-912240-92-0

Sandstone Press is committed to a sustainable future.
This book is made from Forest Stewardship Council ® certified paper.

MIX
Paper from
responsible sources
FSC® C022174

Jacket Design by kid-ethic
Typography by Iolaire, Newtonmore
Printed and bound by Severn, Gloucester

In memory of John Schuler

(Johannes David Schüler, Breslau, 1919 – Banbury, 1997)

CONTENTS

INTRODUCTION

FLIES IN AMBER

Pretty in Amber to observe the forms
Of hairs and straw and dirt and grubs and worms.
The things, we know, are neither rich nor rare,
But wonder how the devil they got there!

Alexander Pope, 'Epistle to Dr Arbuthnot'

I am standing in the Ashmolean Museum in Oxford. In a glass case in front of me are some small, irregular beads of dark, honey-coloured amber. Discovered in a Mycenaean tomb in Crete by Sir Arthur Evans, they date from between 1700 and 1300 BC, the dawn of classical civilisation. At around the same time, in north Wales, hundreds of amber beads were placed in a stone-lined tomb along with a body wrapped in the spectacular gold shoulder ornament known as the Mold Cape, now in the British Museum. Amber has been found in the tomb of Tutankhamun and in the ruins of Troy. The Etruscans imported large amounts of it, which they used to adorn jewellery, as did the Romans after them.

My fascination with the substance began as a child. My father had a small piece of opaque, tawny amber, about an inch long, crescent-shaped and holed in the middle like a bead. I have it on the desk in front of me as I write. It was a relic of his days as an apprentice telephone engineer in pre-war Germany, and he would use it to demonstrate its electrostatic properties. After suspending the amber from a length of thread, he would rub it on his sleeve and hold it over an ashtray, so that flakes of ash would fly up and adhere to the resin, like iron filings to a magnet. It was the Greek philosopher Thales of Miletus, around 600 BC, who first discovered amber's ability to attract seeds, dust and fibres after being rubbed on wool. The ancient Greek name for amber, *elektron*, is the root of the word electricity.

The amber came from the southern and eastern shores of the Baltic, where it was washed up by storms and gathered by local people. It began its existence as resin oozing from the trunks of conifers in the prehistoric forests of northern Scandinavia between 40 and 50 million years ago. Carried downstream by rivers, the resin settled in a layer under what later became the southern Baltic some 10,000 years ago as the glaciers of the last Ice Age receded. In the course of time, it was transformed into amber by the processes of polymerisation and oxidation. Some even made its way into the North Sea to wash up on the shore of Suffolk. Amber is also found in Siberia, the Far East, Mexico and the Dominican Republic. It was Dominican amber that inspired Michael Crichton's 1990 novel *Jurassic Park*, and the Steven Spielberg film that followed. The premise, that a mosquito trapped in amber could contain a sample of dinosaur DNA, appeared far-fetched at the time, but since the discovery in 2015 of the feathered tail of a small dinosaur in a piece of Burmese amber, it seems slightly less improbable.

It is the Baltic deposits, however, that are the most plentiful, producing around 90 per cent of all the world's supply, their chemical composition making them easily distinguishable from amber originating elsewhere. For the ancient Greeks and Romans, these golden nuggets had mysterious properties: cool in summer, warm in winter, they often contained glimmering fragments of plants, insects and even small vertebrates, frozen in the moment they were caught in the trickling honeytrap.

Amber was attributed with healing powers, and gave rise to myth and legend. In his *Historia naturalis*, the Roman writer Pliny the Elder dismissed the old tales in favour of a brisk scientific explanation: 'Amber is formed by the pith which flows from trees of the pine species, as a gum flows from cherry trees and resin from pines.' A remarkable understanding that was to be lost for more than 1,500 years.

But how did amber find its way from the Baltic to the shores of the Mediterranean, a thousand kilometres to the south? Pliny stated that the substance came from 'the islands of the north of the Northern Ocean'. So highly was it prized that the manager of Nero's games sent an emissary to the far north to collect it. Pliny gave an account of the expedition:

> There still lives the Roman knight who was sent to procure amber by Julianus, superintendent of the gladiatorial games given by Emperor Nero. This knight travelled over the markets and shores of the country and brought back such an immense quantity of amber that the nets intended to protect the podium from the wild beasts were studded with buttons of amber. Adorned likewise with amber were the arms, the biers, and the whole apparatus for one day.

In his *Germania*, written around AD 98, the historian Tacitus mentions a tribe called the Aesti who lived 'on the coast to the right of the Suevian Ocean' and collected 'that curious substance' from the shallows. He noted that the Aesti could not see any use for amber and were pleasantly surprised to be paid for the pieces they gathered. For the poet Juvenal, writing in the early 2nd century AD, the popularity of this luxury item was a sign of Rome's decadence: in his Ninth Satire, he associates the fashion for holding balls of amber to cool the hands in summer with effeminacy. The trade was still going in AD 301, when amber was one of the goods specified in the Emperor Diocletian's edict regulating prices.

Many people view globalisation as a recent phenomenon and fear it as a threat to national identity. Yet the world has been criss-crossed by trade routes since the Neolithic. Phoenician seafarers traded tin from Cornwall; Roman coins are found throughout India; Arab silver dirhems in Anglo-Saxon burials in England. Amber is an ideal commodity for long-distance trade – like silk and spices, it is light, portable, and of high value. But is the written evidence of Pliny and others supported by any physical trace of the route it took?

On a wet and blowy Monday night in February 1925, geographers, explorers, historians and archaeologists gathered at Lowther Hall, the headquarters of the Royal Geographical Society on Kensington Gore in London. The distinguished audience listened transfixed as a young scholar, soldier, archaeologist and poet, J. M. de Navarro, tracked the course of an ancient trade route comparable to the Silk Road from China to the Mediterranean. The sheer length of the route, and its duration, from the Neolithic to the fall of the Roman Empire and beyond, were as thrilling as De Navarro's methodical and detailed presentation was convincing.

José Maria de Navarro was born in 1893 into a comfortable, cultured and cosmopolitan milieu. His father Antonio, a New York barrister of Basque descent, had married the American actress Mary Anderson and moved to England, settling in an old house at Broadway in Gloucestershire. 'You, if I may say so, have made yourselves martyrs to the antique, the picturesque,' commented their friend Henry James. 'You will freeze, you will suffer from damp. I pity you, my poor dears.' De Navarro grew up amid his mother's theatrical and literary friends, who included Oscar Wilde, J. M. Barrie and George Bernard Shaw. On the outbreak of the First World War, he interrupted his studies at Trinity College, Cambridge to enlist with the United Arts Rifles, completing his degree after the Armistice.

Elected a fellow of his college, De Navarro embarked on his groundbreaking study of the Amber Route, travelling through Germany, Czechoslovakia, Austria and Hungary. Significant work had already been done by European scholars such as the Swedish archaeologist Oscar Montelius and the German Karl Schumacher, but De Navarro was the first – literally – to put the Amber Route on the map. The glass lantern slides he showed to the RGS plotted a trail of evidence – worked and unworked pieces of amber, and the Roman coins and jewellery for which they were exchanged – from the shores of the Baltic through the Alps and down into Italy.

Like most ancient lines of trade, the Amber Route did not consist of one well-trodden path but several, which were used at different periods or times of year according to the prevailing conditions. It is unlikely that many people ever travelled the entire route, like Nero's emissary; rather they would take a consignment of amber as far as the next trading post, where they would sell it on to another merchant who would carry it on the next stage of its journey.

The main route followed the River Vistula inland from the Baltic. From there it headed south to cross the River Odra at Wrocław, once the eastern German city of Breslau, before continuing into what is now the Czech Republic, and down the River Morava to join the Danube at the border of Austria and Slovakia. Near the confluence of these two great rivers stand the ruins of Carnuntum, the Roman frontier town where Marcus Aurelius composed part of his *Meditations*. From here, a Roman road, the Via Gemina, ran south through the Hungarian plain before descending the Julian Alps to the Roman city of Aquileia at the head of the Adriatic, where the raw material was crafted into jewellery.

As I unfolded a large Freytag & Berndt map of Europe to

trace the route, the places it passed through sparked another connection. Not only was Breslau, the city where my father was born in 1919, one of the most important staging posts on the Amber Route; the central section, from Gdańsk to Vienna, ran like a string of beads through a number of smaller Polish towns where my ancestors lived and worked, studied and worshipped. For many years, I knew little of this. My grandfather left Germany in 1936 to escape the Nazis, and obtained a job in Genoa, where he lived with my grandmother and their younger son. Against all advice, my father stayed in Dresden to finish his apprenticeship. In 1937, while he was visiting his parents in Italy, a friend's mother wrote to warn him that it was unsafe to return to Germany. After a series of adventures that took them to Yugoslavia, my father and his brother eventually arrived in London.

With the family scattered by Nazism and divided by the Cold War, I grew up in a Britain in which it was odd to know that your ancestral home was a city that could not be found on any modern map, and of which few people had even heard. The imperative was to fit in, to be as English as possible, yet I was obscurely aware of a connection to something else. Only with the fall of the Iron Curtain in 1989 was I able to meet my relatives in East Germany and begin to explore Central Europe. Then a stout parcel arrived in the post – a family history compiled by my cousin Irene Newhouse in the United States – and I began to have some idea of the social and historical background that made me.

As I studied the map, an idea took shape, and a sense of adventure began to stir. An epic journey beckoned: I would follow the Amber Route by whatever means were available, by bus, train or boat, along river valleys, though forest paths and along Roman roads. Winding its 2,500-kilometre course through 12 countries and three millennia, the route traces some of the deepest fault-lines in European history: between

Romans and Vandals, Teutons and Slavs, the Habsburg and Ottoman empires, and the former Iron Curtain. This is no coincidence. The very topography that made it a viable trade route – navigable rivers, fordable crossings, passes through the mountains – also afforded passage to invaders, from Attila the Hun to the mechanised legions of Hitler and Stalin.

One country looms large in this story, though the route does not cross one square metre of its present territory: Germany. Though the main deposits now lie beyond its borders, amber still washes up on its shores, on the sandy beaches from Rügen to Usedom where my family used to take holidays between the wars. (Old photo albums show them relaxing in *Strandkörbe*, those hooded basketwork chairs still used by German holiday-makers to shield themselves from the Baltic wind.) Moreover, much of the route passes through a phantom Germany, those regions lost after two world wars that now form parts of Russia, Lithuania and Poland.

It was the political situation in Europe that prevented De Navarro from following up his researches: 'The Iron Curtain and the Iron Age proved incompatible bedfellows,' he observed ruefully. Travelling through the Russian Federation and the new EU member states almost three decades after the fall of the Berlin Wall, I found them still scarred by the detritus – physical and moral – of the Soviet Union, and struggling to come to terms with the legacy of the past. At times, especially in Russia, I felt it wise to alter people's names and other details that might identify them; in some cases I was asked to do so. Readers may draw their own conclusions from this.

In recent years, however, the Amber Route has become a symbol of hope and renewal, passing as it does through many of the newest EU member states. Wherever you go in Central and Eastern Europe, you will find amber: *Yantar* in Russian, *Meripihka* in Finnish, *Merevaik* in Estonian, *Dzintars* in Latvian, *Gintaras* in Lithuanian, *Bursztyn* in Polish, *Bernstein* in German, *Borosty'n* in Hungarian and, in Italian, *Ambra*. In Lithuania, amber is the raw material for a tradition of craft jewellery rooted in the country's landscape. In Poland, it became identified with the Solidarity movement, and a symbol of national liberation.

In 2007, the Council of Europe designated the Amber Road as a Cultural Route, one of a series of transnational itineraries such as the pilgrim road to Santiago de Compostela that are 'illustrative of European memory, history and heritage and contribute to an interpretation of the diversity of present-day Europe'. It would run from St Petersburg to Venice, and gave rise to conferences, cross-border projects between museums, and even a long-distance cycle route from Gdańsk to Croatia. At a conference in Vilnius in 2012, the project's director, Dr Eleonora Berti, spoke of the need to promote 'artistic, cultural, commercial and political links' in order to 'transcend the cultural and political barriers which marked Europe during and after the great conflicts of the twentieth century'.

Little did I know, as I set out on my journey, how soon and how severely those brave ideals would be challenged, or how sharply the region's historic fault-lines would reopen.

PART I

THE AMBER COAST

ST PETERSBURG TO KALININGRAD

The English are not like the Russians – not any more. They were like the Russians at the time of their Queen Elizabeth I, when they produced their Shakespeare. But not now.

Anthony Burgess, *Honey for the Bears*

CHAPTER 1

THE MYSTERY OF THE AMBER ROOM

The night was cold, the lane a dark crevasse between stone tenements. A light drizzle slicked the pavement. Though it was not yet 11pm, there were few cars about, and fewer pedestrians. The only signs of life came from a couple of dimly lit basement bars. Crossing an old bridge over the Griboyedov Canal, I inhaled a miasma of damp plaster, methane and the throat-catching rasp of brown coal. Along an embankment lined with spindly, blackened lime trees, bright interiors could be glimpsed through windows, their golden light reflected on the water. To my right, a red neon sign reading SEX SHOP in English was mirrored in the wet asphalt.

No sign advertised the guesthouse, so I scanned the dimly illuminated numbers over the dark archways. Each number referred to a tenement or *dom*, comprising not just the five or six floors of apartments fronting the street, but the warren of houses in the courtyards beyond. Eventually I located an inconspicuous grey building, its steel door scarred, rusting and graffiti-etched. An entryphone admitted me to a dilapidated stairwell, with a once-elegant wrought-iron banister and worn mahogany rail; the landings were littered with beer cans, vodka bottles and cigarette ends. A small lift occupied one corner, but a torn scrap of paper taped to the door read *Nye rabotayet* – not working. On the fourth floor, another steel door opened to admit me. Zina, the old lady delegated to let me in, brusquely informed me that the manageress would be around in the morning to register my visa with the police.

The journey had taken me through three time zones. After an hour in transit at Riga, I climbed aboard an alarmingly small, propellor-driven Fokker 500 for the final leg to St Petersburg. The ever-more tedious security checks and immigration controls are all too familiar to any traveller; in addition, because I was self-employed, the Russian consulate in London had demanded three months' bank statements. I thought of Stefan Zweig's evocation of the vanished era before the First World War. 'There were no passports, no visas,' he recalled, 'and it always gives me pleasure to astonish the young by telling them that before 1914 I travelled from Europe to India and America without a passport and without having seen one.' After that cataclysm, he added, humiliations once devised 'with criminals alone in mind' were imposed on every traveller.

Zweig, as he himself acknowledged, grew to adulthood in a rare interval of peace and security in Europe. For Elizabeth Rigby, a Victorian traveller arriving in St Petersburg in the 1840s, the experience was less civil:

> A rush of fresh uniforms boarded us from another vessel, who proceeded to turn out the gentlemen's pockets and the ladies' reticules, and seemed themselves in most admirable training for pickpockets ...

From the airport at Pulkovo, I took a battered 113 bus to Moskovsky. Passengers threw the 26-ruble fare on to a greasy rug on the transmission box, which groaned and juddered every time the driver changed gear. We passed under a labyrinthine interchange, along wide streets of Soviet buildings overlaid with the illuminated signs of the new consumerism. As we drew up at a set of traffic lights, I looked into a neighbouring bus and caught sight of a woman in late middle age, clasping a shopping bag, her drawn, anxious face framed by relaxed young people in baggy jeans, cocooned in another world by the white leads trailing from their ears.

When the bus pulled up opposite an enormous, floodlit granite obelisk, I realised with a start that I had been here before – decades before, when the city was known by another name. This was the Monument to the Heroic Defenders of Leningrad. In September 1941, the German high command issued a chilling directive: 'The Führer has decided to have Leningrad wiped from the face of the earth. The further existence of this large town is of no interest once Soviet Russia is overthrown.' It was the beginning of a gruelling siege that lasted almost 900 days. Despite supplies brought across the 'Road of Life' – the frozen waters of Lake Ladoga – up to 1.5 million soldiers and civilians died of hunger.

Walking away from the monument, I passed through a shopping arcade to the metro, bought a jeton from a woman behind the counter, and let it fall with a clunk into the turnstile. The escalator – a grandiose example of Stalinist classical moderne – was the longest and steepest I'd seen, its bronze neo-Roman torchères on fluted columns casting their beams to the vaulted ceiling. No one bothered to walk up, and few to walk down. The St Petersburg metro is the deepest in the world, on account of the marshy ground – and the expendability of labour in Stalin's Russia.

I emerged into Sennaya (Haymarket) Square, a large oblong flanked by 19th-century buildings and packed with market arcades occupied by late-night cafés, liquor shops, convenience stores, and stalls selling pirate DVDs. Dostoyevsky's *Crime and Punishment* was set here, and the area still had an edgy feel, as hipsters drank in fashionable bars while disabled veterans of Russia's wars in Afghanistan and Chechnya begged on the streets outside. The Soviets cleaned up the neighbourhood, renaming it Ploshchad Mira (Peace Square) and sweeping away the market, though the old police station, where Dostoyevsky's guilt-stricken protagonist Raskolnikov surrendered to the authorities, still stood at an angle across one corner. Now the market was back, along with the old name.

Once Zina had scuttled off, I found myself alone in the guesthouse. My room was basic but clean, and looked on to a bleak lightwell with tiled walls. I unpacked, and set out my maps, guidebooks and notes on the table. The location, in the dark heart of St Petersburg, seemed an appropriate base from which to explore the city.

St Petersburg did not exist in the heyday of the Amber Route, yet it is inextricably associated with it on account of the presence – or rather the absence – of the Amber Room in the Catherine Palace at Tsarskoye Selo. Looted by the Nazis in 1941, it disappeared at the end of the Second World War, and had now been painstakingly recreated – though there are those, both in Russia and abroad, who have never given up the search for the original.

I had last set foot here in February 1983. We arrived on the overnight train from Moscow, after a long journey through seemingly endless, snow-covered pine forest. A samovar of tea bubbled at each end of the carriage. Leonid Brezhnev, the granite-faced General Secretary who presided over two decades of stagnation, had recently expired. His successor, Yuri Andropov, was a former head of the KGB who, despite his role in crushing the 1956 Hungarian uprising, was hailed as a reformer. When he died suddenly 15 months later, power reverted to the old guard in the shape of the moribund Konstantin Chernyenko.

In those days, it was only possible to visit the USSR under the guidance of Intourist, the state tourism agency. Now privatised, it was then in effect an organ of the KGB, and visitors were closely supervised. The tour had to be booked months in advance; I had planned it with my then girlfriend, but by the time our visas came through, the relationship had chilled to the temperature of the Russian winter. Our fellow travellers were the usual suspects: left-leaning journalists, writers, trade unionists and a moderately well known actress. None would have called themselves an apologist for the Soviet system, but I think it fair to say that they all had some lingering sympathy for its original ideals, however much these had atrophied.

I had a personal motive for visiting, having grown up with half my relatives on the other side of the Iron Curtain. My great-uncle Georg Honigmann, a journalist and pre-war member of the German Communist Party, had married Litzi Kohlmann, a glamorous Hungarian-Jewish revolutionary from Vienna. The only keepsakes Litzi possessed were a few photographs of her parents and 'an English student with a pipe in his mouth, very good looking...' The enigmatic Englishman was Kim Philby, to whom she had been married for 12 years. Honigmann and Litzi's daughter Barbara later rediscovered her Jewish faith and emigrated to the West, where she is now an acclaimed novelist. In her memoir *Ein Kapitel aus meinem Leben*, she recalls how she had no idea of her mother's past until their Berlin home was besieged by British journalists after her ex-husband defected to the Soviet Union.

I spent the next day getting my bearings. Peter the Great's 'window on the West' was founded on 16th May 1703, on land conquered from Sweden, to give Russia the port it needed to become a European power. Between 10,000 and 20,000 serfs and prisoners of war were forced to work in the mosquito-ridden marshes, while the aristocracy were ordered to transport stone – in short supply in a sandy river-mouth – to the site to build palaces. Situated in the Neva delta on 40 islands linked by 400 bridges, St Petersburg was dubbed 'the Venice of the North' by Alexander Menshikov, Peter's sidekick and the city's first governor, sealing its reputation as an alien transplant. Largely

designed by foreign architects, what eventually rose from the mud
was a cityscape of soaring spires and elegant colonnades, long
vistas and grand public spaces, in sharp contrast to Moscow's
huddle of brick battlements and onion-domed churches.

St Petersburg radiates from the point where the River Neva
divides around the Strelka, the pointed tip of Vasilyevsky Island.
In that bleak Cold War February, we found the Neva frozen so
solid you could drive a tank across it, yet leaning against the
stone revetments, a woman was sunbathing in a bikini, her fur
coat held open like a flasher's mac to shield her from the Arctic
wind. Across the ice, the slender golden spire of the Peter
and Paul Fortress glimmered in the wintry sunlight. There
were few cars except for the heavy black Zil limousines of the
party apparatchiks. For most of the time we were shepherded
through a numbing succession of propagandist museums: the
Museum of Communications, the Exhibition of Economic
Achievement, the First Five-Year Plan Palace of Culture . . .

We were not encouraged to roam the city, but with a little
ingenuity – and a few backhanders – it was possible to slip the
leash, to mix fleetingly with young people desperate for jeans
and Western pop music, see the long queues for tired vegetables
on the half-empty shelves of drab shops, and catch a glimpse
though an archway into filthy courtyards where men washed
themselves at standpipes like a scene from Depression-era
Britain. This dour, sclerotic gerontocracy was the socialist
utopia in which so many had believed so fervently and for so
long.

My uncle, who with Honigmann's assistance had crossed
from the British to the Russian sector of Berlin, hoping to
build a better society on the ruins of Hitler's Reich, used to tell
an old Soviet joke: Lenin, Stalin and Brezhnev are travelling
together on a train when it stops, inexplicably, in the middle
of nowhere. 'The only thing that will get us moving again,'
declares Lenin, 'is a new economic plan.' A new economic

plan is devised, but the train remains stationary. 'Bah!' declares Stalin. 'You can't make an omelette without breaking eggs.' He steps out of the carriage, and shortly afterwards a shot is heard from the driver's cab. Still the train refuses to budge. 'I have an idea,' says Brezhnev, and pulls down the blinds. 'Look,' he says. 'We are moving again!'

Now, more than two decades after the dissolution of the Soviet Union, there was nothing to prevent me wandering as I pleased. Superficially, Nevsky Prospekt remained as it was when I had last seen it, an imposing boulevard flanked by a mixture of 19th-century neoclassicism and early 20th century Art Nouveau. But the streets were now crowded with mobile phone shops and sushi bars, the skyline bristling with satellite dishes and Pepsi adverts. By far the most noticeable contrast was the traffic. Rust-bucket Ladas spluttered and bellowed like beasts of burden as drivers punished their engines in an attempt to outpace the sleek BMWs and chunky 4x4s on either side. If the silent grandeur of Leningrad appeared to preserve, in the amber of a command economy, the historic aspect of St Petersburg, this was an illusion. In the years before the Russian Revolution, the city was industrialising fast, and the brash commercial metropolis described in Andrei Bely's 1905 novel *Petersburg* bears an uncanny resemblance to its post-communist incarnation:

> The motorcars' roulades in the distance, the rumble of the red and yellow trams ... In the evening the Nevsky is flooded by a pall of fire. And the walls of many buildings burn with gemstone light: words composed of diamonds sparkle brilliantly: *'Coffee House', 'Farce', 'Tate Diamonds', 'Omega Watches'.*

Beyond the Nevsky, in striking contrast to the neoclassical Kazan Cathedral, the brightly painted, turbanned domes of the Church of the Saviour on Spilled Blood brooded beneath a leaden sky. The embankment narrows where the apse juts into the canal, allowing the altar to rest on the exact spot where Tsar Alexander II was fatally injured by a bomb thrown by the anarchist group *Narodnaya Volya* (People's Will) in March 1881. His assailant, Ignacy Hryniewiecki, also died of wounds sustained in the explosion, making him one of the first recorded suicide bombers. Around the exterior, plaques listed the murdered tsar's achievements, a combination of relentless territorial expansion – the conquests of the Amur, the Caucasus and Central Asia – and liberal reform: the abolition of serfdom in 1861, relaxation of press censorship, greater autonomy for Finland and the establishment of schools throughout the empire.

Alexander was killed not in spite of his reforms, but because of them. Liberalisation might have prevented, or at least delayed, the revolution; a reactionary backlash, on the contrary, would hasten it. If the intention was to provoke one, it succeeded. With its dumpy columns, ogee windows and asymmetrical domes, the church embodies a 19th-century revivalist vision of medieval Muscovite architecture, as if trying to stamp an 'authentic' Russian identity on this polymorphous city conjured out of the marshes by a tsar hell-bent on Westernisation. Its construction presaged a wave of Russification that would outrage nationalist sentiment in Finland and the Baltics, creating a cauldron of resentment that erupted in the uprisings of 1905. Pogroms were launched against the Jews, so that between 1881 and 1914, an estimated three million fled Russia, mainly to the Unites States and the East End of London.

The Catherine Palace, home to the legendary Amber Room, is located some 25 kilometres south of the city centre. The minibus was scheduled to depart from Gostiny Dvor, an elegant yellow and white shopping arcade on Nevsky Prospekt.

There has been a market here since the 18th century. Once these covered passages were thronged with bearded peasants and kaftaned Jews; now they were sleek with high-end international chains: Prada, Gucci, Louis Vuitton, Donna Karan. The many jewellers on the upper floor displayed a plethora of amber: beads, pendants, brooches, rings. Much of it, I was informed, came from Kaliningrad, the Russian exclave on the Baltic that contains the world's largest amber mine.

When I arrived at the bus stop, there was no one there but the driver Pavel, our guide Alitsiya, and a young Frenchman visiting his Russian girlfriend. A party of tourists had been delayed. After much phoning, Pavel agreed to collect them outside Moskovsky station. Edging through the gridlock on Nevsky Prospekt, we picked them up, five elderly Indians from Hertfordshire, just off the train from Moscow, before driving out through the industrial fringes of the city. Beyond the ring road, a scrubby landscape of small trees rose gently to a range of low hills, crested by two rusting howitzers that marked the limit of the German advance in the Second World War. Beside the road was a military graveyard; a small Orthodox church, in the traditional style, had recently been built beside it. Descending the hill, we entered Pushkin, a town with a population of 100,000. The original name *Saarskaya Myaza*, Finnish for Island Farm, was later corrupted to Tsarskoye Selo, or 'Tsar's Village'. The Soviets renamed the place in honour of Pushkin, who attended the lycée here, and although the palace had reverted to its original name, the town was still called after the poet.

As we passed through an Egyptian-style gate into expansive parkland, the palace came into view, a long façade of white, blue and gold, with gilt atlantes and caryatids flanking tall arched windows. Originally built for Catherine I, the wife of Peter the Great, between 1718 and 1724, Tsarskoye Selo owes its Rococo exuberance to the empress Elizabeth, who had it completely refashioned by her favourite architect Rastrelli in the 1750s.

We ascended a sweeping staircase of white Carrara marble to the imperial apartments. The Throne Hall was a riot of white plaster, gilt curlicues, candelabras and mirrors beneath a fiendishly clever *trompe l'oeil* ceiling that queasily shifted perspective as one moved around the room. Vladimir Putin holds receptions here for world leaders; oligarchs hire it for their weddings. The profuse gold leaf looks unnervingly new, as indeed it is. On 22nd June 1941, the day Hitler's armies invaded the Soviet Union, the young curator of the palace, Anatoly Kuchumov, received the order to pack up its treasures for evacuation. On 17th September, Tsarskoye Selo fell to the Germans. By the time the siege of Leningrad was lifted in January 1944, the building was a wreck; wartime photographs show this enfilade of rooms gutted to the brickwork, snow drifting in through shattered windows.

Catherine the Great thought Elizabeth's love of Rococo extravagance vulgar: 'These people had merchants' taste,' she reportedly said, before commissioning the Scottish architect Charles Cameron to design a suite of rooms in a more sober, classical style. And there it was: the Amber Room. It was smaller than I expected, and with the light refracted from glowing nuggets of amber, mirrors and gilt sconces, it felt like being submerged in a jar of marmalade. Théophile Gautier, who visited in the 1860s, experienced the same sense of disorientation and wonder:

> The expression 'The Amber Room' is not just a poetic hyperbole, but exact reality ... The eye which has not adapted to seeing this material, applied in such scale, is amazed and blinded by the wealth and warmth of tints, representing all colours in the spectrum of yellow, from smoky topaz up to a light lemon. The gold of carvings

seems dim and false in this neighborhood, especially when
the sun falls on the walls and runs through transparent
veins . . .

Gradually the room resolved into its component parts. The
wall on the window side was plain; the other three were faced
with traditional tripartite panelling, covered in an intricate
jigsaw of amber, clear and cloudy, tawny and honey-coloured,
backed with gold foil to reflect the light. Cartouches enclosing
the monograms FR – (Fredericus Rex) with the single-headed
Prussian eagle, and EP (Elizaveta Petrovna) with the double-
headed Russian one, bore testimony to the room's evolution:
commissioned by the elector Friedrich III of Prussia, given to
Peter the Great, and set up here by his daughter Elizabeth.
The wall panels were divided by mirror-surfaced pilasters
framing four marble mosaics by the Florentine artist Giuseppe
Dzokki, depicting the senses, *Sight*, *Taste*, *Hearing* and *Touch
and Smell*. Panels of clear amber were engraved with delicate
intaglio seascapes; others had relief carvings of biblical scenes.
In the frieze at the top, gilt putti frolicked lewdly amid swags
of carved drapery.

The room underwent many transformations in its long
and troubled history. When Friedrich's wife Sophie Charlotte
commissioned Andreas Schlüter to design the interiors of her
palace at Charlottenburg in Berlin in 1696, the architect found
dozens of chests filled with raw amber from the Baltic in the
cellars. He summoned the craftsman Gottfried Wolfram from
Copenhagen to create a room panelled with the substance.
Wolfram devised a method of softening amber in hot water
laced with honey, linseed oil and cognac so that it could be
extruded to wafer thinness, and produced 12 large panels, each
four metres high, ten smaller panels, and twenty-four sections
of amber-covered skirting board.

But then the project stalled. Sophie died suddenly of

pneumonia in 1705, and in 1707, Schlüter was exiled after a tower he had built for the Berlin Mint collapsed. Friedrich Eosander, a young architect then in favour at court, was appointed in his place. When Wolfram refused to hand over the panels, Eosander broke into his workshop and stole them. Wolfram instigated legal proceedings against Eosander, who counter-sued and had the craftsman jailed. By the time Friedrich died in 1713, the room had yet to be assembled. His son and successor, Friedrich Wilhelm I, had no interest in this expensive and troublesome project; he sacked Eosander and had the panels put into storage.

In November 1716, Peter the Great paid Friedrich Wilhelm a visit in Berlin. Peter had long been fascinated by amber, having bought a copy of Philipp Jacob Hartmann's book *Succini Prussici* ('Prussian Amber') in Königsberg back in 1696. To cement their alliance, Friedrich gave him the panels, which were packed up in 18 crates, loaded on to carts and dispatched to St Petersburg; in return, Peter gave Friedrich fifty-five giant soldiers and a goblet he had made himself. The following summer, the panels arrived at Peter's new Summer Palace on the Neva. When Menshikov supervised the unloading, he encountered a flatpack nightmare: many pieces were broken or missing, and there were no instructions on how to reassemble them. The Amber Room went into storage again, and there it remained until 1743, when Elizabeth commissioned the sculptor Alessandro Martelli to install it in the Winter Palace. As the panelling was not sufficient for the room she had in mind, mirrored pilasters were used to pad it out.

In 1755 she decided to move the room again, this time to her new palace at Tsarskoye Selo. Here, it was reassembled in an even larger room; as there was no money to pay for more amber, fake panels and yet more mirrors were used. After Catherine the Great ascended the throne in 1762, she decided that the Amber Room was in need of renovation. More than

900 pounds of amber were shipped from Samland, and four carvers hired from Königsberg to replace the fake sections with the real thing.

There the Amber Room remained until 1941. It was not among the treasures moved to Siberia to escape the German advance; judging the panels too fragile to dismantle, Kuchumov hid them behind false walls. It was a terrible mistake. When the Russians were finally able to return in January 1944, there was no sign of the Amber Room. The Germans had crated it up and sent it to Königsberg, where it was exhibited in the castle until it disappeared, in circumstances still shrouded in mystery, during the closing days of the war.

In the decades that followed, the pursuit of the missing room became an obsession, with the KGB pitted against the East German Stasi, and assorted freelance treasure hunters joining the fray. Several suffered mysterious deaths. Two British journalists, Catherine Scott-Clark and Adrian Levy, spent years investigating its fate, publishing their findings in a 2004 book *The Amber Room: The Untold Story of the Greatest Hoax of the Twentieth Century*. Neither their conclusion that the Amber Room no longer existed, nor their portrayal of the Russian bureaucratic obfuscation they encountered in their search for it, won them many friends, even among the liberal intelligentsia of St Petersburg. 'Even if their findings are basically correct,' one woman told me crisply, 'their approach was somewhat unsympathetic.'

What I was looking at was a replica, the work of modern craftsmen and women who laboured for more than twenty years to recreate this 'symbol of Russian cultural and art losses'. Only one colour photograph, an autochrome dating from 1917, exists of the original room, but detailed drawings and black-and-white photographs – assisted by computer modelling to calculate the depth of the relief – enabled the restorers to recreate it in painstaking detail. Even the names of the makers and repairers, scratched here and there in the shadow of a decorative moulding, were reproduced, to which the restorers, with justifiable pride, added their own. Six tons of amber from Kaliningrad were used in the work, which was eventually completed in 2003 at a cost of €12 million, with financial support from the German energy company Ruhrgas. The room was finally unveiled by President Putin in the presence of the German Chancellor Gerhard Schröder and other world leaders on 31st May that year, the tercentenary of the founding of St Petersburg.

The four marble mosaics were recreated from the original watercolour designs, which survive in the Museum of the Opificio delle Pietre Dure in Florence. Then, in 1997, one of the originals, *Touch and Smell*, was offered for sale in Bremen by a man called Hans Achtermann, whose father, a former Wehrmacht officer, had looted it during the war. Achtermann was arrested, and the panel was returned to Russia. Apart from some slight variation in colour, where the restorers seem to have matched the original cartoon more closely than their 18th-century counterparts, it proved remarkably similar to the recreation, inspiring confidence in the accuracy of the rest of the restoration work.

Except that it all looked too new. It was not just a question of the colour, which would mellow in time, but the accuracy of the joins, the perfection of the fit. The original had been moved and damaged on several occasions. The backing boards had warped, pieces of amber had shrunk and fallen off, and the whole was patched and repaired many times. The reconstruction represents a state of perfection that the original never attained. It is a Platonic ideal of the Amber Room as it existed in the imagination of its seekers. It is also a labour of love and pride, and it is hard not to be moved by the skill and dedication of the craftsmen and women who devoted decades of their lives to the fulfilment of this impossible dream.

The installation of the Amber Room at Tsarskoye Selo necessitated the establishment of a workshop to make running repairs. When not busy maintaining the room itself, the artisans turned their hand to smaller pieces such as chess sets, caskets and figurines. Fortunately these items survived the war, having been taken to Novosibirsk for safety, and are now exhibited in a modern gallery on the ground floor of the palace. There is a delicate little samovar of clear amber dating from the 1790s, and even a set of gentleman's toiletries commissioned by Catherine the Great for her lover Grigory Orlov. The domesticity of these items is touching: the amber-handled shaving brush, soap dish, studs and pomade flasks are not far removed from the kind of present a woman might give the man in her life today. When the decision was taken to recreate the Amber Room, the workshop was re-established, and its craftspeople once again began to create icons, goblets, caskets and candlesticks, which were displayed alongside the work of their 18th-century predecessors.

Leaving the museum, we walked through the grounds in the gathering dusk. Catherine had two gardens created here, one in the French style, with formal parterres and geometric avenues of trees, the other in the English landscape tradition, with lakes and pavilions set amid undulating lawns and woods. As our party headed back towards the bus, I looked up at the lighted windows of the long green façade to see the tawny glow of the Amber Room radiating into the night.

What other amber, beside the Room, could be found in St Petersburg? The Hermitage seemed the obvious place to look. One of the world's greatest art galleries, it was set up in the Winter Palace in 1764 when Catherine the Great bought a collection of Flemish and Dutch paintings from a Berlin art dealer, and opened to the public in 1854. In the classical galleries, which most visitors hurry through on their way to the Renaissance paintings, my eye was caught by a Roman sarcophagus from the 2nd century AD, depicting the fall of Phaeton. Ovid's *Metamorphoses* tells how Phaeton begged his father, the sun god Helios, to let him drive his chariot. Unable to control the horses, the youth careered about the sky, scorching the earth until Zeus struck him dead with a bolt of lightning. His body fell into the River Po, where his sisters, mourning on the riverbank, were metamorphosed into poplar trees. In Arthur Golding's Elizabethan translation:

> Now from these trees flow gummy teares that Amber men
>   doe call,
> Which hardened with the heate of sunne as from the
>   boughs they fal
> The trickling River doth receyve, and sendes as things of
>   price
> To decke the daintie Dames of Rome and make them fine
>   and nice.

It was a powerful, intense, dynamically rendered scene: Phaeton tumbles headlong, his hair ablaze, amid flailing horses and shattered fragments of his chariot while his sisters weep and his friend Cygnus, transformed into a swan, dives into the river to retrieve the smouldering corpse. A few rooms further on, in the Pompeian gallery, I found some of the 'gummy teares' themselves, a set of chunky, dark honey-coloured faceted amber beads, dating from the 1st to 3rd centuries AD, from northern Asia Minor.

Upstairs, crowds of visitors were marvelling at the old masters. Few ventured into a grey side-corridor where a collection of 'trophy art' was furtively displayed. These paintings were war booty, in some cases twice looted, first by the Nazis and then by the Red Army; they were not included in the Hermitage's online catalogue, and could not be exhibited abroad for fear of confiscation. The small but stunning collection of Impressionists and Post-Impressionists included works by Renoir, Monet, Manet, Sisley, Gauguin, Van Gogh – a lovely landscape with a house – and Cézanne – a self-portrait and one of his Mont St-Victoires. The insistence that the missing Amber Room still exists in a cave somewhere in Germany is believed by some to be a bargaining ploy against demands for the return of these works.

I wandered through an endless succession of imperial apartments, overwhelmed by their scale. In the Malachite Room, the doorknobs were faceted globes of amber held in brass eagles' talons. The room was a triumph of power over taste, a demonstration of the tsar's ability to have two tons of this richly veined green mineral hauled hundreds of miles from the Urals in the days before railways. It was amid this brooding splendour that Alexander Kerensky's impotent Provisional Government vacillated as the cruiser *Aurora*, moored just across the Neva, fired the shot that gave the signal for the storming of the Winter Palace.

As I looked out of the window across the river, the two Roman-style rostral columns on the Strelka gave out a burst of flame, like a summons to move on. I made my way across the Palace Bridge to Vasilyevsky Island, past the columns and the university, to Peter the Great's *Kunstkammer* – his cabinet of curiosities. The green and white church-like building was built to house his collection of curios: conjoined foetuses preserved in jars of alcohol, skeletons of children with two heads, deformed animals and so on. Grotesque as it seems, Peter assembled the collection not out of morbid curiosity but to spread scientific understanding and banish old superstitions, at a time when Puritan settlers in New England were burning innocent women for witchcraft.

Up the winding stair into the tower was a monument to another great Russian moderniser, a recreation of the laboratory established here in 1748 by Mikhail Lomonosov. A fisherman's son from the far north, Lomonosov was a man of extraordinary versatility: a chemist whose *Elementa Chymiae Mathematica* (1741) anticipated Dalton's theory of the atomic structure of matter; a ceramicist who revived the art of mosaic in Russia; and a poet, playwright and grammarian who laid the foundations of the modern Russian literary language. The circular, vaulted chamber was dominated by the large round table at which the St Petersburg Academy of Sciences met in the 18th century. Around the room were scientific instruments of the period: retorts, a large burning lens and an electrostatic generator operated by a crank handle. On a leather-topped chest of drawers stood Lomonosov's pen and inkwell, his brass microscope, and a box of mineral samples including pieces of malachite and amber.

It was in this room, in 1757, that Lomonosov unveiled a crucial discovery about the nature of amber. In the course of sixteen years' study, he had noticed that its specific gravity was close to that of pine resin, and that the plant and animal inclusions found within it were all associated with a forest environment. His chemical analyses showed that 'water separated from amber smells of succinic acid, a property of growing things.' His speech to the Academy established conclusively that amber was not, as was then believed, solidified petroleum but the resin of ancient trees.

Back on the southern side of the Neva, just north of Nevsky Prospekt, between the Griboyedov canal and the Bolshoi, the yellow neoclassical Mikhailovsky Palace now houses the Russian Museum. The collection originated in Russia's first ethnographic exhibition, held in 1867 in the Manège in Moscow. The mannequins in the traditional dress of the various peoples of the empire posed against painted backdrops of national scenery exuded tsarist paternalism. 'Very natural looking and rather typical,' was Alexander II's approving comment. After the collection was moved here in 1948, the Soviets continued to develop it, the perspective modified only slightly: the Russian people, the revolutionary vanguard, were now 'elder brother' to the other nationalities of the Union.

'Amber ornament is a certain part of the national dress of the Baltic peoples,' proclaimed the label beside a collection of chunky beads and pendants of clear and cloudy amber created between 1950 and 1980 in the Latvian cities of Liepāja and Riga, and Klaipėda and Vilnius in Lithuania. The dates were telling: the Baltic states, which had achieved independence in 1918, were forcibly annexed into the Soviet Union in 1939. There were also several pieces of raw amber on display: fist-sized chunks, gnarled and rough-surfaced, one shaped like a crab shell, and a number of smaller pieces with flies and mosquitoes trapped inside. These colonial trophies were a reminder that that amber is not just a beautiful substance but, like any material of value, a commodity that people have fought over, and that the Amber Route ran through some of the most bitterly contested regions of Europe.

I returned to the guesthouse with my soul out of place, as the Russians say. In the stairwell, the flaking blue distemper was adorned with graffiti inspired by American rap: BLAZIN UP THA WEED – SLAP THAT BITCH. The rain picked up, hammering on the metal roofs and gurgling down the wide tin drainpipes, forming rivulets through the uneven cobbles and pitted asphalt.

As I descended the echoing stairs the next morning, two young women, the brevity of their skirts at odds with the weather, stood at either end of the first-floor landing, smoking furiously and studiously ignoring each other. The apartment was occupied by a clinic specialising in minor cosmetic surgery: liposuction, electrolysis, Botox ... The sign had disappeared from the lift, which was still not working.

CHAPTER 2

CROSSING THE GULF

The morning was exhilaratingly bright and cold. A seagull perched atop the double-headed imperial eagle that crowned a granite obelisk commemorating a visit by the Empress Alexandra in 1833. The yellow stucco of the town hall glowed in the winter sun, which sparkled off the domes of the Orthodox cathedral on its rock above the bay. Down by the jetty, a couple of old men were belting out the theme from *Love Story* on a battered trumpet and accordion as an excited crowd watched the arrival of a flotilla of coastguard boats. Seabirds wheeled around the boats and a juvenile herring gull, in its brown winter plumage, waddled along the quay.

You are never far from the sight, sound or smell of the sea in Helsinki. This agreeable low-rise city is spread across a rocky, starfish-shaped peninsula in a wide natural harbour fringed by islands. After mist-shrouded St Petersburg, its breezy, maritime air lifted my spirits. This small capital of just over half a million was an easygoing place where almost everyone seemed to speak English. It clung to the southern shore of a long, thinly populated country that stretched 1,500 kilometres to the north, beyond the Arctic Circle. The entire population of this nation was just 5.5 million, similar to that of St Petersburg.

I had hoped to arrive by ship, but the service had been discontinued. Instead, I took the Helsinki express from St Petersburg's Finland Station. The moment I stepped on board,

I was in a different world: from the rackety streets of post-communist Russia to the egalitarian prosperity of Nordic social democracy. The train filled up quickly, mostly with Finns, though there were a few Russians. At Vyborg, the last town on the Russian side, the intercom announced that the dining car and lavatories would be locked until the crossing was complete. 'Please prepare yourself for a customs and border inspection.'

For five centuries, Finland was ruled by Sweden, with Swedish the language of the administration and social elite; it is still spoken by a minority and recognised as an official language. It was a Swedish king, Gustavus Vasa, who founded Helsingfors, as it was then called, in 1550, but the city failed to develop. The capital remained at Turku on the west coast, and Helsingfors was abandoned to the ravages of the Great Northern War, which brought plague in its wake, killing two-thirds of its inhabitants in 1710.

This was the first in a series of conflicts that destroyed Sweden's position as a European power and culminated in Russia's annexation of Finland in 1809. As a grand duchy within the Russian Empire, Finland had its own constitution and parliament, giving it limited autonomy. Alexander I commissioned the German architect Carl Ludwig Engel to rebuild the city centre in a style appropriate to a capital, including the monumental Senate Square, dominated by a vertiginous flight of steps leading up to the gleaming white Lutheran cathedral, which mirrored its redbrick Russian Orthodox twin across the harbour.

At first, the Russians encouraged the use of the Finnish language in order to weaken the country's ties to Sweden. As nationalism gained ground, the government of Nicholas I became alarmed and, in 1850, banned the language. Under the 'tsar liberator' Alexander II, the native tongue was encouraged once more; Alexander's statue in Senate Square is the only monument to a Russian ruler not taken down after independence. In the backlash that followed his assassination, the pendulum swung the other way again. Writing in 1885, the Russian anarchist Peter Kropotkin noted that 'the small dose of liberty enjoyed by Finland' was infuriating to 'the Reactionists now in power in Russia':

> A country where people travel without passports, and the dvorniks (porters) do not listen at the doors of lodgers, appears to them a hotbed of revolution. Even the industrial development of this small country renders them uneasy.

Kropotkin's warning that 'the longing for a complete independence will be redoubled by the attempts ... against Finland's autonomy' proved correct. Standing beneath Alexander's statue, I recalled that it was here, on 16th June 1904, that the Russian governor-general Nikolai Bobrikov was assassinated by a young nationalist. The event reverberated across the world, in another small country seeking freedom from its larger neighbour. 'Was it you shot the lord lieutenant of Finland between you?' J. J. O'Molloy asks Myles Crawford and Stephen Dedalus in James Joyce's *Ulysses*. 'You look as though you had done the deed. General Bobrikoff.'

The industrial and economic development observed by Kropotkin was evident to visitors. Arriving in the 1890s, the British journalist and travel writer Mrs Alec Tweedie found a bright, modern capital 'very advanced in its ideas', with 'electric light everywhere, telephones in each house', and noted the emancipation of women and the fact that the press was less heavily censored than in St Petersburg. Her contemporary A. M. C. Clive-Bailey, in his *Vignettes from Finland* (1895), wrote that:

> It would be difficult to find a town of 80,000 inhabitants in England so clean, so bright, with such museums, libraries, and public buildings. Even Bedford is not as educational

as Helsingfors nor is Brighton so well served with social amusements, concerts and theatres.

Shaken by the 1905 Revolution, the government of Nicholas II was forced to reinstate Finland's parliament. The new legislative body was notably progressive, the first in Europe to grant women the vote. Another period of reaction followed, however, and it was only after the Russian Revolution of 1917 that Finland broke free of its overbearing neighbour.

As I headed south along Kaptensgatan, the city's calm and friendly atmosphere belied its turbulent history. The long grid-plan streets, framed by tall early 20th-century buildings in brick and brownstone, with trams clanking up and down the hillside, were reminiscent of San Francisco. After stopping for coffee in a pretty tree-lined square, I caught an unexpected glimpse of my ultimate destination: in the window of an antique shop was a small oil painting, dating from around 1790 at a guess, depicting a Venetian scene. Beneath the craquelure, a gondolier was rowing two figures in beaked carnival masks past the white domes of San Giorgio Maggiore.

As I studied the painting, the shop's owner invited me to look around. A youngish man, in his late thirties perhaps, comfortably dressed in a check shirt and wearing fashionable narrow spectacles, he would not have looked out of place in Camden or the Cotswolds. On his trips into the Finnish countryside, he had assembled an impressive selection of rustic furniture – long-case clocks, pine chests and reed-bottomed chairs – that once graced farms and rural manor houses. Other, more sophisticated pieces, mostly originated in Stockholm prior to 1809, and St Petersburg thereafter. He enthusiastically opened an 18th-century writing box, with its inkwell and recesses for pens and paper, describing it as 'the laptop of its day'. Two elegant Empire dressers looked to date from the reign of Alexander I. Apparently Russians had been 'buying back their history' in recent years, though this had tailed off since the economic crisis.

I asked him if he ever came across amber – *meripihka* in Finnish – but he said that he did not see it often. A phone call to a friend who specialised in jewellery confirmed that it had not been much used in Finland. This was a disappointment: the substance does wash up on the shores of the Gulf, if not in the quantities found further south, so I would have expected more evidence of it in a country with such a rich tradition of craftsmanship.

He suggested that the best place to pursue my search would be the National Museum, so I headed north along Mannerheimintie, past the parliament building, an imposing edifice in honey-coloured stone. In front of it stood an eques-trian statue of Carl Gustaf Mannerheim, the wily old cavalry officer who secured Finland's independence by skilfully playing off Hitler and Stalin against one another. The museum was itself a monument to the country's national aspirations. Built by Eliel Saarinen, Herman Gesellius and Armas Lindgren between 1905 and 1910, when independence was beginning to look like a realistic proposition, it is one of Finland's grandest examples of National Romantic architecture. The granite façade, soaring tower and steep-roofed wings give it the appearance of a great Hanseatic guildhall.

It was the prehistoric galleries that drew my attention. Prominently displayed amid the flint tools and shards of pottery were eight amber pendants. The largest, about 3 centi-metres across, was a dark, rich honey colour. Most striking, however, was a wedge-shaped pendant found in a burial near Metsäpirtti, on the shores of Lake Ladoga in what is now Russian Karelia. With a few deft strokes, the sliver of pale, opaque amber had been carved into a stylised face, its deep-set eyes peering out beneath a chiselled brow. Though small, it radiated power. Who did it represent: a warrior, a hunter, a shaman? And was it made in Karelia, or imported from lands further south?

The first settlers arrived here after the end of the last Ice Age some 10,000 years ago, as the Baltic Sea began to develop at the southern edge of the retreating glaciers. The Neolithic, which lasted from around 4000 to 2000 BC in the region, was marked by the emergence of pottery. The vessels were decorated with wavy lines incised in the wet clay with a comb; their makers, known as the Comb Ware Culture, are thought to be the ancestors of the Finns and Estonians. Their burials often contained personal ornaments of amber, along with flint points and animal sculptures of wood, bone and soft stone.

By the late Iron Age, the peoples of southern Finland had a flourishing trade with Rome, as evidenced by coins, brooches and other objects found in the region. The collapse of the Roman Empire does not seem to have curtailed the traffic: a Migration-Era amber sword bead was found in a grave at Lägpeltkangas, near the west coast, while Merovingian amber beads found in a cemetery at Käräjämäki, further inland, suggest that the trade was still going strong well into what used to be called the Dark Ages.

As I left, I bought a postcard of the Metsäpirtti pendant, hoping that this ancient, enigmatic face would serve as an amulet as I crossed the Gulf of Finland to the amber-rich Baltic Republics.

There can be no finer way to arrive in Tallinn than by sea. A quiet, overcast Sunday morning brightened as I walked to the ferry terminal in Helsinki. Beside the harbour, a rocky outcrop was festooned with a spectacular display of icicles. It was still possible to take the catamaran – a bright red Australian-built craft called the *Merilin* – as there was no sea ice yet; a week or two later I would have had to make the 80-kilometre crossing by slow ferry. Ahead, in the harbour mouth, lay the wooded islands of Luoto and Blekholmen, with its elaborate green-roofed boathouse. This was home to the Nylands Yacht Club, where Arthur Ransome berthed when he visited Finland's 'trim stone-built capital' in the early 1920s to buy ropes, hooks and clips for his yacht, besides 'bread, butter, cheese, apples, Swedish oatcake, tobacco, stocking-caps and a Finnish sheath-knife, a gorgeous piratical thing with a horse's head for a hilt'. Best remembered as the author of the *Swallows and Amazons* books, this avuncular, pipe-smoking, quintessentially English figure led a bizarre double life. As Moscow correspondent for the *Manchester Guardian*, he witnessed the Russian Revolution, became a fervent supporter of the Bolsheviks, married Trotsky's secretary, Evgenia Shelepina, and worked as a double agent for both the Russian Cheka and MI6. In the early 1920s, he had a ketch, the *Racundra*, built for him at Riga, and undertook a number of sailing trips around the Baltic.

The *Merilin* turned in the harbour and made its way past a scattering of rocks before navigating the channel between the boatyard island of Särkkä Längören and the lighthouse-church on the fortress archipelago of Suonemlinna. Then the water became choppy. Up on deck, the sharp south-westerly was bracing. The cat shook free of the last scattering of islets and skerries and picked up speed. About 55 minutes into the crossing, the low, wooded island of Prangli appeared on the port side; beyond it, a red and black lighthouse stood on an isolated rock. Before long, the coast shimmered into focus, with the soaring spire of St Olai's church as tall as the high-rise buildings on the city's outskirts. As we passed between Aegna Island and the Vilmsi peninsula, the domes and spires of the Old Town solidified out of the haze. To their left, monotonous ranks of Soviet apartment blocks stood like rows of dominoes; to the right, the cranes and gantries of the dockyard.

The catamaran docked beside a crumbling concrete

ziggurat, once the V. I. Lenin Palace of Culture and Sport. Although built as recently as 1980 for the sailing events of the Moscow Olympics, its rotting concrete was a scene of unspeakable dereliction. There were no customs or passport control; I simply crossed a grass-verged dual carriageway to the medieval Sea Gate, which guarded the entrance to the town. In a grassy park to one side was a black marble monument, shaped like a broken arc, to the 852 people who drowned when the ferry MS *Estonia* sank in the Baltic on its way to Stockholm in 1994.

I passed under the Gothic arch and hauled my luggage up the rattling cobblestones of Pikk, the long medieval street, lined with steep-gabled merchants' houses, that leads to the heart of the Old Town. At the back of St Olai's, a macabre skeleton was carved on a tomb in a wall niche, a toad on its chest and serpent round its skull. In the window of a tiny souvenir shop, I could see several strings of amber. Further on, a narrow passage beside the Church of the Holy Spirit, with its astronomical clock, led me into Town Hall Square. Across an expanse of cobbles fronted by medieval and Renaissance houses, the lancet arches and dragon waterspouts of the Raekoja – the Town Hall – stood bright in the wintry sunlight, its high steeple piercing the pellucid sky.

Although the present structure dates from 1402, there had been a town hall on this site since the 13th century, when Reval, as the city was then called, was ruled by Denmark. In 1248 it joined the Hanseatic League, a mercantile alliance of north European ports stretching all the way to King's Lynn in Norfolk. The Danes sold Tallinn, along with their other lands in Estonia, to the Teutonic Knights in 1346. The Knights fortified the city, building the walls and towers that still ring the Old Town. In 1561, northern Estonia was conquered by Sweden during its brief ascendancy as a European superpower, and it was among the territories lost to Russia in the Great Northern

War at the beginning of the 18th century. But whoever ruled in the Toompea, the windy citadel that looms over the town, the city's mercantile class remained stolidly German, the descendants of settlers who came in the wake of the Teutonic Knights; in consequence, Town Hall Square still looked, in the words of Arthur Ransome, 'like one of those night-cap-country towns that old German wood-engravers used to put into their backgrounds'.

From Town Hall Square, I set off in search of my hostel, wheeling my luggage downhill towards the Estonian Drama Theatre, a fine Art Nouveau building from the early years of independence; its relief carvings and shingled roof embodied the same National Romantic aspirations found in Finnish architecture of the period. Immediately opposite, the hostel shared an imposing five-storey Secession-style building with the Ministry of Culture, a property management company and various other businesses. A plaque informed me that it was designed by no less an architect than Eliel Saarinen. I climbed a steep flight of steps to a double door, beyond which a tinny lift took me up to the fourth-floor reception. An unsmiling young woman informed me that my room was number 59, on the fifth floor, and handed me the keys. Climbing the stairs, I was puzzled to find that the sign on the landing only listed rooms up to 58. After exploring the maze of corridors, I solved the mystery; room 59 had recently been partitioned off from a landing, bisecting a fine bay window. Looking out over undulating leaden eaves on to a courtyard, the room was sparsely furnished with two rickety pine beds, coverless duvets and wall lamps with trailing leads. It was clean enough, though, and had that East European feel I remembered from visits to relatives in the old DDR, and which was rapidly disappearing everywhere.

I returned to the main square to find it almost deserted, with just a handful of people wandering its ice-dusted cobbles under a sky glittering with stars. The windows of the jewellers' shops glowed with amber necklaces, charms, brooches and pendants. Round a corner, in the ground floor of an old house, I stumbled on La Casa del Habano, a 'smoke-easy' designed to get around the anti-smoking legislation that Estonia, like many other European countries, had introduced. You bought a drink – and a cigar, if you wished – and took them through a glass partition into a cosy sitting room with comfortable chairs and low tables, under a marvellous old ceiling of deeply fissured wooden boards. A powerful, almost silent air conditioning system kept the atmosphere sweet. It had the air of a slightly louche private club, an establishment discreetly catering for forbidden pleasures. Regulars kept their own bottles of spirits in a locked cabinet, for which they had keys.

The clientele was a mixture of Estonians, Britons, Swedes and Germans. Business was transacted in hushed tones: import-export, art dealing, property. Fragments of conversation insinuated their way into my consciousness with the tendrils of cigar smoke:

'They're willing to invest, but . . .'

'Tallinn is a village – you can go out to dinner with anyone and they'll know someone you know.'

'Basically, what it comes down to is I'm going to have to bribe him . . . '

A couple of dotcom entrepreneurs invited me to join them. Paul was from Wexford, Louis from Austin, Texas. Young high-fliers – LSE, Harvard, MIT – they had been investing heavily here, mostly in IT start-ups. Home to the inventors of Skype, the country had been dubbed 'the Silicon Valley of the Baltic' by the *New York Times*. After decades of isolation, Tallinn was busily resuming the role it once played as Reval, a thriving mercantile city with international business connections.

A few flakes of snow were falling as I set out in search of coffee the next morning. On a narrow, crooked alley called

Voorimehe (formerly Kleine Rittergaße), 'The Wild Irish Rover' was booming out of an Irish-themed pub. I browsed in a couple of antique shops; their contents – ormolu clocks, Russian icons, Tsarist banknotes, Soviet and Nazi weaponry – formed a potted history of the city. I climbed the narrow, cobbled streets towards the Toompea, where a steep stair led though a Gothic arch with a heavy, iron-studded door, into a neat, orderly quarter of Baroque and neoclassical buildings.

The Toompea was dominated by the Cathedral of Alexander Nevsky, built in 1900 in the Russian style, its onion domes surmounted by gold crosses. After independence in 1917, it was seen as a symbol of Tsarist oppression, and there was talk of demolishing it. Ransome thought it 'monstrous ... breaking with a touch of Byzantium the Gothic and Scandinavian outlines of the place'. Today, however, the church seems to have settled into the architectural mosaic of Tallinn's complex history. Inside, I was transported back to Russia. Light filtered through clouds of incense from high windows around the dome, where the four Evangelists looked down from the pendentives. A handful of worshippers prayed before the gilded iconostasis. To the right of the entrance, two marble plaques commemorated the sailors killed on the Russian battleships sunk by the Japanese at the Battle of Tsushima in 1905. The ships of the Baltic fleet – Admiral Rozhestvensky's flag battle-ship *Knyaz Suvorov,* the *Nakhimov,* the *Imperator Aleksandr III,* the *Borodino* and the *Navarin* – had sailed half way round the world, and their loss was a crushing blow to Russian morale that helped precipitate the 1905 Revolution.

Despite the fact that Alexei, the Patriarch of Moscow and All Russia, who died in 2009, hailed from Tallinn and was ordained a bishop in this church, the atmosphere was subdued, defensive even, as if this were the citadel of an embattled minority. For many Estonians, the Russian-speakers are an unwelcome remnant of a brutal 50-year occupation during which their language and culture were suppressed, and tens of thousands of their compatriots were killed or deported to the gulags. When Estonia became independent in 1991, Russians who had moved there during the Soviet occupation – some 30 per cent of the population – were required to demonstrate knowledge of the country's language and history in order to qualify for citizenship. Non-citizens could not vote, obtain a passport or travel abroad, a state of affairs that drew sharp criticism from the United Nations, the Council of Europe and Amnesty International.

By now, the snow was falling steadily. Immediately opposite the cathedral stood a pink neoclassical palace, built in the reign of Catherine the Great. It was now the seat of the Riigikogu, the Estonian parliament. The ancient white cathedral nearby, topped with a black Baroque cupola, dated back to Danish times. The adjacent ramparts offered what Ransome called 'the finest view to be obtained in any of the Baltic capitals':

> down sheer precipice on the ancient walls of the lower town, with the round grey towers that rose above them and the dark spire of the church of St Nicholas of the Sailors, and far over the roofs of the town ... the harbour with the ships coming and going.

The snow continued its soft, relentless descent, blanketing the roofscape below me. As I braced myself against the cold, I was approached by a man in a warm jacket and woolly hat. Tall, well built, with chestnut curls reaching to his shoulders, he introduced himself as Kulno. It transpired that he was a photographer, a promoter of local bands with a bag full of CDs to sell and, in a small way, a dealer in amber. When I told him the purpose of my journey, he pulled a bracelet of yellow, cloudy amber from the depths of his rucksack. He could get me more, he said, but warned me that the amber on sale here was mostly from Kaliningrad.

I asked about the CDs in his bag, and he told me that he was involved in the Tallinn Song Festival, which was held every summer. The festival, he explained, played a crucial part in Estonia's struggle for independence, which became known as the 'singing revolution'. In June 1987, more than 10,000 people packed the festival to sing patriotic songs banned by the USSR. By September the following year, their numbers had swelled to 300,000. Each year, the protests grew in strength until, after sending in tanks, the crumbling USSR finally recognised Estonian independence on 24th August 1991.

It is sometimes said that the best way to get to know a city is to get lost in it; as I made my way back down through the winding streets to the Old Town, I had no difficulty in doing so. And then, just as inadvertently, I got my bearings again, and found myself back on Pikk. Where the long street joined Olevimäg stood a tiny chapel, with icons visible through the windows; built in 1909, in the reign of Nicholas II, it was little bigger that a telephone kiosk. A classy jeweller's shop nearby displayed a selection of work by modern Estonian designers, including a neck-band with a large amber pendant. The young woman in the shop confirmed what Kulno had just told me, that all the amber on sale was imported.

A few doors along, the medieval Great Guild Hall was now home to the Estonian History Museum. Its Gothic vaulted chambers were filled with artefacts from every era, from the Stone Age to the 20th century. As in Finland, amber had been found in prehistoric burials across the country. In a glass case in front of me glistened three such pendants, one a long shard of cloudy amber, another light golden, and one, about five centimetres across, darker, reddish and rounded. During the Iron Age, amber was one of the main trading commodities with the Roman Empire; a display in the adjacent room included a number of Roman coins found in Estonia, alongside Islamic and Saxon currency brought here by the Vikings.

The museum was itself the product of the German bourgeoisie who dominated the mercantile and cultural life of the city. In 1842, 37 teachers, lawyers, doctors and clerics got together to form the Estländische Literärische Gesellschaft. They devoted themselves to the study of local history, culture, language and folklore. Gertrud Elisabeth Mara contributed the manuscript of a poem by Goethe, which he had dedicated to her back in 1771; the widow of a local artist, G. A. Hippius, donated Mozart's manuscript of the cadenzas from one of his piano concertos, which her husband had obtained from the composer's piano tuner. Rosaries strung with small, dark amber beads testified to the Teutonic Knights' monopoly of the trade in the Middle Ages.

The distinctive culture of the Baltic Germans, which flourished for six centuries, came to an abrupt end in 1939 when the Molotov-Ribbentrop Pact assigned the Baltic republics to the Soviet sphere of influence, and they were 'repatriated' to the Reich by the Nazi government. In June 1940, the Red Army occupied Estonia, snuffing out the independence the country had won from Russia just 22 years earlier. A year later the Nazis invaded, to be driven out in 1944, when Estonia was forcibly incorporated into the Soviet Union.

The next day, I explored the working city of offices, shopping centres, tramlines and traffic intersections that lay beyond the Old Town walls. The steel and glass towers that rose out of the Gulf of Finland as I arrived by ferry now loomed above me, their mirrored surfaces reflecting the watery Baltic sunlight, a symbol of the city's renewed commercial confidence. Just north of the port was the Rotermann Quarter, a complex of workshops and warehouses built by the industrialist Christian Barthold Rotermann in the late 19th century. Andrei

Tarkovsky's film *Stalker* was partly shot in an old chemical factory here. After decades of neglect, the buildings had been turned into a fashionable quarter of shops, restaurants and bars, but a few corners still retained the air of dereliction that drew the director of *Andrei Rublyev* and *Solaris* here in the 1970s.

The screenplay, by Boris and Arkady Strugatsky, was loosely based on their science-fiction novel *Roadside Picnic*. Something has happened, possibly a nuclear accident; no one knows for sure, but an area known as the Zone has been cordoned off by the military. Somewhere within it is a mysterious room where people are confronted by their innermost desires. The Stalker ekes out a living by guiding clients to this room. His vocation, according to Tarkovsky, is 'to serve people who have lost their hopes and illusions'.

The director was the heir to a long Russian literary and artistic tradition: his father Arseny Tarkovsky was a distinguished poet and translator, a friend of Osip Mandelstam and lover of Marina Tsvetayeva. In his book *Sculpting in Time*, the younger Tarkovsky consciously aligned himself with the Dostoyevskian tradition, and lamented the neglect of such ideas in Soviet Russia:

> There are several reasons for this: first, their total incompatibility with materialism, and then the fact that the state of spiritual crisis experienced by all Dostoyevsky's characters is also viewed with misgiving. Why is this state of spiritual crisis so feared in contemporary Russia? I believe that it is always through spiritual crisis that healing occurs . . .

This enigmatic film was the last Tarkovsky would make in the Soviet Union. While working on his next, *Nostalgia*, in Italy, he decided not to return to his homeland. Since the fall of the Soviet Union, his films have deepened in resonance and found many followers among a new generation struggling to live without ideological certainties. In one powerful scene, the Stalker, played by Alexander Kaidanovsky, recites one of the elder Tarkovsky's verses as he leans against a cracked window in this industrial wasteland:

> All that might've occurred
> Like a five-fingered leaf
> Fluttered into my hands,
> But it isn't enough.

It gets dark early in the Baltic winter. As I walked back up to the Old Town, two very drunk Estonian girls staggered giggling across the square. Behind the picturesque, Tallinn had its seamy side. The stag-night trade had largely moved on, but a couple of 'international' bars in the city centre still exuded an air of seedy desperation. Sitting in one of these dives, I found myself watching an absurd catwalk show of 'Paris's craziest designs' on a flatscreen TV. The barmaids were fresh-faced Estonian girls caked in foundation and lip-gloss, a travesty of femininity that seemed just steps away from the modern slavery of the sex trade. Women from the economically depressed, largely Russian-speaking areas of north-east Estonia are trafficked into Tallinn to meet the demand, and HIV rates are high.

I took refuge in the Casa del Habano, where I met a Swedish publisher called Torsten, who was here to set up a graphics studio for his publishing house in Stockholm. His Estonian girlfriend would run it. Estonia, he said, had a well-educated workforce who were cheaper to hire than their Swedish counterparts, and living costs were lower. While many older people who grew up under the Soviet system had difficulty adapting, those in their thirties and younger had great entrepreneurial flair. He believed that the tension between Estonians and

Russians was dissolving: the younger people had all learnt Estonian, and a process of assimilation was under way. I was not entirely convinced: unemployment was still twice as high among Russian speakers as among Estonians, Russian-speakers accounted for 58 per cent of Estonia's prison population, and had a higher incidence of respiratory diseases, alcoholism and drug addiction.

After a while, our conversation touched on a troubled passage in the country's history. When the Soviets invaded in 1940, many Estonians fought for the Germans, including Torsten's girlfriend's grandfather, who was taken prisoner by the Russians and never heard of again.

'It affects many families in Estonia,' said Torsten as the smoke of his Cohiba curled around the table lamp, 'but they don't talk about it.'

When the Soviets reoccupied the country in 1944, many took to the woods, where they waged a guerilla war against the occupying forces. Known as the Forest Brothers (though there were women among their ranks), they carried out acts of sabotage, assassinated Russian officers and killed Estonian collaborators. On Estonian national holidays, the blue and white national flag mysteriously appeared fluttering from church spires.

The career of Alfons Rebane embodies the complexities of the situation. For many Estonians, he was a hero of the resistance to Soviet tyranny; for others, a Nazi collaborator. An officer in the army of independent Estonia between the wars, Rebane took to the forests during the Soviet occupation of 1940–41 to lead a partisan unit fighting the invaders. After the Germans pushed the Red Army out of Estonia, he joined the Estonian Legion of the Wehrmacht, and in 1944 his unit was merged with the Waffen SS. After the Soviet victory, Rebane fled to Britain, where he was recruited by the SIS to direct the anti-Communist resistance.

Their struggle, however, was fatally undermined by Kim Philby, who provided information that enabled the KGB to infiltrate and destroy many units. When the failure of the Western powers to support the 1956 Hungarian uprising made it clear they could expect no help from that quarter, most of the Forest Brothers gave up. A few held out much longer: Kalev Arro was killed in an exchange of fire with the KGB in 1974; August Sabbe survived in the forests until 1978, when he drowned himself in a river to evade capture; while J. Lindemann died a natural death in the woods as late as 1981.

In the late 1980s, the historian Mart Laar began travelling from village to village, collecting oral testimony from surviving Forest Brothers. It was a courageous venture even in the glasnost era. By the time his book *War in the Woods: Estonia's Struggle for Survival, 1944–1956* appeared in 1992, Laar was Prime Minister of a newly independent Estonia. In 1999, during his second term, the ashes of Rebane, who had died in Germany in 1975, were returned to Estonia for reburial with full military honours. Ethnic Russians demonstrated outside the Riigikogu, and the Russian government registered an official protest.

After exchanging business cards with Torsten, I wandered back to my hostel. Overnight, the temperature rose, and the snow turned to sleet. Around noon, I took cover from a sudden shower in a bar on Town Hall Square; when I emerged, the snow had washed away. The city had resumed its workaday aspect, and people were returning to the streets. Down by the walls, a market was in full swing, selling cheap clothing and ironmongery, much as it did in Ransome's day, when it was called the 'Lousy Market'. I had intended to travel to Haapsalu the next day or the day after, but suddenly, with the roads clear, I felt the urge to move on.

CHAPTER 3

EXILES IN THEIR
OWN LAND

The sky was full of stars: the reclining figure of Andromeda
nursing the ovoid blur of the Great Spiral Nebula in her lap,
the Milky Way streaming down to meet the water. Beyond the
brightest stars were smaller ones, and beyond them smaller
ones still, receding ever deeper into infinity. A band of pale
green glowed on the western horizon. The inlet was lined with
reeds, its shallows crusted with ice. Geese called in the distance.

The little port of Haapsalu stands at the westernmost edge
of the Estonian mainland, in the county of Lääne, where the
Gulf of Finland meets the Baltic and the coast turns a right
angle from east-west to north-south. Here the Eurasian land-
mass breaks up into an archipelago that sprawls across the
Bay of Riga. Over the water are the wild, windswept islands
of Hiiumaa, Saaremaa and Muhu – known to Germans and
Scandinavians as Dagö, Ösel and Moon – and their countless
smaller companions. Back in the Neolithic, the region's inhabitants buried their dead with carved amber figurines of birds,
snakes and other animals.

The last part of Estonia to be conquered by the Livonian
Order, the archipelago was for centuries a lawless haven for
smugglers, wreckers and pirates. In 1839, the Russian ship
Nikolai I was lost off Saaremaa on its way from St Petersburg
to Lübeck. The following year the steamer *Vulture*, sailing

for St Petersburg, sank off the southern coast of the island. Rumours went around Lloyd's of London, whose underwriters sustained substantial losses, that the islanders had put out false lights to lure these ships on to the rocks. In 1850, on its maiden voyage from Blackwall on the River Thames to St Petersburg, Tsar Nicholas I's brand-new 400-tonne steam yacht *Peterhof* struck a reef off Saaremaa in strong winds. All on board were saved, but it proved impossible to salvage the ship, valued at more than £20,000.

The tree-lined promenade took me round the curve of the bay, past an ornate wooden Kursaal that exuded the faded gaiety of a 19th-century resort. Leaving my bags on a stone bench, I moved toward a street lamp to check the map. As I returned, I could hear music, a lilting melody that tried to become a waltz but kept falling back on itself. It appeared to be emanating from my luggage. I tried to think what might be responsible, until the tune came into focus and I recognised the 5/4 *Allegro con grazia* from Tchaikovsky's *Pathétique* symphony. Triggered by my movement, the music was coming from the bench itself, which I now saw was embellished with a bronze relief of the composer, in commemoration of an 1867 visit when Gapsal, as it was then known, was one of Tsarist Russia's most popular holiday destinations.

The hotel was not far. The heart of the complex was a 19th-century turreted villa, but I was put up in a modern chalet at the water's edge, with a verandah looking on to the sea. I woke the next morning to an extraordinary sight: the wide expanse of Haapsalu Bay under an eggshell sky, the low sun casting an orange tint on to the few clouds. The shallows were full of waders and seabirds; a roll like thunder signalled a flight of swans taking off. After breakfast, I took a walk around town. The old quarter stood on a peninsula with a lake in the middle, and it was hard to tell where the land ended and the water began. Everything was of wood: wooden houses with wooden shutters, wooden picket fences and woodpiles in the yards; wooden jetties and old wooden fishing boats, all nestling amid wizened ash and birch trees. Woodsmoke hung in the air.

The town centre was ranged round a green under the walls of the combined castle and cathedral. In 1279 the town became the seat of the Bishopric of Ösel-Wiek, a semi-autonomous principality that was part of the Livonian Confederation. The castle was destroyed by Russian forces during the Great Northern War, but the church still stood amid forbidding ramparts, a fortified outpost of Christendom from the days when paganism was being suppressed by the sword. The few other stone buildings seemed equally alien: German-style villas recalling the spa craze of the 19th century, imperial Russian administrative offices that could have been transplanted from St Petersburg. Ransome moored his ketch here in 1923, coming ashore for bread, milk and matches. Like me, he arrived in autumn, and found a quiet little town recovering from the 'alien but profitable bustle of the summer'. Haapsalu was not, he noted, like an English resort, 'where whole families go to the seaside for a tumultuous fortnight', but a place where 'men plant out their wives and children ... for the summer, to get brown, take mud baths and cure imaginary diseases, while they run down by train from Reval for the weekends.'

Towards the northern end of town stood the Museum of Estonian Swedes. The old wooden building was locked and unattended, but as I approached the door, a black-and-white cat mewed at my feet, and a young woman emerged from the house opposite to open the museum. Estonia was ruled by Sweden before the Russians conquered it, and many Swedes settled on its western shores and islands. Their descendants continued to live here, fishing and boatbuilding, until the Soviet takeover in 1944, when most left for Sweden, though a few elderly residents still kept the culture alive, meeting at the museum once a week to weave tapestries. I found the old photographs, handicrafts and fishing boats and nets curiously moving; this all but vanished people, clinging tenaciously to the remnants of their culture, seemed to embody so many of those dispossessed by the conflicts of the past century.

Now it was the Russians' turn. Throughout the Cold War, Haapsalu and the islands were a military area, off-limits to visitors even from the Soviet Union. Just four kilometres south-west of town, the Tokhaapsalu air base was home to the 38 MiG-23 jets of the 425th Interceptor Aviation Regiment until it was decommissioned in 1991. As I walked north, the peninsula divided into two prongs; the eastern one was occupied by the yacht club, while the western part was a dismal scene of abandonment: a long row of crumbling, Soviet-era industrial premises, half demolished, burnt out, with packing cases stencilled with Cyrillic script rotting amid the detritus of more recent, unofficial occupation: decomposing trainers, used condoms, hypodermic syringes . . .

Back in Castle Square, a secondhand camera shop offered a selection of old Russian Zenits and Lubitels, while the window of a small antique shop displayed a bedraggled fur stole, some big pink and blue tsarist banknotes, and an old necklace of dark, blood-red beads, with a ticket on which was written, in a neat, old-fashioned hand, the single word *Merevaik*: amber.

After a few days' ferry hopping through the beautiful, desolate Moon archipelago, I arrived at Kuressaare, the only settlement of any size on Saaremaa. The pretty market town was readying itself for winter: workmen were putting up Christmas lights, and grit was being spread on the roads. At the tourist office, I learnt that there was no ferry to Ventspils on the Latvian coast in winter, which meant I would have head back to the mainland, lengthening the journey by at least 250 kilometres. I am reluctant to use a car when travelling; there is less opportunity to meet people or observe the surroundings, and it is impossible to take notes with one's hands on the wheel. But in the circumstances, the only thing for it was to hire one.

I drove into Pärnu just as it was getting dark. Located on the estuary of the river of the same name, the city was an early member of the Hanseatic League, trading in timber, amber, furs and salt fish with ports as far afield as Lübeck and King's Lynn. Since the development of its mud baths in the mid-19th century, it had been primarily a resort, but its busy harbour and thriving university generated enough activity to avoid the lassitude that steals over such places in winter. I wandered the grid of streets lined by weatherbeaten timber houses and neoclassical Russian churches in search of the Hotell Bristol, only to find a note on the door announcing that it was closed, and redirecting guests to the Hotell Victoria round the corner. This turned out to be a stroke of luck: the Victoria was a beautiful Art Nouveau mansion, built in the 1920s as the Grand Hotell and looking on to a small park laid out around a statue of the 19th-century Estonian poet Lydia Koidula, whose portrait adorned the 100-krone banknote until Estonia joined the Eurozone in 2011. My room was large and pleasingly irregular, with sloping ceilings and a rickety glazed door opening on to a wrought-iron balcony.

The bar was a long, elegant room painted sage green, with a faded, old-world elegance. I was ordering a drink when I noticed an odd group in the corner: a woman in a burgundy evening dress, chiffon scarf and elbow-length gloves, who looked as if she had just stepped out of a production of *The Cherry Orchard*, accompanied by a girl of about 11 or 12 and an older woman with short-cropped hair and a businesslike demeanour, speaking Russian together. A few minutes later, the two women got up, went over to the piano and began a recital of Russian songs to an audience of about a dozen, most of them elderly Russian ladies. I recognised Tchaikovsky's 'None But the Lonely Heart', the letter scene from *Eugene*

Onegin, and songs by Glinka, Dargomyzhsky and Milyutin. It was quite unexpected and very beautiful, filled with sorrowful pride and nostalgic yearning.

Afterwards, I thanked the singer and asked if she spoke English. She did, a little, and apologised as she went to get changed. While she was gone, the girl sat at the piano and played a melancholy Rachmaninov étude with proficiency and feeling. Her mother returned, wearing jeans and a cardigan, and gave me her card, dismissively pointing out that it was in Estonian, as if this were a distasteful necessity. Born in Volgograd, she had come to Estonia as a child and studied music at the Georg Ots Academy in Tallinn. She now managed the vocal studio of Pärnu Russian Cultural Society, which received a small grant from the Estonian government.

As 20 or so well-dressed Estonians from the local wine club gathered at a long table to hear their chairman expound the merits of terroirs and vintages, she explained that her daughter had been studying piano for six years, and was now at the music school in Pärnu. Keen to practise her English, the girl – who must have been born several years after Estonian independence – told me, with fierce pride: *'I am Russian!'*

The coastal A1 to Riga, the Via Baltica, was a smooth, modern EU-sponsored road. There was little traffic, and almost before I knew it I had crossed the Latvian border – since the Baltic republics joined the Schengen group, the checkpoints had been dismantled. Where the road hugged the shoreline, I could see breakers rolling in through a line of pines.

The approach to the city took me through gritty outskirts of dusty Soviet housing blocks, interspersed with older buildings in various stages of disrepair, amid a tangle of tramlines and trolleybus gantries. The great metropolis of the Baltics was a bustling, grimy place, the scars and glories of its turbulent history cheek by jowl on every street. Past the neo-Byzantine

Russian Orthodox cathedral, the road followed the embankment of the river Dvina. I found a parking place near the
Latvian riflemen statue, and booked in to a chic little hotel in
a 16th-century merchant's house on the edge of the Old Town.

Sitting by an open fire, I scanned the listings in the *Baltic
Times* and saw that there was a concert that night at the
Great Guild. Setting out, I noticed that Russian was more
widely spoken than in Estonia, and that the language was
more visible on advertisements and public notices. Beneath the
shop windows aglow with amber necklaces, however, many
Russians were begging on the streets. Russian-speakers made
up almost 30 per cent of Latvia's population and, with similar
language laws to those in Estonia, half of them could not
get citizenship. The head of the Latvian parliament's foreign
affairs committee, Aleksandrs Kirsteins, had described them
as 'civilian occupiers', and called for them to be put on trains
back to their 'ethnic homeland'.

The Great Guild, built in 1384 as the meeting place of the
city's mercantile elite, dominated the northwestern corner of
the main square. It was heavily restored in the 1860s, though
the Münster room, with its Gothic vaults and musicians'
gallery, preserved its medieval appearance. Around the walls
were painted the arms of all the cities of the Hanseatic League,
including London and Ipswich. I made my way into the auditorium, amid a crowd which, in contrast to the predominantly
elderly audiences who attend classical concerts in Britain,
seemed drawn from all age groups and walks of life.

The Latvian National Symphony Orchestra took the stage
under the baton of the Gibraltarian conductor Karel Mark
Chichon; with the young Latvian pianist Lauma Skride, they
gave a lyrical reading of Schumann's piano concerto. The
real drama, however, was reserved for the second half, with
Tchaikovsky's *Pathétique* symphony (it seemed that Pyotr
Ilyich was to be my travelling companion on this leg of the

journey). From the opening notes, deep in the double basses and bassoons, it was clear that Chichon had little truck with any notion of Tchaikovsky as a sentimental composer. This was a powerful, coherent reading – the march was particularly effective, beginning skittishly and building through heroic swagger until it became a relentless juggernaut. It took us to the threshold of the terrifying world of Shostakovitch, and the despair of the finale was as glacial as anything by the later Russian composer.

As I stopped to admire the towering redbrick cathedral after the concert, I was approached by a Russian couple. The man was apologetic: 'I'm not KGB, not Mafia, not al-Qaeda.' Yuri had lived in Riga for 40 years, and was now in a hostel, as they couldn't get a flat on his pension of 55 lats (about £50) a month. He told me he was 50, but he looked 65. His wife, Elisaveta, was a small woman in a white quilted jacket, her delicate features careworn. Decent, dignified people left high and dry by the receding tide of the Soviet empire.

The next morning, I walked out past the railway station and the market, housed in a row of 1930s Zeppelin hangars. On one side loomed the Academy of Science, a Stalin skyscraper identical to the ones in Moscow and Warsaw; opposite, the pretty onion-domed Church of the Annunciation, a relic of an earlier era of Russian rule. Just up the road, I came across the ruins of the synagogue, destroyed by the invading Nazis in 1941. Behind it stood a monument by the sculptor Elina Lazdina, unveiled in July 2007. A falling wall was held up by columns inscribed with the names of those 'who risked their lives to save more than 400 Jews from death'. Someone had left a single red carnation at the foot of the memorial; others had left pebbles.

I picked up the car and headed out of the city across one of the wide bridges that span the Dvina. West of the river, you enter the province of Kurzeme – known in English as Courland, in German as Kurland. For more than two centuries, tiny Courland was an independent state and even, briefly, a player on the world stage. When the old Livonian Confederation was carved up between Sweden, Denmark and Poland in 1562, the last Master of the Livonian Order, Gotthard Kettler, managed to secure a new power base here. Under Kettler and his descendants, the Duchy of Courland and Semigallia, though nominally a vassal of Lithuania, was effectively autonomous. It reached the zenith of its power and prosperity during the long rule (1642–82) of Gotthard's grandson Jacob. An educated, energetic man who had travelled widely in Western Europe, Jacob built up the Duchy's merchant fleet until it was one of the largest in the continent. Trading out of the Baltic ports of Windau (now Ventspils) and Libau (Liepāja), it exported timber, grain, fish and amber as far afield as England. During the English Civil War, Jacob sent a fleet of warships to the aid of King Charles I. In the 1650s the duchy even established colonies on St Andrew's Island in Gambia, and in Tobago.

On Friday 11th December 1663, in a London coffeehouse, William Harrington, an English merchant trading in the Baltic, told his friend Samuel Pepys:

> The great entertainment and sport of the Duke of Corland, and the princes thereabouts, is hunting; which is not with dogs as we, but he appoints such a day, and summons all the country-people as to a campagnia ... and so making fires every company as they go, they drive all the wild beasts, whether bears, wolves, foxes, swine, and stags, and roes, into the toyle; and there the great men have their stands in such and such places, and shoot at what they have a mind to ...

It was not to last. In 1655, the Swedish army invaded Courland, and in 1658 they took the Duke prisoner. While he was in captivity, his colonies were occupied by the Dutch and his ships destroyed. After his release in 1660, he rebuilt his fleet and recaptured Tobago, but the glory days were over. Maybe the Duchy, with just 200,000 inhabitants, was too small to sustain such global ambitions. As Harrington told Pepys, 'They are not very populous there, by reason that people marry women seldom till they are towards or above thirty; and men thirty or forty years old.' At the mercy of its powerful neighbours, Courland maintained a precarious independence until it was annexed by Russia in 1795.

A straight, single-lane highway took me through forests of pine and birch, past a village where women were selling apples and potatoes by the roadside. As the woods gave way to open country, a fine mist settled on the broad fields where cylindrical bales of hay stood blackening in the autumn damp. Then, for the first time in the three-hour drive, the terrain became hilly, before sweeping down to the coast. It was an exhilarating drive. Some 20 metres below, the Baltic was a startling Aegean blue, with white-topped breakers rolling in to a sandy beach.

From here, the Amber Coast curves down towards Liepāja, where the 'gold of the north' starts to be washed ashore in significant quantities. At the little town of Jūrkalne, a white-washed 18th-century church overlooked a steep, sandy bluff where wind-blasted pines leaned precariously over the edge; the bleached skeletons of their fallen companions lay on the beach below. Jūrkalne, or Feliksberg as it was then known, was the scene of a curious naval engagement during the Napoleonic Wars. On 15th May 1809, Captain Joseph Baker, in command of the frigate HMS *Tartar* out of Leith, ran a Danish sloop aground here. After a shoot-out on the dunes, Baker's crew boarded the abandoned vessel, to find that the Danes had left a candle burning in the powder magazine. With just half an inch to go before the flame reached the explosive, one of Baker's men snuffed out the light.

At Pāvilosta, a sleepy harbour where the river Saka joins the Baltic, I walked down to the beach to make my first attempt at finding amber. A solitary person – it was hard to tell if man or woman – was combing the beach. Swathed in a windcheater and a woollen hat, eyes fixed on the sand and shoulders braced against the wind, the figure stalked the tide-line, occasionally picking up a small object and stowing it away in a pocket. He or she was obviously having more success than I was. Everything that caught my eye turned out, on closer inspection, to be nothing more than an orange pebble. Thinking I might learn something by observing a more experienced amber-hunter, I followed at a discreet distance, but the figure moved away on my approach. After an hour or so, ears and fingers numb with cold, I decided to call it a day.

I was heading for the port of Liepāja, but rather than follow the main highway, which ran inland, I took a minor road connecting the coastal settlements. For much of the way, the track ran through dense pine forest, deeply rutted and churned to mud by timber lorries. Ziemupe was little more than a few farmhouses round a duck pond, a Hansel and Gretel village in the woods. A narrow track led through a juniper grove to a simple, whitewashed Lutheran church on the edge of the dunes, its sober 16th-century interior enlivened by a Baroque altar and pulpit. How much longer it would stand here was anyone's guess. The coast was subject to severe erosion, and about 10 metres had disappeared into the sea in recent years. As I stood on the dunes, the setting sun formed a bar of red in the west. To the north, the beam of the Akmeņrags lighthouse swept the Baltic; to the south, the harbour lights of Liepāja cast their glow into the darkening sky.

Driving on through forests of birch, I was startled by a deer scampering across the road in the beam of my headlights. Then, as I rounded a bend, the trees opened on an astonishing sight: a huge Russian Orthodox cathedral, its gilded domes lit by floodlights. I had arrived in Karosta, the northern suburb of Liepāja founded in 1893 by Tsar Alexander III as a naval base, and used as recently as 1991 by the Soviet military. The road wound down towards a swing bridge across the ship canal that separates Karosta from Liepāja. It was unattended, and its gates padlocked; it had been that way for more than a year since a Georgian tanker ran into it in a storm, obliging residents to make a detour of several kilometres and reinforcing Karosta's isolation.

Liepāja's official tourist brochure tried to make a virtue of Karosta's 'enchanting brutality', waxing lyrical about 'the sweet smell of wild roses among the hard cold steel of twisted barbed wire'. In reality, it was a dismal place, riven by unemployment and drug addiction, its streets dark and deserted on a Saturday night. This was where most of the city's Russian-speaking population lived, the ancillary workers brought here to service the naval base, now stranded and largely jobless in a country that did not want them.

Navigating the empty streets, I eventually found the main road into town. As I stopped at the flashing red light of a level crossing, a long train of blue petrol tankers crossed, the logo of the Russian energy company Gazprom stencilled on the side of each. The Mercedes in front of me sported, beneath its number plate, a small Soviet flag and the initials CCCP. The train passed, the gates lifted, and I drove across the bridge into Liepāja. I found a hotel on a narrow street of wooden houses behind a redbrick Gothic church, opposite a market selling cheap clothes and Soviet memorabilia.

The town straddled a narrow spit of land between Lake Liepāja and the sea, its weather-worn wooden houses laid out on a grid alongside a ship canal lined with freighters, tugs, derricks, warehouses and factory chimneys. With a population of 69,000, Liepāja is Latvia's third city, and its eventful history and commercial importance were evident in its assortment of architectural styles. The neo-Gothic spires of St Joseph's Catholic Cathedral and the Baroque belfry of the Church of the Holy Trinity looked down on fin-de-siècle boulevards, grey postwar concrete and a spanking new pedestrian precinct of neon-lit bars and glass shopping arcades.

The city began as Liva, a fishing village occupied by the Livs, and was Germanised as Libau by the Teutonic Knights. In the 17th century, Jacob Kettler turned it into a major port. Amber was one of its main exports and, although city regulations banned Jews from engaging in commerce, many were active in the trade, either collecting amber themselves or purchasing it from local farmers before selling it on in Memel or Danzig. The quantities involved were substantial: a Memel tradesman, Filip Ebert, was offered one and a half barrels of choice amber on a single occasion. In a letter dated 7th February 1700, a Jewish merchant named Isaac Wulf petitioned the Duke of Courland for the right to conduct trade in the Duchy on the grounds that he had been standing in for his relative Zacharias Daniel as *Stradvogt*, or shoreline supervisor. Daniel, to judge from the letter, had held the post for about 10 years.

The plague that accompanied the Great Northern War, however, killed a third of the population, and the port only regained its importance after its annexation by Russia in 1795. The zenith of its prosperity arrived in the early 20th century, when its parks were laid out, its tramways constructed and many graceful Art Nouveau buildings erected. Liepāja, as it was now called, even became capital of Latvia for a few months at the end of the First World War, when Riga was occupied by the Bolsheviks and the government of the fledgling state holed up here under British protection.

On 22nd June 1941, the day Hitler attacked the USSR, Liepāja was heavily bombarded, devastating its historic centre; on 29th June, German troops entered the city. The genocide of its Jewish population began a month later when groups were marched to the dunes at Šķēde, seven kilometres north of the town, and shot. Within a year, there were just 800 left. A single block of the city was fenced off with barbed wire to form a ghetto and, on 1st July 1942, they were moved into it. Just over a year later, on 18th October 1943, the ghetto was 'liquidated', and the inmates transported to the Kaiserwald concentration camp near Riga. Fewer than 80 survived. After the war, the Soviet Union tightened its grip on the Baltic, and some 940 of the city's inhabitants were deported to Siberia. Because of its naval base, Liepāja became a closed city on Stalin's express orders; even villagers from the surrounding countryside needed a permit to enter. Only with the advent of *glasnost* in the 1980s did Liepāja re-establish contact with the outside world.

Walking around town the next morning, I was struck by the mix of architectural styles; either side of a one-storey, typically Scandinavian wooden house was a Gründerzeit stucco apartment building of the kind to be found in any German city, and a redbrick villa that would not have looked out of place in a London suburb. The grandest building was once the headquarters of the Russian-East-Asian Shipping Line – Liepāja was one of the main ports of departure for emigrants to the United States, with a direct line to New York from 1906. Amber was in evidence everywhere. The Museum of Art and History, located in a mullioned neo-Gothic villa, displayed a large collection of archaeological and ethnographic amber exhibits. Campaigns encouraging townspeople to collect amber on the beach and donate it to the city had resulted in a 123-metre string of beads (the world's longest), and a tall, hourglass-shaped amber clock on the promenade.

I headed to the beach – separated from the town by a long strip of park – to see if I could find some for myself. As the dunes completely screened the town, it seemed oddly remote. There were just a handful of walkers: a few couples, a middle-aged woman walking a dog. Bracing myself against the wind,

I set off along the shore, eyes on the pebble-strewn sand. After a while, I passed a solitary man in a windcheater scanning the tideline. He studiously avoided me. Amber hunters were clearly a reclusive breed. After a couple of hours, I had nothing to show for my efforts except a few pretty stones and a bad cold.

I retreated to the shelter of town to pass an aimless afternoon in bookshops and cafés. During the night, my sleep was disturbed by heavy rain clattering on the metal roofs and gurgling in the gutters until it was driven away by strong winds, howling across the city over the sound of waves rolling in on the beach. I awoke early to a blustery day, with a long, low band of grey cumulus scudding across a pale blue sky, seagulls keening around the church steeples and the smoking chimneys of the wooden houses, and church bells ringing.

I set off around 10am, driving out of town between the reed-fringed expanse of Lake Liepāja, part natural wilderness, part industrial wasteland, and a line of pines crowning the dunes. After Rucava, the forest grew denser and darker, hemming in the road on either side. A few kilometres further on, I crossed the border into Lithuania, and turned off the main road towards the fishing village of Šventoji. The harbour is mentioned in 13th-century chronicles, and appears on 16th-century maps. Amber had been in use here since the Stone Age: archaeological excavations conducted between 1966 and 1976 uncovered a large quantity of Neolithic amber beads and figurines. The finds were now in the National Museum in Riga and the Amber Museum at Palanga, the next stop on my route. In the 18th century, local people paid the lord of the manor a fee for the right to collect amber; in 1739, Šventoji had 10 licensed nets.

Grim ranks of Soviet housing blocks led from the main road to a resort area of chalets and log-cabin style restaurants, all shuttered for the winter. The maritime quarter was charming, however, with its red and white lighthouse and the striking

Modernist church of St Marijos-Juru, an angular building that jutted from the pines like a ship's prow, its slim red steeple visible far out at sea. Beside it, the Šventoji river wound a serpentine path through the dunes.

I reached Palanga by noon, as the rain was turning to sleet. A bronze, bewhiskered bust of Jonas Basanavičius, architect of Lithuanian independence, gazed balefully down the street that bore his name. Leading down to the pier, it was now lined with bars, amusement arcades, casinos and strip clubs. Originally a fishing village, Palanga was first mentioned in written sources in the 13th century. As an outpost of Lithuanian territory separating Livonia from Prussia, it was coveted – unsuccessfully – by the Teutonic Knights, who wished to unite their two domains. During the 16th and 17th centuries it developed into a major port, frequented by Dutch, Swedish and English vessels, and exporting large quantities of timber, flax, grain and amber. A commission sent by the Duke of Prussia reported in November 1581 that Jews were active in the amber trade. In 1701, however, during the Great Northern War, the port was destroyed by the Swedes, and never regained its importance. After the Third Partition of Poland in 1795, Palanga found itself close to the Russo-German border, and became a nest of smugglers; later in the 19th century, its position made it a hotbed of Lithuanian nationalism as pamphlets were smuggled in from Germany.

In 1824, a Polish-Lithuanian count, Mykolas Tiškevičius, tried to revive the port; his heirs had more success when they set about developing the village as a bathing resort, with hotels, sanatoria and spas. Then as now, amber jewellery was a popular souvenir; by the end of the 19th century, some 500 workers were employed in the industry. Nowadays, Palanga is Blackpool on the Baltic, heaving in summer and, on this wet winter day, deserted and forlorn. Miraculously, the Amber Museum was open, in the pink neo-Renaissance palace built by Felix Tiškevičius in 1897 amid landscaped parkland. After the family were forced to flee in 1941, the house became derelict. It was eventually restored in 1957, and the Amber Museum was established here in 1963.

With more than a quarter of a million pieces, this is thought to be the world's largest collection of amber, but it was not the scale that impressed me so much as its magnificence and diversity. Amber was displayed behind powerful magnifying glasses, allowing you to look deep into its glowing interior. There were small, smooth pebbles, and large pieces several inches across. With a diameter of 20 centimetres – almost the size of a football – and weighing 3.5 kilograms, the Sun Stone is the third largest piece of amber in Europe (the other two are in Berlin and Kaliningrad). It had been stolen and recovered twice, most recently in September 2002.

Many of the pieces were clear and golden, others opaque and rough-textured. Some had a flaky surface, almost like a worked Stone Age flint. Many contained amber within amber – droplets caught in later resin, forming subtle striations; others bore the impression of bark or leaves. Then there were the inclusions, fragments of plants and animals trapped within the resin: flies, beetles, moths, ants, spiders, centipedes, dragon-flies, and even vertebrates, the most stunning of which was an entire gecko. Amber with reptile inclusions was so prized that pieces were often forged as early as the Middle Ages.

Apart from natural amber, there were the artefacts made from it. One room was devoted to replicas of the Neolithic carvings found at Juodkrantė on the Curonian Spit in the 19th century – beads, amulets, circular charms, pendants and human figures – beautiful pieces, eloquent in their simplicity. There were amber rosaries, monstrances and other devotional artefacts made by Lithuanian craftsmen in the 17th and 18th centuries, and some bizarre Soviet trophies including a bust of Lenin and even a model tractor. A display showed how goods and coins from as far afield as Rome, Byzantium and Smolensk had been found in the region, traded in exchange for Baltic amber.

From Palanga, the Amber Route continues south to Klaipėda. Just south of Kretinga, an impatient driver leaned on his horn as I slowed the car to a crawl in the nearside lane. By my calculations, I had just crossed what was once the boundary between the empire of the Tsar of all the Russias and that of the German Kaiser, but I could see no trace of it – no monument, no plaque, not even a line on the tarmac. I have an old postcard, dated 1900, that shows the frontier post with its barrier, customs house, and sentry-box painted in chevrons. It looks peaceful enough, a sleepy country crossing. Just 14 years later it was the front line between two empires at war. The first fighting took place on Monday 3rd August 1914, when a column of Cossacks made a raid across the border here and was repulsed by the garrison at Memel. The main Russian advance, however, came further south, in the fierce, swiftly moving campaign described by Solzhenitsyn in his novel *August 1914*.

Amid the gleaming glass on Potsdamer Platz in Berlin, nothing but a line of cobbles marked the course of the wall that divided the city for decades. It was now possible to drive from Derry into Donegal up an ordinary road, where once you would have met the watchtowers and armoured cars of the British Army. Here too, in the flatlands north of Klaipėda, there was nothing whatever to mark this once-momentous division – just waterlogged fields.

Yet I was entering one of the most contested slivers of land in European history. Memelland, as it once was, was the northernmost part of East Prussia. The pagan Old Prussians who lived here in the 13th century paid allegiance to the Grand Duchy of Lithuania, then at war with the Teutonic Knights. Around 1252, the Knights invaded, initiating two centuries of conflict that only ended in 1422, when a weakened Teutonic Order made peace with a united Poland-Lithuania at the Treaty of Melno. Memelland was one of the few gains the Knights were able to extract from the agreement, establishing a border that was to remain in place until 1918.

The Knights styled themselves the Lords of Amber, and exercised total control of the trade, supplying rosary beads to much of Europe. They enforced their lucrative monopoly with an iron hand, forbidding the collection of amber from the beaches on pain of death. After their last Grand Master converted to Lutheranism in 1524, Memelland became a part of the Prussian state and eventually, in 1871, the most north-easterly outpost of the German Reich. Throughout the centuries of German rule, the territory had a substantial Lithuanian-speaking population, known as Prussian Lithuanians or *Lietuvininkai.*

I turned on to a narrow road towards Karkle, a fishing village reputed to be a good place to find amber, through the ubiquitous pine and birch forests, magically spangled with snow. Records show that back in 1540, Karkelbeck, as it was then called, was a substantial town; now it had dwindled to a cluster of houses nestling around a pond in the woods. I walked down a wooden stairway to the beach, a wide curve of sand and pebbles dusted with snow and ice. The wind was bracing. A handful of people strolled along the foreshore, their eyes on the tideline. A more serious amber hunter, carrying waders and a net, strode purposefully past me into the distance. I headed north, picking through clumps of seaweed. From time to time, my eye was caught by some bright object, but before I had picked it up I realised it was just a pretty piece of golden quartzite. After a couple of hundred yards, I came to a fast-flowing stream that carved a deep channel through the dunes before describing a hairpin across the foreshore and disgorging into the sea. A couple of young men roared past me on quad bikes, fording it easily, but I realised that without waders, it marked the northern limit of my exploration. I headed back the way I came, scanning the tideline.

Amber hunting is not as easy as it might appear. The stuff doesn't sit around in heaps waiting to be picked up, nor do polished specimens lie gleaming in the sun's rays. To spot a piece of amber on the beach, you need gimlet eyes, knowledge of the many colours and forms it takes, and an understanding of its properties. Amber is light enough to float in salt water, but the Baltic is so mildly saline that a piece of the stuff is only marginally buoyant in it. Agitated, it will float; left to settle, it will sink. Pieces of amber are borne in on the waves but, unless something detains them, the sea will draw them back again. That is why amber hunters don waders to stand waist-deep in icy water to catch these fugitive fragments of Baltic gold.

If there is such a thing as beginner's luck, I wasn't having any, so I decided to take a more systematic approach, scanning the shallow pools where a piece of amber might be stranded. And then, suddenly, there it was, lying in the lee of a ridge of sand and pebbles that had blocked its return to the sea. It was not large or lovely, but it was indisputably amber: a cylindrical segment broken from a stalactite of resin, like an icicle, or a drip of wax from a candle, just over a centimetre long and about half a centimetre in section; a semi-opaque tortoiseshell colour, and on one side it bore the imprint of the bark of the tree from which it had oozed some 50 million years ago.

CHAPTER 4

SHIFTING SANDS

Flaky snow started to fall as I drove across a wide modern bridge over the River Danė and into Klaipėda. The Old Town was an appealing jumble of cobbled streets, neoclassical stucco and gabled brick warehouses that gave some idea of what the rest of the city must have looked like before it was devastated in the last months of the Second World War.

The city's location was crucial. It was here, on the narrow strait that connects the Curonian Lagoon to the Baltic, that Poppo von Osterna, Grand Master of the Teutonic Knights, built a castle in 1252 to control access to the lagoon and the River Nemunas – known to Germans as the Memel – which empties into it. The Curonian Spit, the 100-kilometre sandbar that divides the lagoon from the sea, provided an easier means of communication with the Knights' domains in Prussia than the marshy mainland. The town that grew up around the castle was peopled by German settlers. Admitted to the Hanseatic League in 1254, it became a major entrepôt for timber (much of it exported to England), grain, leather, furs – and amber. Customs documents record that 27 Prussian *stein* (almost 300 kg) of amber was exported from here in 1677.

But the location also made it a target. The Swedes captured the city in 1628, and in 1757, during the Seven Years War, a 70,000-strong Russian army advanced on Memel. After a five-day artillery bombardment that could be heard 100 miles away in Königsberg, the city surrendered. The Russians held the town until 1762, when the Empress Elizabeth died and her successor, Peter III, withdrew from the conflict.

I checked in to an elegant hotel, the Europa, on the main square, an expanse of cobbles dominated by a cream-stuccoed neoclassical theatre. Surveying this gracious civic space, I struggled to banish from my mind a flickering newsreel of Hitler standing on the theatre's swastika-hung balcony on 23rd March 1939 to announce, with Chaplinesque gesticulations, the return of Memel to the Reich. The hotel was built in 1854, and used to be called the Hotel de Russie; after the Russians besieged the city (again) during the First World War, it was renamed the Baltischer Hof. My room, papered in dark red and furnished with a heavy mahogany desk, bedstead and wardrobe, exuded the lugubrious comfort of Middle Europe.

After the First World War, the Treaty of Versailles placed Memelland under League of Nations jurisdiction, enforced by a contingent of French troops. On 11th January 1923, Lithuanian nationalists expelled the garrison, and the following May the city was annexed by the new Republic of Lithuania, and thenceforth known as Klaipėda. German-speakers, who called themselves Memellanders, still made up almost 50 per cent of the population. They managed to maintain reasonably cordial relations with their Lithuanian neighbours until, in the 1930s, local Nazis began to agitate for reunification with Germany. As Hitler steamed toward Klaipėda aboard the pocket battleship *Deutschland*, the Lithuanian government had little choice but to relinquish the territory. Many Lithuanians, particularly those who had played an active role in the city's political and cultural life, fled. So too did 8,000 of its Jewish inhabitants, whose presence dated back to 1567. Of those who remained, the majority perished in the Holocaust. The synagogue and Jewish graveyard were destroyed in 1939; a plaque at the end of Synagogue Street, in the southern part of the Old Town, marks the site.

By the autumn of 1944, Soviet forces had encircled Memel, and in January 1945, they captured the city. Those Germans who had not fled were expelled. Initially, the area was administered as part of the Kaliningrad region, but in 1948 it was transferred to the Lithuanian Soviet Socialist Republic. At the time, this seemed little more than a piece of internal reorganisation, but on the break-up of the Soviet Union it ensured that Klaipėda would become part of independent Lithuania. The northernmost ice-free harbour in the eastern Baltic, it was now Lithuania's third city and main port.

Given its history, it is not surprising that the region has long held a powerful emotional resonance for both Lithuanians and Germans. In a small public garden stood the Monument to the United Lithuania. Set up in 2003, it took the form of an incomplete colonnade: a large square pillar, representing Lithuania Major, supported one end of the pediment; a smaller Doric column, representing Klaipėda, held up the other; while beyond it, the pediment broke off in a jagged edge to evoke the lost region that now forms the Kaliningrad *oblast* of Russia. The monument was inscribed with a quotation from the *Lietuvninkai* poet Ieva Simonaitytė, who was born in 1897 under German rule and died in 1978 under that of the Soviets: 'We are one nation, one land, one Lithuania.'

For the Germans, the region's importance was enshrined in the lyrics of what was to become their national anthem, Hoffmann von Fallersleben's 'Das Lied der Deutschen'. The opening line, *'Deutschland, Deutschland über alles'*, has become notorious, but when it was written in 1841, a united Germany was no more than an ideal, and the song was intended as a paean not to military expansionism but to the political union of a fragmented people whose homeland stretched *'Von der Maas bis an die Memel'* – from the Meuse to the Memel.

I woke the next morning to find the town silent under snow. In one of the old warehouses on the bank of the Danė, I came across a crafts and antique shop selling books, handicrafts and amber jewellery. I bought a German guide to the Curonian Spit, and a book of old photographs of Memel in the 19th and early 20th centuries. Many were reproduced from postcards. On one, dated 1st April 1904, a British visitor had written:

> Very best wishes for a happy Eastertide. Had a most awful time coming here, not so ill, as frightened! Never thought the ship would weather the storm. Think I must return by train. Couldn't possibly go though such an experience again. I was five nights instead of three on the sea. It is like a nightmare to me. Hope you are all well ...

I hope the writer had a safe journey home. His fears were by no means exaggerated. In October 1900, *Lloyd's List* reported: 'A Memel telegram states that a capsized vessel is stranded and totally wrecked at Karkelbeck. The fate of those on board is not known.'

Only a narrow strait separated the city from the Curonian Spit, whose wooded shore was visible across the water. The old postal route connecting Berlin with St Petersburg ran down the Spit, and in January 1717, the panels of the Amber Room trundled along it in 18 crates loaded on to carts on their way from Berlin. In Memel, the consignment was received by Pyotr Bestuzhev-Ryumin, Lord Steward (and lover) of the Duchess of Courland, the future Empress Anna Ioannovna; from there it was sent under military escort via Riga to St Petersburg.

My plan was to drive the length of the Spit and across the Russian border into Kaliningrad. I manoeuvred the car up the clanking metal ramps on to the car ferry behind a big Toyota 4x4 with tinted windows and Russian plates. The ferry turned round in the channel and, almost before I knew it, we had arrived at Smiltynė on the far shore. As I drove between forested dunes, with the mainland visible to the left across the widening lagoon, the contrast was surreal: all around me was natural wilderness, but beyond the water rose the tall new buildings and dockyard cranes of Klaipėda. And then, as the shipping terminal slid from view, all I could see was the low, wooded shore of the mainland.

The dunes and forests of the Spit shelter elk, wild boar, roe deer, brown hare, foxes and smaller predators such as pine marten, stoat and weasel; its skies are patrolled by sea eagles, white-tailed eagles, black kites, buzzards and ospreys. The waves that crash into the Baltic shore are skimmed by black-headed gulls, black and common terns, oystercatchers, red-throated divers and ringed plovers, while thousands of waterbirds and waders winter in the shallows of the lagoon. Wilhelm von Humboldt, who visited the Spit in 1809, observed that it 'is so peculiar that if you don't want your soul to be missing a wonderful impression, you must see it, just like Spain or Italy.' The Spit is designated a UNESCO World Heritage Site.

I drove gingerly along the narrow, ungritted road – all the more gingerly after passing a car that had skidded into the ditch; the driver, mercifully uninjured, was calling for help on his mobile. Not far beyond, two redbrick 19th-century buildings stood to the left of the road: barracks built to house French PoWs from the Franco-Prussian War, who were put to work planting trees on the dunes. A few kilometres further on, I stopped and walked down to the edge of the lagoon. The landscape, under snow, was almost absurdly beautiful, the sun casting a golden glow on the reeds that skirted the brown, brackish water. The air was bracing, and rich with the scent of pine; all I could hear was the wind in the trees.

Just before Juodkrantė, on the lagoon side, I came to a secluded cove fringed with reeds, lined with fishing boats and littered with all the appealing junk of a working boatyard: oildrums, rope, old tyres and planks. This was Amber Bay, a sleepy place today, but once the site of a substantial mining operation. In 1857, after dredgers employed by the Prussian government to deepen the lagoon for shipping began turning up pieces of amber, two businessmen from Memel, Wilhelm Stantien and Moritz Becker, saw an opportunity and offered not only to do the work at their own expense, but also to pay a daily rent in return for any amber they might find. They began dredging with just four machines, worked by horses, but the operation expanded rapidly, and at its peak employed 1,000 labourers and more than 20 steam dredgers, two tugboats and about 100 lighters or barges. The operation yielded up to 70 tonnes of amber a year and brought prosperity to Juodkrantė, then known by its German name of Schwarzort. By the 1890s, however, the deposits were worked out, and the firm of Stantien und Becker transferred its operations to Palmnicken (now Yantarny) on the Samland coast.

While dredging the lagoon, workers uncovered a large hoard of Neolithic amber artefacts dating back to the 3rd millennium BC: beads, amulets, circular charms, pendants, human and animal figurines, together with many pieces of raw, unworked amber. At first, the company officers gave the figurines away to visitors as souvenirs, but as they began to attract the attention of scholars, the firm called in Professor Richard Klebs, a geologist from the University of Königsberg, to examine the finds. Klebs managed to collect and catalogue 434 pieces, publishing them in his book *Der Bernsteinschmuck der Steinzeit von der Baggerei bei Schwarzort* (*Stone Age Amber Adornments from the Mines at Schwarzort*) in 1882. The Schwarzort Treasure, as it became known, was exhibited in Berlin, London, Chicago and St Petersburg. After Klebs's death, the collection was bought by Königsberg University. In the destruction of that city at the end of the Second World War, most of it was lost; just five pieces loaned to the University of Göttingen survived. Thanks to the meticulous illustrations in Klebs's book, however, it was possible to make the replicas I had seen in the Amber Museum at Palanga.

South of Juodkrantė, the road turned sharply to the right and crested a high dune. I got out and walked to the summit, from where I could see across the swaying tops of the pines to the Baltic, blue-green with white-crested waves under fast-moving grey cumulus. It was perishingly cold. To the east, on the lagoon side, the trees surrendered to a landscape of fearsome barrenness, a Saharan sweep of sand startling at this northerly latitude. This was the Nagliai Reserve, one of the remaining areas of unplanted, unstabilised sand, stretching some 10 kilometres to the south. There were three main peaks: the nearest was the Ariu Dune, known to the Germans as the Scharfenberg; beyond it rose the Nagliai (Negeln) and Vingkope (Wingkap) dunes. Sculpted by the wind into curves of severe, geometric beauty, they cascaded down to the very edge of the lagoon, engulfing everything in their path.

The Curonian Spit was formed by wind-blown sand around 7,000 years ago, a shifting, volatile landscape that was stabilised by forests of linden that sprang up in prehistoric times. By the mid-18th century, however, the demand for timber for the shipyards at Memel had stripped the peninsula of most of its woodlands. By the end of the century, just 10 per cent remained. Without trees to break the force of the wind, and without their root systems to hold the friable soil in place, the restless dunes broke loose once more, engulfing whole villages, while any remaining trees in their path were sandblasted to whitened stumps.

Between 1675 and 1934, 14 villages were lost. One of them, Negeln, bequeathed its name to the dune under which it lay buried. After the original settlement was engulfed in 1675, the village moved further south three times until finally, in 1836, it was abandoned, and the displaced inhabitants founded Preila and Pervalka further down the Spit. Travelling through here in 1860, the Königsberg geologist Julius Schumann found a freshly uncovered churchyard, with skulls, bones and fragments of coffins strewn amid the sand. In the 19th century, an intensive programme of reforestation was initiated, and a continuous dune wall was built along the Baltic side. As a result, forest, mostly pine and birch, both natural and planted, now covered some two-thirds of the Spit. But it remained a fragile ecosystem, under constant threat from erosion, and dependent on untiring management for its survival.

From here on, the main road ran down the middle of the Spit; as all the settlements sheltered on the lagoon side, they had to be reached by secondary roads. A few kilometres further on, the road to Pervalka led off to the left; beside it, atop a tree-clad dune, stood a strange monument carved from the trunk of an ancient oak. It commemorated the poet and folklorist Liudvikas Rėza (Ludwig Rhese), whose home village of Karwaiten (Karvaiciai in Lithuanian) lay beneath the dunes to the south. By the time Rėza was born in 1776, Karvaiciai was already doomed: the dunes had engulfed the forest by the edge of the village, and the sand reached halfway up the windows of the deanery. The villagers struggled on until 1795, when the last families relocated to Juodkrantė. The wooden bust of Rėza scanned the dunes as if in search of his buried home; beneath it were inscribed a few lines from his poem 'The Drowned Village':

> Dear Traveller, stop at these wretched ruins!
> Several years ago gardens blossomed around the cottages,
> And the village extended from the forest to the lagoon.
> Alas! What do you see today? Only the wind-drifted sand.

By the time I arrived at Nida it was growing dark. It was a fairly sizeable place – more a small town than a village – but almost completely closed out of season. The Hotel Jurate, where I had booked a room, was an imposing gabled edifice set back from the road; it was rebuilt in the later 19th century, so there was sadly no trace of the window on which Queen Luise, in flight from Napoleon's army in 1807, scratched a few lines from Goethe's *Wilhelm Meister* with her diamond ring:

> Wer nie sein Brod mit Thränen aß,
> Wer nicht die kummervollen Nächte,
> Auf seinem Bette weinend saß,
> Der kennt Euch nicht, ihr himmlischen Mächte.[1]

I was the only guest. The room was small and spartan, but clean. The furniture – wardrobe, desk, bedside table – was all modern. Just one item stood out: an old-fashioned, dark-varnished birch chair, with a fabric-covered seat. I was looking at a piece of the old Soviet Union. I upended it and, sure enough, a mimeographed label glued to the underside carried the logo of the USSR and the address of a factory in Siauliai. Below was the word стул – chair in Russian; I could also decipher the 'Index' followed by a number, 'Article' (ditto), and a series of prices. The date was 1979 – had the chair been British or West German, I would have dated it to the 1950s.

The next morning was fiercely cold, and a light snow was falling. There were few people about. A cultural centre attached to the tourist office displayed a small exhibition of local art; the café there, and the Kursis around the corner, were the only places open. Fishing boats and yachts were moored in the harbour, though the yacht club was closed for the winter. In a wooden hut, under a flickering fluorescent tube, a red-faced woman in a yellow sou'wester was selling freshly caught fish: cod, sole, halibut and sprats from the Baltic, pike-perch *(sterkas)* and eels from the lagoon. For all its charm, Nida was a dead end. On

---

1 Who never ate their bread with tears,/ Who never spent nights full of care/ Weeping on their bed,/ Does not know you, you heavenly powers.

one side was the lagoon; two kilometres in the other direction, the Baltic; four kilometres to the south, the Russian border. The only way out was back, 50 kilometres to Klaipėda.

The town, known in German as Nidden, is first mentioned in documents of the Teutonic Knights in 1437; the post station was transferred here from Pilkoppen – now Morskoye on the Russian side – in 1745. By the 1880s it was a flourishing resort, and a meeting place for artists and writers. The artistically inclined hotelier Hermann Blöde gathered around him such people as the poet Karl Zuckmayer, the composer Engelbert Humperdinck and the painters Lovis Corinth and Max Pechstein. A leading member of the Expressionist group Die Brücke, Pechstein came here in 1909; his powerful paintings of the strange landscape of the dunes represent a key moment in his development. The psychoanalyst Karl Abraham, who visited in August 1917, wrote to his mentor Sigmund Freud:

> We too have landed in a remote corner, the most north-easterly of the fatherland. Nidden is about in the centre of the Spit of land about 100km long, on the Kurian lagoon, on the shore of which I am sitting writing. In absolutely wonderful weather we are enjoying nature in this secluded Spit of land with its huge forests and sand-hills . . .

I walked north up Pamario Street to the church, which stood amid pine trees atop a steep dune; a tall redbrick building with a slim tower and a steep roof, dating from the 1880s. In the graveyard under the trees, Germans and Lithuanians lay at rest together. The wooden grave markers of the fisherfolk, with their strange bird and animal forms, looked oddly pagan amid the more conventional wrought-iron crosses. Blöde, who died in 1934, was buried here alongside his parents. Here too were the graves of Fritz and Dorothea Fröse, whose forebears – fishermen, postmasters and later hoteliers – had lived in Nida since

1720. Their son Johann Michael introduced electricity to the town in the 1920s, but the entire family fled during the Second World War, and were now dispersed throughout Germany and the USA.

One side of the church was covered in wooden scaffolding. As I approached, a yellow-jacketed roofer called down to me in English, asking if I wanted to see inside. I nodded vigorously, and he clambered down and showed me in through the main door, genuflecting before the altar before making his way to the vestry to turn on the lights. The whitewashed interior, with its fine hammer-beam roof, was beautiful in its austerity. On the soffit of the chancel arch was painted, in Gothic letters, a verse from the Gospel of St Matthew (5:8), in Luther's translation: *'Selig sind, die reinen Herzens sind, denn sie werden Gott schauen.'* (Blessed are the pure in heart, for they shall see God.)

Andrius was a sturdy, weatherbeaten man in his fifties, missing the final joints of three fingers on his right hand. He and his colleague had been re-tiling the roof for the past month, and hoped to finish the job the following week. They were not local, but from a town in central Lithuania. As I was about to leave, he suddenly asked if I wanted to see the view from the top. We ascended the stone stairs to the gallery, passed through the organ loft and climbed a set of rickety wooden steps through the belfry and into the roof space. Stacked on the boards were a number of simple wooden crosses from the churchyard, dating mostly from the early 20th century; most of the names were German. I stepped gingerly on to a flimsy duckboard and peered through a skylight half obscured by snow at the view across the treetops to the lagoon. Andrius slapped one of the stout oak beams and said approvingly, 'Very good construction. Very strong.' It would have had to be to withstand the winds off the Baltic and the heavy snowfalls.

A little way beyond the church, on a high dune overlooking the lagoon, stood Thomas Mann's two-storey summerhouse.

Painted in the oxblood, blue and white characteristic of the region, it was one of the few houses in Nida to retain its thatch; most were now tiled. The curator, a German woman in her forties, spoke no English, so we conversed in her native tongue. Mann, she told me, first visited Nida in 1929, the year he won the Nobel Prize for literature, and was so taken by the place he commissioned the house to be built. A photo showed him and his wife Katya arriving in a horse-drawn *fiaker* as the locals line the street to greet them.

The unique landscape of the Curonian Spit made a powerful impact on him, as he explained in a talk to the Rotary Club back in Munich in 1931:

> The impression is elementary and almost oppressive, not so much when you stand on the heights and can see both bodies of water, as in the steeply enfolded areas. It is a trackless waste: just sand, sand, and sky ... The sea and the shore have a primitive, elemental nature ...

An outspoken opponent of the Nazis, Mann emigrated to the United States in 1939, settling at Pacific Palisades near Los Angeles. When the Germans occupied the Spit, the house was appropriated – with one of those coarse ironies in which the Nazis specialised – by Hermann Göring as his hunting lodge. After decades of post-war neglect, it was painstakingly restored, and reopened as a museum in the 1960s.

Glazed double doors opened on to a room with a grand piano and windows looking out through pine trees to the lagoon. Other rooms were given over to displays of photographs, newspaper cuttings and editions of *Joseph and his Brothers*, on which Mann worked here. In the visitors' book, one comment, in German, read: 'I visited Pacific Palisades last year. It is clear how much he loved a sea view.'

In the afternoon, I drove across to the Baltic side in the hope of finding more amber. As soon as I left the cover of the trees and clambered down the wooden stairs to the shore, I was caught in a relentless north-easterly, which whipped up the sand so that it ricocheted off the back of my jacket. In the distance, to the south, the sun broke through the cloud, illuminating a high dune and a steel watchtower that marked the border with Russia. The waves rolled in ferociously, and the wind detached fragments of foam and sent them scurrying across the sand like small devils. As the rattling on the back of my jacket grew more insistent, I realised that it was not just sand but hailstones, and made a dash for the shelter of the woods. The ground seemed solid, a rich amalgam of leaf mould, lichen, sphagnum moss and toadstools, but the humus was just inches deep; beneath it, starkly visible wherever a tree had been felled by the wind, was sand, a reminder that it was only painstaking forest management that held this landscape together.

By 9.30pm I was ensconced in my room. It was snowing relentlessly. At about 10, the night was split by a sizzling bolt of lightning and a terrific clap of thunder. Eventually, I drifted into sleep, to be woken at intervals by strange, tortured sounds of creaking, cracking and breaking. I awoke to find that three feet of snow had fallen in the night. I had planned to cross the border that day, but it didn't look as though I'd be going anywhere. Men were out with shovels clearing the footpaths, but the hotel drive was still deep in snow. When I pointed to the fluffy white mound that was my rented car, the hotel staff fell about laughing and offered me another night's stay for free. It would take a snowplough to clear the drive, and the team had more urgent priorities: the schools, the clinic and the fire station.

There was nothing unusual about snow in Lithuania, of course, but locals couldn't remember such a heavy fall for a decade or more. People tramped about in gumboots wielding shovels and long poles to dislodge the snow from the trees. A large branch had sheared off the false acacia outside my hotel window under the weight of snow, narrowly missing the car. A wizened silver birch across the road had suffered a similar fate, and up by Thomas Mann's house, several stout pines had shattered, while others had been uprooted and leaned like wounded soldiers on the shoulders of their comrades.

The enforced inactivity gave me an opportunity to observe the life of the town. With few people around, the same faces kept popping up. There was a little crowd from the Town Hall – a modern brick building on the main square – who lunched at the Kursis on the dot of noon. At 1pm, the man from the tourist information centre showed up at the café. I visited the centre twice in the course of the day to email Kaliningrad to explain the delay. The young woman on duty was cheerful, intelligent, and extremely tall. She told me that most local people who weren't employed in the tourist industry worked for the municipality, the clinic, or the National Park; I could recognise the latter by the logo on their windcheaters and the sides of their 4x4s. Many houses were now second homes occupied by weekenders from Klaipėda, and shut up for the winter, the water turned off to prevent the pipes from freezing. Although fishing was no longer the mainstay of the economy, there was still a small fleet. Her father was a fisherman; to her great anxiety, he had gone out on the lagoon two days before, despite the weather.

The next morning, the driveway had been cleared, and I was free to continue my journey. As I drove past the red and white striped lighthouse, the extent of the damage to the forest became evident. Men were out with cherrypickers to collect the broken branches, which were hauled away by tractor to be stacked by the side of the road. I reached the border in minutes. This had only been an international frontier since 1923, when Memelland became part of Lithuania, and seemed like an arbitrary line drawn across the middle of the Spit, but it was in fact an extension of the border formed by the River Nemunas on the landward side of the lagoon, and dated back to the 14th century, when it divided the counties of Memel and Fischhausen.

The Russian guards were brisk but not unpleasant. In response to my enquiry whether anyone spoke English, a woman in khaki uniform with stars on her epaulettes replied with a cheerful *'nyet'*. A helpful Lithuanian driver, who spoke both English and Russian, translated as they checked my visa and car documents. Ten minutes later I was driving past a sign saying 'Welcome to Russia'.

Beyond the frontier, the road narrowed and had not been cleared; the forest, mostly birch, was deeper and wilder. After a couple of kilometres, the dark, shaggy forms of two huge wild boar shambled across the road in front of the car. A little further on, I turned down a narrow lane to Morskoye, the first settlement on the Russian side. Pillkoppen, as it used to be called, was once an important place; in 1283, the Teutonic Knights built a castle here – *pils*, in the Baltic languages, means castle – and a village grew up around it. But the settlement was constantly menaced by the shifting dunes, the castle fell into ruin, and the population was devastated by plague. What was left of the old settlement lay buried beneath the Altdorfer Berg, a large dune that jutted into the lagoon to the south.

Apart from a few householders clearing snow, the village was deserted. Here and there, some redbrick houses were under construction, their style a curious architectural nod to the old German villas of the region. In the garden of a traditional ochre-painted wooden house stood a modern metal sculpture topped with a cross, bearing the inscription, *'Den ehemaligen Bewohnern von Pillkoppen zum Gedenken.'* ('To the memory of the former inhabitants of Pillkoppen.') The house once belonged to Franz Epha (1828–1904), the forest inspector who devoted forty years to stabilising the dunes; his activities saved the village from being engulfed by the mountain of sand that now bears his name.

I drove on, through birch woods shattered by storms, to the next settlement. Rybachy – Rossitten – was situated on a headland projecting into the lagoon; looking back, I could view the Spit as far as the border, the sweep of dark green forest interrupted by snow-clad dunes marching down to the water's edge. Rybachy was a larger, grittier place than Morskoye, its old wooden houses interspersed with low-rise Soviet housing blocks. There was a café-bar, a handful of shops, and a small 19th-century redbrick church on ulitsa Gagarina. The old parsonage opposite was now a school. A potholed track led down to a small harbour lined with derelict industrial buildings.

Near the church, a pink two-storey building housed the Rybachy Biological Station for the study of bird migration. Every year, more than ten million birds, mostly passerines – chaffinches, siskins, goldcrests, willow warblers, great tits and starlings – which dislike crossing large areas of water, follow the Spit during their spring and autumn migration from north-west Russia to southern Europe and Africa. The importance of the Spit as a migratory route was first recognised in the late 19th century by Johannes Thienemann, a German pastor and ornithologist. In 1901, he set up the Vogelwarte Rossitten, the world's first institution to undertake the large-scale ringing of birds. Now run by the Zoological Institute of the Russian Academy of Sciences, it trapped between 50,000 to 100,000 birds a year in mist nets on the dunes before ringing and releasing them.

South of Rybachy, through the trees on my left, shimmered Lake Tschaika (Seagull Lake), the only sizeable body of freshwater on the Spit. Sadly, the seagulls had long since departed; no one seemed to know why. In a lonely graveyard on its shore, both Thienemann and Epha were buried. I was now approaching the narrowest point of the Spit. The wall of sea dunes crept closer and closer to the road on the right; to the left, through the trees, the lagoon was visible a few hundred yards away. Everywhere, the sound of the wind and the sea.

Past Lesnoy – a medium-sized settlement with a big new hotel and some flashy modern villas – the Spit broadened. The dunes shrank away, the countryside became less forested, and the extraordinary landforms of the Spit mutated into something more mundane: flat farmland intersected by broad roads lined with limes – the first mature deciduous trees I had seen for more than 100 kilometres. And yet, if the topography of the region I was entering seemed quotidian, its geopolitics could not have been more extraordinary, for this was Russia's forgotten outpost: the Kaliningrad *oblast*.

CHAPTER 5

BACK IN THE USSR

'You're from London and you're going to Kaliningrad?' a young man in Lithuania asked. 'That's like me going to Mars.'

I drove through a tract of concrete that could have been anywhere in the former Warsaw Pact, down potholed lanes flanked by decrepit industrial premises. Raw, unlovely, it was by far the biggest city I'd been in since Riga. With its Communist street names, Khrushchev-era housing and *Komsomolskaya Pravda* on sale at roadside kiosks, it felt like I was back in the USSR.

Kaliningrad is one of Europe's strangest anomalies, a pocket of territory separated since the collapse of the Soviet Union from the rest of Russia by Poland and Lithuania, both now members of Nato and the EU. Conquered from Germany at the end of the Second World War, the region measures some 200 kilometres from east to west and a little over 100 kilometres north to south – about the size of Northern Ireland – and has just under a million inhabitants.

The car rumbled over bone-shaking cobbles, across a wide modern road and into a gated estate of new villas near the northern end of Gorky Street. The Hotel Albertina was a bizarre rotunda, designed to appeal to German tourists and decorated with memorabilia of the university from which it took its name but from which it was at least two kilometres distant, and with which it had no official connection. Although it was the cheapest hotel my tour operator deigned to recommend, it seemed luxurious after my spartan lodgings in Nida.

I arrived in the late afternoon, having driven across the Samland Peninsula, a thumb of land that juts into the southeastern Baltic, through a landscape of flat fields, redbrick farmhouses, lakes and ponds, where storks' nests perched atop the telegraph poles. Until 1945, this was part of East Prussia, a distant outpost of the Reich, its capital, Königsberg (now the city of Kaliningrad) 600 kilometres from Berlin. Even after Prussia assumed the leadership of the German Empire in 1871, it remained a remote region, with its mysterious forests and amber-strewn coast, where many inhabitants had roots predating its medieval conquest by the Teutonic Knights. Between the wars, the province was separated from the rest of Germany by a strip of Polish territory. At the Potsdam Conference in July 1945, an almost straight line was drawn across East Prussia from Belarus to the Baltic; everything to the south was assigned to Poland, while the territory to the north became the Kaliningrad *oblast* (region) of the Soviet Union.

For almost half a century, Kaliningrad was a forbidden city, heavily militarised, closed to foreigners, and unknown to many Soviet citizens. Even in the 21st century, it attracted few visitors, mostly Scandinavian businesspeople or Germans seeking their roots. In post-Soviet times the area acquired a grim reputation for crime, drug addiction and HIV. This was not enhanced by the nomenclature, which created the impression of a Soviet timewarp. While the rest of Russia reverted to pre-revolutionary names, the region and its capital commemorated Mikhail Kalinin, nominal head of state during Stalin's rule, and its streets were still named after Marx and Lenin. In a region that was part of Germany until 1945, there were no pre-Communist Russian names to revive.

With barely an hour of daylight left, I didn't venture into the centre but explored the neighbourhood on foot. The grey, slushy streets were lined with sinister-looking housing blocks, the entrances covered with graffiti. Nearby was a brand-new Viktoria Supermarket. Founded by two local ex-seamen, the chain was now expanding to St Petersburg. The aisles contained a mix of the familiar – Cif cleaner, Cherry Blossom shoe polish – and the unfamiliar – open freezer chests of scampi and crab sticks that you bagged up with a metal scoop, and three large plastic tanks, one crowded with fat golden carp, another with silver-grey trout and a third in which green langoustine waved their claws despairingly.

The hotel manageress arrived the next morning. After some initial confusion, we realised that we both spoke German. The breakfast room was completely German-themed, with views of old Königsberg and busts of the university's famous alumni, including Immanuel Kant and E. T. A. Hoffmann. It all seemed faintly bogus except for an old upright piano; I lifted the lid to see that it was made by Julius Heinrich Zimmerman in Leipzig. Lyudmila, the manageress, told me she learnt German in the tourism industry. I couldn't suppress a fleeting fantasy that, like Vladimir Putin, she learnt it in the KGB. A raven-haired woman in her forties with a gash of red lipstick, she looked like a glamorous villainess in a Bond movie. I asked her whether it was difficult to park in town.

'*Was meinen Sie, Parkplätze?*' she wailed in blank incomprehension.

It is only when I drove into the city centre that I realised the misunderstanding was not linguistic but cultural. The very idea that one might have difficulty parking, or – heaven forfend – have to pay, was alien to her. The system was very simple: park on the road, park on the pavement, park wherever you damn well please. The authorities had put up signs warning that parked cars would be towed away, but no one I spoke to later had ever had their car towed, or knew anyone who had.

I left the car outside the Town Hall in Ploschad Pobedy

– Victory Square. The new Orthodox Cathedral of Christ
the Saviour was a shimmering vision of white and gold in the
pale sunlight. How rare to see a modern building that actually
enriched a cityscape, bringing grace and dignity back to a grimy,
battered metropolis. Most of the historic centre was destroyed
in the Second World War or demolished in the decades that
followed. On the night of the 29th–30th August 1944, 176
Avro Lancasters of the RAF's No 5 Group, operating at the
limit of their range, dropped 480 tons of incendiary bombs on
Königsberg, leaving the city ablaze.

'Königsberg,' crowed the official RAF report, 'the malig-
nant breeding ground of the arrogant military caste, a town
which has stood unchanged for 600 years, has to the benefit
of mankind, been wiped out overnight.' The raid was clearly
intended as a warning to the Russians: 'Ponder on what would
have been the reaction,' the report continued, 'had the Russians
flown to Bremen before us and utterly destroyed it.'

Beyond the Hotel Kaliningrad was a low hill on which the
castle of the Teutonic Knights once stood. Gutted in the raids,
its ruins were dynamited on Brezhnev's orders in 1970 as a
symbol of German imperialism. This is where the city was
founded in 1255, and where, in 1701, the elector Friedrich III
was crowned King Friedrich I, his queen Sophie at his side
bedecked in amber jewellery. In its place was built the Dom
Sovietov, the House of the Soviets. The builders ignored the fact
that the castle rock was riddled with tunnels, so the concrete
monolith began to subside before it was even finished. Never
occupied, and known to locals as 'the Monster', it stood amid
cracked paving and dry fountains, a dismal monument to a
failed ideology.

Not quite all of old Königsberg had disappeared. From this
bleak rise, I could look down at the 13th-century cathedral on
the island called the Kneiphof in the River Pregolya. Burnt out
in the raids, it remained a shell throughout the Soviet era. The

story goes that Brezhnev, having ordered the demolition of the castle, demanded to know when this 'last rotten tooth of Königsberg' would be pulled. When local officials asked what he proposed to do with the tomb of Immanuel Kant, regarded as a precursor of Marx, he fell silent, and the cathedral was allowed to remain, crumbling slowly into ruin. Now, with financial assistance from Germany, it had been restored to its medieval gingerbread splendour. Against its north-east corner, a plain red sandstone colonnade enclosed the philosopher's tomb. Sadly, the narrow streets that once clustered around the cathedral had not survived, and it stood alone on its island amid dreary municipal parkland.

Although the historic centre was obliterated, the topography of the wider city remained. The Pregolya – Pregel to the Germans – wound from east to west, dividing around the Kneiphof. Two elongated lakes extended north from where the castle once stood, the remnant of a river dammed by the Teutonic Knights to breed fish and power their water mills. Around the inner ring road, a chain of neo-Gothic brick forts built by the Germans in the 19th century were prominent, well maintained landmarks; one, the Dohna Fort, now housed the Amber Museum.

In its circular galleries, some gigantic chunks of raw amber were displayed; the largest, weighing four kilogrammes, was the size of a human head. There were droplets, stalactites, amber with the imprint of bark, and richly coloured pieces with swirls of white and blue. Amber with inclusions was displayed behind magnifying glasses, so you could peer into its depths at fragments of leaves and fern, spiders, flies and mosquitoes, and even grasshoppers that didn't hop out of the way in time.

Among the artefacts were copies of the Juodkrantė treasure and other Neolithic ornaments. There were clocks and smoking accessories made by the Staatliche Bernstein Manufaktur between the wars, while the Soviet era was represented by a 1960 model of the atomic ship *Lenin* ploughing through waves of amber – above it, a slim amber missile bearing the legend CCCP streaked through an amber sky. One room was given over to replicas of panels and carvings from the Amber Room, installed in the castle here after the Nazis stole it from Leningrad, and then lost amid the chaos of war.

The savagery of the conflict became evident when I visited the bunker of General Otto Lasch, the last German commandant of Königsberg. I found it just off ulitsa Proletarskaya, on what used to be Paradenplatz. Planted with horse-chestnut trees, the square was dominated by the Immanuel Kant State University; to the right of the entrance stood a small statue of the philosopher. The original disappeared during the war, and this replica was brought here by Marion, Countess Dönhoff on the back seat of her Citroën when she returned to the city in 1992. In the courtyard was a headless statue of Neptune that once adorned the gardens of Dönhoff's ancestral home, Friedrichstein, an 18th-century manor that stood amid the meadows of the Pregel some 20 kilometres south-east of Königsberg. Almost all Dönhoff's male relatives perished in the Second World War or were executed for their part in the July 1944 plot to assassinate Hitler. In January 1945, as the Russian tanks approached, she fled on horseback – the same means by which her ancestors had arrived 600 years earlier – through the war-torn countryside to the West. By the end of that month, Friedrichstein had burnt down, whether by accident or design. Settling in Hamburg, Dönhoff became one of the most distinguished journalists in West Germany, publisher of the liberal weekly *Die Zeit*, an adviser and friend to politicians and diplomats until her death at the age of 92 in 2002.

Under the trees at the southern end of the square were four bullet-scarred pillboxes, grimly incongruous in this pleasant public space where students gathered to chat and smoke. I felt a chill of foreboding as I descended the dank concrete stair and passed through heavy steel doors into a long corridor lined with small rooms on either side.

On 6th January 1945, Churchill, anxious to relieve the pressure on Allied troops in the Ardennes, asked Stalin when he intended to attack across the Vistula. On the 12th, Chernyakhovsky's 3rd Belorussian Front advanced westwards, bottling up the German Army Group North in the Samland peninsula. The fighting was fierce and confused, with villages taken and retaken several times in a day. On the 19th, Chernyakhovsky himself was killed; his replacement was Marshal Vasilievsky. By the 26th, Königsberg was encircled.

Reports from outlying areas recaptured from the Russians left the inhabitants of Königsberg with few illusions about the fate that would befall them. A total of two million people fled East Prussia during the closing months of the war, and some 970 vessels were mobilised to rescue them; an estimated 25,000 people lost their lives as 144 German ships were sunk by mines, torpedoes and aerial bombardment. Many who remained chose suicide, and the pharmacies dispensed cyanide to anyone who demanded it.

On 6th April, following a massive artillery bombardment, the Red Army fought its way into the suburbs. By then, the city's defenders consisted of little more than the Volkssturm, old men and boys armed with hunting rifles. One of the bunker's rooms displayed a printed leaflet in German, dated 7th April 1945 and signed by Marshal Vasilievsky, which was air-dropped on the city:

> The German forces south-west of Königsberg on the Vistula Lagoon have been utterly destroyed, and their remnants driven into the sea ... Your position is hopeless ... To avoid unnecessary bloodshed, I urge you to lay down your weapons and cease resistance.

On 9th April, Lasch and his staff emerged from the bunker to surrender. Hitler, furious at the loss of Königsberg, sentenced him to death in absentia. Lasch was sent to a Soviet labour camp, where he remained for ten years. In the bunker, his workroom was preserved, complete with desk, maps, typewriter and field telephone. It was an eerie, claustrophobic place.

Königsberg was the first major German city to be captured by the Russians, and after four years of warfare, twenty million deaths and a long, grim advance through territory ravaged by the retreating enemy, its fall was terrible. 'There shall be no mercy – for anyone, as there was no mercy for us,' Chernyakhovsky had told his troops. Marion Dönhoff's cousin, Hans von Lehndorff, was working as a doctor in Königsberg when it fell, and left a nightmarish picture of the stricken city:

> Between flaming ruins, a wildly yelling throng, without beginning or end, was pushing its way along the street . . . We went on towards the castle. Out of the ruins, like an exclamation mark, rose the tower, split all the way down, riddled, hacked by a thousand shells . . . Right and left among the ruins the remainder of the population was creeping about like half-drowned fowls.

His diaries record the murder, looting, arson and rape that followed. After the initial fury of conquest had subsided, many Germans were employed to keep the infrastructure running. In 1947, however, the remaining East Prussians were expelled. They were among 11 to 16 million forced to flee from eastern and central Europe between the end of the war and 1948. The half-century of silence about this ethnic cleansing – known in Germany as *Die Flucht* (the Flight) – is understandable: in Communist countries, criticism of Soviet policy was prohibited, while in the West any sympathy for Germans was considered tantamount to an apologia for the Third Reich. Only since the fall of the Iron Curtain has the subject been widely discussed, and it remains sensitive. When Antony Beevor's *Berlin: The Downfall 1945*, with its painstakingly documented account of the mass rapes perpetrated by the Red Army, was published in 2002, the Russian ambassador in London denounced it as 'an act of blasphemy'.

I set off up Prospekt Mira in search of the tour agency I had engaged to take me to the amber mine at Yantarny, which was off limits to independent travellers. They would also provide me with an interpreter. The lower end of this long street (formerly Adolf Hitler Straße) was lined with early 20th-century neo-classical buildings and a fine avenue of lime trees. After the road curved around the neoclassical portico of the Drama Theatre, the architecture began to look more German. Past the zoo, I found myself in the suburb of Amalienau, with its Jugendstil villas. Beneath my feet, the word FEUERWEHR was set in red capitals on a concrete hydrant cover. A few paces further on, an Art Nouveau drain lid bore the inscription FRANZ MOGENTHIN − LEIPZIG-EUTRISCH.

I located the tour agency in a modern office building behind a pretentious neo-Georgian portico. I was a little early, and a harassed looking young woman suggested I come back after lunch. She recommended a place called *Dvenadtsat Stulyev* (Twelve Chairs) nearby. It looked more like a private house than a restaurant, and I was shown into a dimly lit basement. Named after the 1928 novel by Ilf and Petrov, one of the few satires published during Soviet times, the restaurant had a cosy, bohemian ambience. A couple of businessmen invited me to join them at their table; they spoke good, Russian-accented English, but turned out to be Turkish. Teher and Ali were in construction, and had been doing business in Russia for more than a decade, with offices in Moscow, Kaliningrad and Ryazan.

Then my interpreter breezed in. An ebullient woman in her

forties, Lydia spoke excellent English. A gold Orthodox cross nestled amid a string of amber beads at her throat. We had a quick lunch and then set off for Yantarny, but not before she had exchanged business cards with the Turks. My guide turned out to be voluble, opinionated, passionate and indiscreet. Before we had travelled any distance, I had learnt that she was outraged by the westernisation of Russia, and pitied the younger generation, as represented by her twenty-year-old daughter.

'All they have is their mobile phones and the internet. They read no books, they don't listen to classical music, they have no knowledge of history and no connection with nature. They are a lost generation. All they want is material things – cars, houses, nightclubs, money. They have nothing in here,' she says, striking her chest. 'But Irina just says, "Mum, you're too old fashioned."'

Lydia confided her fear that, like other young women in Kaliningrad, Irina would get drawn into the sex industry. 'She comes home from college and says her friend has got a new car. She earned the money working in a nightclub. With her clothes on? I ask.'

We were driving west along a road lined with lime trees with broad white bands painted on their trunks. 'We call them Hitler's last soldiers,' Lydia said, explaining that they were planted by the Germans and every now and then still claimed the life of an unwary – or vodka-sodden – Russian motorist.

As we drove through the village of Kumehnen/Kumachevo, I noted that the tower of the medieval redbrick church had collapsed, and the crumbling walls were festooned with weeds.

'Nobody worships there any more, and there is no money to maintain the buildings,' Lydia said. 'All people do around here is drink.'

She bewailed the derelict farmland; when we passed three black-and-white cows in a field, she pointed out that they were the only ones we'd seen. Many farmers had slaughtered their herds because they could not compete with the cheap imported meat sold by supermarkets such as Viktoria. I said I didn't think the produce on sale there was all that cheap – prices seemed much the same as in the UK, and given that unemployment here approached 20 per cent, and a teacher earned about 7,000 rubles (£160) a month, it was hard to imagine how Kaliningradtsy made ends meet.

'We live very simply,' Lydia replied. 'We live in small flats, we buy second-hand clothes, we grow our own vegetables and we do without many things.'

There was a widespread feeling that Kaliningrad had been neglected by the new Russia. It might not have been as impoverished as, say Arkhangelsk or Novosibirsk, but the standard of living fell far behind that of Moscow or St Petersburg. Muscovites, it seemed, only came here to build holiday villas in scenic spots. Back in the 1990s there had been talk of turning the region into a European Hong Kong, a hub for trade with its EU neighbours. But the biggest trade seemed to be cigarette smuggling, while entrepreneurs complained that bureaucratic interference from Moscow – and the bribes required to get anything done – were stifling local initiative.

Pre-war maps describe this littoral as *Die Bernsteinküste* – the Amber Coast. The largest deposits could be found at Yantarny – the name is derived from *yantar*, the Russian word for amber – a coastal settlement of old German villas and farms, and the site of a mine that produced 90 per cent of the world's amber. Simonis Grunovii, a Dominican monk, visited Samland in 1519 in search of a nugget of amber to give to the Pope. 'When there is a northerly gale,' he observed, 'all the peasants in the vicinity must come to the beach and run with nets into the sea to fish for floating amber ... but many will drown.' The amber fishers wore leather jackets with deep pockets, and were roped together to prevent them from being carried off by the waves. Large fires burned on the beaches so they could thaw out as they emerged from the icy waters. As Grunovii rode through Elbling, Pillau, Fischhausen and Gross Dirschkeim, he saw corpses dangling from gallows all along the coast. 'The High Master of Prussia,' he noted, 'prohibited the free collection of amber by hanging from the nearest tree . . .'

Security in the 21st century was less draconian, but I still had to report to the mine office. The tiled room, guarded by *militsya* in camouflage fatigues, was redolent of the old Soviet Union. My passport was checked and the paperwork issued before I could drive up a rutted path to a checkpoint with STOP painted on a concrete block and a yellow sign reading PROHIBITED ZONE. A taciturn guard raised the boom barrier, and we climbed to top of a wind-battered bluff crowned with stunted juniper and buckthorn. To one side, the land tumbled down to a long, sandy beach. On the other, a barren lunar landscape stretched almost as far as the eye could see: a vast opencast mine, with troughs and hillocks of sand, and mechanical diggers like toys far below.

The first mine was established at Palmnicken, as it was then called, in 1870 by Stantien und Becker. We could see their pit a short distance away; long worked out, it now formed a broad, deep lake. In 1899 the Prussian government bought the mine, and it had remained the monopoly of the various states – Prussian, German, Soviet and Russian – that controlled the territory ever since, except for an ill-fated attempt at privatisation during the Yeltsin years. The production process had changed little since it was mechanised after the First World War. The 'blue earth' that contained the amber was excavated by mechanical diggers and loaded on to trucks, which carried it to spray houses where high-pressure hoses separated the resin.

As we left, a guard conducted a desultory search of the car. Theft was a still a problem, although the Wild West atmosphere of the 1990s, when more amber was stolen than sold through official channels, appeared to have been tamed, and there was enough left to sustain production for another 300 years.

Lydia suggested we visit an artist and musician friend of hers who lived nearby. We stopped in the village and she jumped out to buy some biscuits to take with us, before driving up to a low range of old German farm buildings on a bluff overlooking the sea. Kostya came out to greet us; in his late thirties, with long, light brown hair, he was wearing paint-spattered jeans and a sweatshirt, and had a dreamy, abstracted air. He ushered us through a low doorway – the heavy old farmhouse door was held in place by ancient barrel hinges with elaborate finials – to join his mother, Margarita, in a low-ceilinged room dominated by a tiled German stove. On every shelf and ledge was something from the sea: shells, whitened driftwood, large, smooth pebbles, and pieces of amber. We sat at the table and drank hot black tea sweetened with home-made blackcurrant jam, accompanied by dry, smoky Baltic sprats on small rounds of white bread, and gritty, flavoursome pears from the garden.

The two women exchanged samples of the handicrafts they made: leather purses, pendants of driftwood and amber, bottles covered in leather and studded with amber. You need equipment – tumbling and polishing machines – to produce shiny round beads with a neatly drilled hole, but using chalk and paraffin, they managed to achieve a smooth matt finish, and a hot needle made a good enough piercing to hang a pendant. I found these hand-crafted pieces far more appealing than the industrially-finished amber jewellery on sale throughout the Baltic.

Our conversation was interrupted by the ringtone – Ravel's *Bolero* – of Lydia's mobile. The caller was a man in Denmark called Hans. Did she know anyone who could provide him with 8,000 tonnes of Königsberg cobblestones? Apparently the cobbles that still paved many of the city's streets were in great demand for restoration projects in Western Europe. Yes, she did know someone... How much was he prepared to offer? Two euros apiece? They could fetch as much as nine. She'd get back to him.

Kostya talked about the moral decline of Russia and the need for enlightened people to provide vision. As Lydia translated, I was unsure where his statements ended and her commentary began, so close were their views. Both shared a loathing for consumer culture and a belief in the need for spiritual regeneration. For them, capitalism and communism alike were states of slavish dependency and spiritual bankruptcy. Only closeness to nature, an awareness of God and faith in Holy Mother Russia could offer a way forward.

Kostya picked up a guitar and began to strum. As he sang in his light, husky baritone, Lydia translated: 'It is better to go hungry than to feed on poison.'

'This is for you,' he said as we were about to leave, and pressed into my palm a small handful of amber he had collected.

The next day, beside the Dom Sovietov, I came upon an archaeological excavation. No one was working, but there were explanatory panels, and apertures in the hoardings allowed me to peer in. Stone walls descended a couple of metres below ground level to a flagged floor. This was the torture chamber of the Teutonic Knights, later used as the wine cellar of a restaurant called the Blütgericht – 'Blood Court'. I had seen an old newsreel of the place bedecked with swastika banners and Teutonic kitsch. Directly above it was the Knights' Hall, where the Amber Room may have been stored before its disappearance.

In May 1945, the Council of People's Commissars dispatched Professor Alexander Ivanovich Brusov to track it down. He found the ruined city still smouldering. On 10th June, in a municipal building nearby, Brusov discovered 10,000 pieces of amber, some in boxes, some loose on the floor. An inventory made clear that this was part of the collection of Königsberg

University. Other boxes had already left in the care of Karl Andrée, director of the Institute of Palaeontology and Geology and the author of several books on amber. The rest, including the Juodkrantė treasure, had disappeared. The Amber Room was not among the finds. One day Brusov came across Alfred Rohde, the former curator of the castle museum, wandering deranged amid the ruins. Rohde told him that, after the RAF raids, he had the Amber Room dismantled and packed into crates, awaiting transport to a safe place in rural East Prussia or the mines under Saxony. In the ruins, Brusov discovered the charred remains of cornices, mouldings and hinges from doors taken from Tsarskoye Selo at the same time as the room. His report was bleak: 'We should give up looking for the Amber Room.'

This was not what his masters wanted to hear. Too much national pride had been invested in the room – and it was a valuable card to play in negotiations with western governments over the return of works of art looted by the Russians. The following year, they appointed Anatoly Kuchumov, the Leningrad curator in charge of the Amber Room before the war, to lead a further investigation. Paul Feyerabend, the manager of the Blütgericht, told him under interrogation that the Knights' Hall had survived the fall of the city, but had been burnt out soon afterwards. Kuchumov dismissed his testimony, reporting that the Germans must have removed the Amber Room to an unknown destination. The hunt was on once more.

The obsessive quest for the missing room seemed entirely in keeping with this enigmatic place. All cities reinvent themselves; few have been reinvented so catastrophically as Kaliningrad – or Königsberg, or Królewiec in Polish, Karaliaučius in Lithuanian, Kenigsberg in Russian. There have even been proposals to rename it Kantgrad, after its most famous son. This Kafkaesque proliferation of Ks offers a glimpse of the

city's multiple identities. It had become a city of the imagination, a place that meant different things to different people, who
refashioned it according to their own memories and desires.
For the Nazis, Königsberg was a rampart of Teutonic civilisation against the barbarous east. For the Russians, it was the
citadel of a Prussian military elite, and had to be obliterated.

Older residents, who had arrived from Russia, Ukraine or
Belarus, remembered that much of the city was still in ruins
in the Fifties and Sixties. Of its previous occupants they knew
nothing. 'History for us began in 1946,' Lydia told me. 'We
didn't know any of the old names.' Marion Dönhoff called
one of her volumes of memoirs *Namen die keiner mehr nennt*
('Names no one mentions any more'), lamenting the loss of
place names such as Quittainen, Arklitten and Trakehnen.
These strange, lyrical, archaic names are more Baltic than
German – so much so that years before the wholesale renaming
by the Soviets, the Nazis had already 'Germanised' many of
them, turning the town of Eydtkuhnen into Ebenrode. Only
now were the inhabitants of the region – few of whose great-
grandparents were born here – beginning to reclaim that past,
and many now referred to the city as 'Kenig'.

As with the names, so with the physical fabric. Dmitri
Navalikhin, chief architect of post-war Kaliningrad, wanted to
turn 'a capitalist city devastated by air raids and artillery fire'
into one fit for 'a new progressive and leading culture'. To what
extent he succeeded can be judged by Dönhoff's comment when
she returned in 1990, for the first time in almost half a century:
'If I had been parachuted into this city and asked where I was,
I might have answered, in Irkutsk.'

Yet the romantic views of old Königsberg produced for
German tourists are also an imaginative construct. Pre-war
photographs show that the medieval streets around the cathedral had largely made way for modern developments by the
1920s and 1930s; there was even an eight-storey Constructivist

high-rise in the Altstadt. The main tower of the castle, which features so prominently in these illustrations, was a 19th-century pastiche. If any part of the city centre looked much as it did before the war, it was the western end of Ploschad Pobedy. One might easily mistake the classical-moderne colonnade of the North Station for a Soviet construction, but it was actually built in 1930. The dour courthouse and City Hall, built in 1923, also preserved their original appearance. Countess Dönhoff would have had no difficulty recognising this part of town, though she might not have recalled it with the same fondness as the Altstadt.

At the other end of the square, the golden domes of the Orthodox Cathedral signalled a more recent architectural reinvention. The region had been Russian for more than half a century, but for most of that period, the architectural expression of this was Soviet. Now, as religion and nationalism filled the ideological void left by communism, Orthodox churches were springing up everywhere, particularly beside war memorials, of which there were many in a region so bitterly fought over. Not far from my hotel, I noticed a small yellow sandstone church so traditional in style that it could have stood in an ancient Russian city for centuries; in fact, it was brand new. For the first time in its history, this corner of Europe was beginning to *look* Russian.

The forts on the inner ring road were mirrored by an outer circuit of 15, sited one kilometre apart beyond the city limits. They were built after the Franco-Prussian War, in part by French PoWs, and funded from the five billion francs of war reparations paid by France. Seldom visited, they had been used for the past fifty years to store vegetables, and were slowly crumbling away. Most were dangerous, and some were still surrounded by unexploded mines. But Fort No 1 – named Fort Stein after the Prussian statesman of the Napoleonic era – was looked after by a volunteer caretaker who lived there with his family. One afternoon, Lydia and I drove out to visit him. The polygonal fortification stood on a low, tree-covered hill, amid neglected farmland to the east of the city. It was surrounded by a deep, dark moat, which we crossed by a drawbridge, covered from both sides by gun embrasures.

A tall, rangy man in his mid-forties opened the massive iron door and greeted us. Stanislav first came here in 1991, when a co-operative, 'The Old City', was set up to restore Kaliningrad's historic buildings. They rented the fort from the organisation that stored vegetables and grain there. Then, with the help of volunteers, they started to restore the building. When he was evicted from his flat in town, he moved in, and had squatted the place for the past 15 years.

Stanislav introduced us to his friend Sergei, a young man in combat fatigues who belonged to one of the Patriotic Clubs, military enthusiasts who sought out the remains of fallen soldiers to give them a proper burial. At first, it was difficult to find the information necessary for an accurate restoration, but then two sons of former German commandants visited and explained many aspects of the building. The last commandant was killed by his own troops when he refused to surrender. 'He's buried out there,' Stanislav said, pointing to the rampart.

Stanislav's office occupied one of the barrack rooms; he and his family lived in another. There was no running water except for a well; beside the broken stump of an old iron standpipe, a modern electric pump had been rigged up. If they needed electricity, Stanislav had to cycle to the nearest filling station with a jerrycan to fuel the generator. This had not stopped the electricity and water companies from presenting him with enormous bills.

'The officials who made out the bills knew perfectly well that we have no mains water or electricity,' he explained. 'They just expect you to pay a bribe. One day they'll probably take the building and we'll be on the streets.'

A glass-fronted bookcase stood along one wall of the office; on the others were maps, photographs and charts. A wood-burning stove in the corner was the only source of heat. In the bookcase were a number of smaller artefacts: cartridge cases, a dagger, and an aluminium belt buckle with a swastika surrounded by the words GOTT MIT UNS. As I translated, Sergei fidgeted with the bolt of his sub-machine gun while Lydia hissed: *'The Devil was with them!'*

We emerged on to the gun platform on top of the fort, which was grassed over, with trees growing from it. An amphitheatre in the centre – originally a drill square – was now used for musical events. The eerie ambience made it a magnet for bikers, Goths, neo-pagans and 'dark folk' bands – even shamans from Siberia had performed here.

'Do you know Tarkovsky's film *Stalker*?' Stanislav asked as we were about to leave. Somehow I understood what he was saying before Lydia had time to translate. 'This is the Zone,' Stanislav said, gesturing around us.

After giving Sergei a lift back into town, Lydia and I stopped for dinner at a small Ukrainian restaurant. Under the influence of the live music and the wine, she grew nostalgic. 'I love these Ukrainian songs,' she said. 'I love the Ukrainian language. It's such a shame they had to make that Orange Revolution. They sold themselves to the Americans. These fucking Americans, they try to come between Slavonic peoples and drive them apart. At least it won't happen in Belarus. The President there is strong.'

To anyone in the West who took an interest in such matters, Viktor Yushchenko, leader of Ukraine's Orange Revolution, was a democratic hero, while Aleksandr Lukaschenka, the President of Belarus, was 'the last dictator in Europe'. But people saw things differently here.

'In the West,' she said, 'you like Gorbachev. For us, he was a dog, a monkey, a puppet of the Americans. He ruined everything.'

Buffeted by the intensity of the views I'd encountered, I spent the next day making a solo circuit of the Samland peninsula. As I drove north from Kaliningrad, the first place I came to was Svetlogorsk. Formerly the German spa town of Rauschen, it seemed to have come through the war physically unscathed. Amid its steep, narrow streets of old German houses, it was hard to believe I was still in Russia. The shops and cafés had signs in German, and 'Bernstein' was offered for sale everywhere.

I was trying to make for the north-westernmost tip of the peninsula, the Brüster Ort, but there was no direct road, so I ended up a few kilometres to the south at Donskoye. On the outskirts of town was a large barracks, and I passed several convoys of military trucks on the road. A pale sun shone low through the trees, glinting off the domes of a little blue and gold Orthodox church; here and there a bonfire smouldered amid scrubby farmland. To the north I could see two headlands jutting out into the sea. But I could go no further: the Brüster Ort was a military zone.

Instead, I followed the coast road south; alongside it, a rash of new villas had appeared. Several had large cars with Moscow plates parked outside, and guard dogs straining at the leash. The road took me back to Yantarny, where I parked the car and made my way down to the beach. A bleak cairn, with a black marble plaque in Russian and Hebrew, commemorated the inmates of Stutthof concentration camp murdered here in January 1945. As Soviet troops advanced into East Prussia, the Nazis force-marched some 7,000 prisoners, many of them women, through Königsberg to Palmnicken. Half-starved and clad only in rags, just 4,000 survived the icy conditions. On the night of 31st January, they were herded on to the beach by the SS and driven under machine-gun fire into the sea. Martin Bergau, then a 15-year-old member of the Volkssturm, watched in horror from the cliff-top. 'I could not believe my eyes. Between the ice floes,' he wrote in his 1994 book *A Boy from the Amber Shore*, 'the water was thick with countless floating bodies.' Just 15 survived.

The lagoons between the cliffs and the strand were relics of a failed attempt to mine sea amber on an industrial scale. I walked along the tideline, and almost immediately picked up a piece, not large, but smooth and golden. The next took longer to find, and at first I was unsure it wasn't a golden-brown shard of glass. But as it grew warm between my fingers, I could feel its resiny texture. The third and last – by now the light was failing – was scarcely larger than a grain of Demerera sugar, but unmistakably the real thing.

From Yantarny, I headed south towards Primorsk. It was dark now, and after a while it struck me that the road was poor even by Kaliningrad standards. It came to an abrupt end at a pair of locked gates. Beyond them stood a low, darkened building and a communications tower with a red light on top. The entire coast was bristling with military installations, and I had an alarming vision of spending the night as a guest of the Red Army. I turned round and drove all the way back to Yantarny, where I found the point where my track had diverged from the main road, and headed back to Kaliningrad.

I was woken by the phone at eight the next morning, with Lyudmila demanding, in her shrill German, that I move the car because the builders working on a villa next door needed to get a truck through. When I reached the car, the front nearside tyre was completely flat. I had thought the wheel was rattling badly as I came into Kaliningrad, but put it down to the cobbles; the damage must have been inflicted by one of the potholes on the road south from Yantarny. It couldn't have happened at a worse time. The rental agreement required me to return the vehicle in Lithuania that day. Not wanting to retrace my steps, I had agreed to drop it off in Kaunas, which had the advantage of allowing me to travel the length of the Kaliningrad *oblast*.

It was Lyudmila who saved the day, swiftly enlisting the foreman from the building site. He removed the old tyre, fitted the spare, bundled the damaged wheel, along with me and a small girl with a violin case, into his car and set off. After dropping the girl at her violin lesson, he drove me to a tyre shop off Gorky Street, where they battered the dented wheel back into shape and fitted a new tyre. It came, to my surprise and relief, to just 500 rubles. I offered the foreman another 500 for his trouble, but he wouldn't accept more than 200.

I was off by 12, and out through the checkpoint east of the city, along the valley of the Pregel. The first place I came to, Gvardeysk, was once known as Tapiau, and despite a large aluminium statue of Lenin, the main square still looked much like an old Prussian market town. Beyond Gvardeysk, the landscape became hillier – I had left the Samland peninsula and was now on the East Prussian mainland – and the road narrowed. In places, it was little more than a cobbled track; it was hard to believe that this was the main road to Moscow, some 1,200 kilometres to the east.

Chernyakhovsk was a fair-sized town, its church steeple visible from a distance. The former Insterburg, it was one of the main transport hubs of East Prussia and suffered heavy bombing in the war. On the outskirts, new retail parks gave way to rows of *Khrushchobi* and then, on the sloping cobbled streets of the centre, old German houses and Prussian administrative buildings. A painted German advertisement for the building firm H. Osterroht was fading but still visible on a wall. A busy market was in full swing. A 19th-century redbrick church was now the Orthodox Cathedral of St Michael; in the churchyard, three gilt onion domes stood on wooden frames, looking as if they had just landed from outer space. Down by the railway yards, a heroic statue of Chernyakhovsky commanded a roundabout.

I reached the border at Chernyshevskoye (formerly Eydtkuhnen), where I waited behind a long line of Russian trucks travelling to the 'mainland'. In the rear-view mirror, a purple sunset broke through gunmetal clouds; above hung a crescent moon with Venus a bright, blazing point of light beneath it. As I reached the checkpoint, an excitable woman guard found something amiss in my documents, and disappeared with my passport. Fortunately a young man who spoke English then appeared, delighted to have the opportunity to practise it. Any misunderstanding was soon cleared up. On the Lithuanian side, I was ushered through swiftly while the Russian truckers were given the third degree. Dostoyevsky came through here by train in 1862 on his way to Berlin, Paris and London. This gave rise to a strange thought: 100 years ago, travelling in the same direction at exactly this point, I would have been *entering* the Russian Empire from Germany; now I was *leaving* Russia to enter the European Union. It was as if the world had been turned inside out.

I arrived in Kaunas about 8pm. My hotel was luxurious, the receptionist spoke perfect English with an American accent, and there was a business centre with blisteringly fast internet access. Why did I find myself missing gritty Kaliningrad? The following morning, I looked around the Old Town, a jumble of pretty Baroque architecture and soulless postwar building. On a wall, I saw a fading Russian advert that must have dated back to Tsarist times, a cousin of the ghost sign I saw in Chernyakhovsk. Nearby, the pretty blue-and-white 19th-century synagogue had – amazingly – survived.

After checking out of the hotel, I drove to the Ninth Fort. Part of a ring of fortifications around the city – a mirror of Königsberg's – it was used by the NKVD to liquidate their opponents after the Molotov-Ribbentrop pact assigned Lithuania to the Soviets. Then, when the Nazis invaded in 1941, it became a place of execution for the inmates of Vilnius's ghetto, and for Jews deported from Germany. Among them was the medieval historian Willy Cohn, an old friend of my grandmother. An equally ardent Zionist and German patriot, he kept a diary through the years of the Third Reich; hidden throughout the war, it was only published in 2012. I had hoped my path might cross that of this singular man at an earlier, less desperate point in his life's trajectory, but history and geography dictated that our journeys should intersect here. On 21st November 1941, Cohn was deported from Breslau along with his wife and two youngest daughters; on the 25th they were brought to the Ninth Fort where, along with 2,000 other Breslau Jews, they were machine-gunned on arrival.

The brick walls and towers, topped by barbed wire, stood on a windswept hill between motorway interchanges. A large Soviet memorial was formed of two broken metal shards leaning towards one another; on closer inspection, they were made up of faces and fists. A bunker-like museum exhibited photographs and personal effects – spectacles, razors, pocket knives – of victims retrieved from the site, along with possessions taken into the gulags by Lithuanians deported by the Soviets. What was unsettling was not just the atrocities perpetrated here, but their appropriation for political ends. Just as the Soviets had commemorated the 'victims of fascism' without acknowledging that the majority were Jews, independent Lithuania now gave priority to the crimes of the communist regime. This would be a desolate place on a bright summer's day; in the fitful snow of a bleak November morning, it was unspeakable.

After returning the car to the rental company, I sat in a café listening to sickly Western Christmas songs until it was time to board the bus. It took a more northerly route than the one I had come by; though less direct, the roads were better. There weren't many passengers: about nine men, mostly Russian workers, and one middle-aged woman. The road followed the valley of the River Nemunas as it wound through meadows hazed with mist, dividing around islands before converging again. From its source in Belarus, this mighty river flows west for 950 kilometres until it discharges itself into the Curonian Lagoon.

Eventually, the lights of Sovetsk appeared across the river. We crossed a pontoon bridge over a smaller arm of the river and arrived at the Lithuanian checkpoint. A guard collected everyone's passports and disappeared for about 20 minutes before eventually returning them. The bus then crossed the Queen Luise Bridge, named after the Prussian queen who brokered the Treaty of Tilsit, signed on a raft in midriver by Napoleon and Tsar Alexander I in 1807. We passed through a floodlit neo-Baroque portal to the Russian border control, where we queued to have our credentials checked again.

The next morning, I rang the tour agency to confirm arrangements for the afternoon's excursion to the naval port of Baltiysk. Lydia was unavailable, so I was introduced to a new guide, Maria. A blonde woman in her fifties, she spoke English well, but with an accent that I couldn't place. It emerged that, though born in Tversk, she was half Polish and spoke fluent German. We headed west out of Kaliningrad, through dacha gardens, along roads laid by Napoleon's soldiers on their way to Moscow.

Maria was well travelled for a resident of Kaliningrad: she had relatives in Poland, and had visited England a few years before. She told me how the accession of Poland and Lithuania to the Schengen group had made journeys to and from 'mainland' Russia difficult. Air travel was too expensive for most people, and the boat from St Petersburg took three days. The Amber Train to Kaliningrad left Moscow at 2pm; at 2am the next morning, staff woke everyone up for a 40-minute customs and immigration check on the border with Belarus. When the train arrived at the Belarus-Lithuania border at 3am, the procedure was repeated. At 4.15am, at Vilnius, there was a 20-minute halt with random checks. On Lithuania's border with Kaliningrad, passengers underwent another 40-minute check before the train eventually arrived at 10.45am. I was struck by the similarity of the situation – sealed trains with border checks in the night – to that of East Prussians between the wars, when the region was cut off from the rest of Germany.

As we approached Baltiysk, we were stopped at a check-point where I had to produce my passport; the area was still a restricted military zone. The port stands at the northern end of the Vistula Spit, a narrow sandbar that runs all the way to Sztutowo in Poland, enclosing the Vistula Lagoon, like a mirror image of the Curonian Spit to the north. Formerly known as Pillau, it is Russia's only ice-free port in Europe, and the headquarters of its Baltic Fleet.

About 50 per cent of the town was destroyed in the war, but a cluster of buildings preserved a corner of old Pillau: the church, the Town Hall, some redbrick barrack blocks and a 1904 officers' casino. The old Lutheran church was now an Orthodox one. Inside, the air was thick with incense, the east end obscured by a wooden iconostasis. Maria lit a candle for her son, who was taking exams. We walked across a wide parade ground, flanked by old houses, with a large war me-morial. On the waterfront was a blue-painted hotel, the Golden Anchor; a plaque on the wall proclaimed that the poet Joseph Brodsky had stayed there as a young journalist in the 1960s. On the head of a statue of Peter the Great, a naval cadet had positioned a cap at a jaunty angle.

Then to the ferry port, to make the crossing to the Spit. The orange and white ferry, the *Vistula*, was an old Caledonian MacBrayne vessel that had been in service in the Western Isles of Scotland as recently as 2001. In a cloud of diesel fumes, it edged into the channel. A watery sun shone weakly through a pewter haze. Beyond the Spit, I could make out the ghostly shapes of huge concrete hangars, reminding me of the 'pagodas' used to test bombs on Orford Ness, for many years another forbidden military zone.

Tensions between Russia and the West had been exacerbated since the Kremlin announced that Russia would position missiles in the Kaliningrad region in response to Nato's defence shield. Some locals thought the missiles had already arrived, others that they had been here all along. One Kaliningradtsy told me they had seen them while out picking mushrooms on the Spit. All agreed on one thing: if Nato could locate its missiles in Poland and Lithuania, right on their borders, why shouldn't they put theirs here?

We jumped out quickly at the other side, as we had to return by the same ferry – there wasn't another for two hours. There was just time for a brisk walk around the only settlement, a small village of ochre-painted houses nestling amid scrawny ash trees. Thus far, and no further. There was no border crossing on the Spit; missiles or no missiles, parts of it were – and, at the time of writing, remain – militarised. To continue along the Amber Route, I would have to double back and follow the landward shore of the lagoon into Poland.

On the cliff above us stood a huge equestrian statue of the Empress Elizabeth, during whose reign (1741–61) the Russians briefly took control of this area (they didn't regain it until 1945). Set up in 2003 on this westernmost point of the Russian Federation, it was clearly modelled on the Bronze Horseman in St Petersburg, and was claimed to be the largest equestrian statue of a woman in the world. Looking up, however, what was most prominent was her mount's enormous *membrum virile*, as if the Empress has been endowed by proxy with the machismo to challenge the West.

PART II

ANCESTRAL VOICES

GDAŃSK TO VIENNA

'Why you? Why us for that matter? Why anything? Because this moment simply is. Have you ever seen bugs trapped in amber?'

'Yes.' Billy, in fact, had a paperweight in his office which was a blob of polished amber with three lady-bugs embedded in it.

'Well, here we are, Mr. Pilgrim, trapped in the amber of this moment. There is no why.'

Kurt Vonnegut, *Slaughterhouse-Five*

CHAPTER 6

THE DELTA AND
THE LAGOON

Rome drew its frontiers at the Danube and the Rhine; the postwar boundary between Poland and Germany was defined by the rivers Oder and Neisse; but in Poland's northeastern corner, the border with Russia drawn up in 1945 runs almost ruler-straight from Goldap to Braniewo, bisecting what was once East Prussia. The vast delta of the Vistula, Poland's largest river, extends on either side of this frontier, feeding into the Vistula Lagoon. Like the Curonian Lagoon to the north, this shallow body of water is separated from the Baltic by a narrow strip of sand. West of Gdańsk, another, shorter spit terminates at Hel, completing the symmetry.

The pike swim in the brackish creeks, the storks build their ramshackle nests on chimneys and telegraph poles, and birds migrate along the Curonian and Vistula spits, oblivious to the checkpoints and barbed wire ... and amber destined for the rich lands to the south passed this way for centuries. Exiled to Poland as a result of the Reformation, Olaus Magnus, cartographer and titular archbishop of Uppsala, depicted this coast in detail in his *Carta Marina*, a magnificent map of northern Europe and Scandinavia published in Venice in 1539. On the Vistula Spit, he put a man with a spade, and a row of small barrels of the type used to gather amber. An inscription reads *ripa svccini* – Amber Coast.

Though the western half of the bay is dominated by the great conurbation of Gdańsk, Sopot and Gdynia, known locally as the Tromiasto or Tri-City, most of the delta is a sparsely inhabited landscape of white, sandy beaches where shards of amber are washed up amid the bladderwrack, of winding rivers and shallow lakes, forests of birch and pine, and flat fields of rich alluvial soil bounded by ditches lined with coppiced willows and alders. The southern shore of the lagoon was ringed by the strongholds of the Teutonic Knights – Braunsberg (Braniewo), Frauenburg (Frombork), and Elbling (Elbląg) – from which they controlled the amber trade. It used to be possible to travel between these towns on a scenic railway that offered wonderful views across the lagoon, but the introduction of a market economy resulted in the closure of many rural lines, and the route was axed in 2006. The abandoned station at Frombork now stands forlornly beside the harbour, grass growing between the tracks, so travellers wishing to follow this stretch of the Amber Route must come by car or take the bus.

At Braniewo, a market town five kilometres from the Russian border, all that remained of medieval Braunsberg was a stretch of city wall with one or two bastions still standing, but Frombork, a few kilometres to the west, was more impressive. Above the small lakeside town, the redbrick walls of the Teutonic Knights' fortified cathedral rose sheer from a wooded hill. In the courtyard stood a gigantic 600-year-old oak, its hollow trunk held upright by steel cables. The castle was dominated by the soaring, pinnacled cathedral, built between 1329 and 1388 and dedicated to the Virgin Mary; the town's German name, Frauenburg, means the fortress of Our Lady. Surmounting all the other castle buildings was the mighty, cupola-topped belfry known as Radziejowski's Tower. The views from the top were well worth the climb. Looking out across the lagoon to the Spit, it was not hard to see why the Knights chose this commanding spot for their fortress; any comings and goings by land or water could be observed.

If the little town seemed peaceful nowadays, its turbulent history reflected that of a region contested by Germans and Slavs for almost a millennium. Conquered from the pagan Prussians – a Baltic people related to Latvians and Lithuanians – by the Teutonic Knights in the 13th century, the Duchy of Warmia (Ermland in German) stretched inland beyond Olsztyn, broadening out from a narrow strip of coast. Over the years, its mixed population of Prussians, Poles and German settlers came to find the rule of the Teutonic Knights increasingly oppressive. In 1454, they rose up against the Knights and allied themselves with Poland. The Thirteen Years War that followed resulted in the withdrawal of the Knights into East Prussia, and the absorption of Warmia and West Prussia into Poland, albeit with a degree of autonomy. Frombork remained in Polish hands until 1772 when the region was annexed by Prussia in the first of the three partitions that would erase Poland from the map until 1918.

In a corner of the castle enclosure stood the stout, square Copernicus Tower, which the great astronomer is thought to have used as his observatory, though his equipment was long gone, carried off by the Swedes in the Thirty Years War. Born in Torún, Copernicus moved to Frombork around 1510, became a canon of the cathedral, and – apart from five years at Olsztyn – spent the rest of his life there. By 1514, his observations had led him to conclude that the earth and other planets revolved around the sun. Knowing how controversial his ideas would be, Copernicus was reluctant to publish them until he had worked out the mathematical proofs, which were not revealed until his *De revolutionibus orbium coelestium* appeared shortly before his death in 1543.

Copernicus was encouraged to publish by the Austrian

mathematician Georg Joachim Rheticus, who arrived at Frombork in May 1539. 'I heard of the fame of Master Nicolaus Copernicus in the northern lands,' Rheticus wrote, 'and did not think I should be content until I had learned something more through the instruction of that man ... I regret neither the financial expense nor the long journey nor the remaining hardships.' Determined to persuade 'this venerable man to share his ideas sooner with the world', Rheticus went to Danzig, where the mayor gave him financial assistance to publish his *Narratio Prima*, or 'First Report' on the discoveries of Copernicus. It concluded with an essay 'In Praise of Prussia', extolling the region's natural resources, including its orchards, lakes and fields, its game and fisheries and, above all, its amber, the 'special gift of God, with which He desired to adorn this region above all others'.

The Bishop's Palace, a white gabled building to the right of the cathedral, was now a museum. The ground floor displayed ecclesiastical treasures: silver and gilt monstrances and crucifixes, including one 19th-century example with four faceted pieces of amber around the pedestal. The first floor was devoted to the life and work of Copernicus, with a series of portraits – none contemporary – and replicas of the instruments he would have used. The view of the cosmos that Copernicus challenged was represented by an early printed edition of Ptolemy's 2nd century AD astronomical treatise *Almagest* in Greek, and the German humanist Peter Apian's *Cosmographia* of 1524, open at the diagram showing the geocentric system. Copernicus was a true Renaissance man, and there are exhibits on his work as a doctor – he recommended tincture of amber for cardiac irregularities – and as an economist. He was also a skilled cartographer, and assisted Rheticus and his friend Heinrich Zell – a pupil of the German cosmographer Sebastian Münster – in producing the first detailed map of Prussia, published at Nuremberg in 1542.

Travelling west from Frombork in a little local bus, between the hamlet of Narusa (population 95) and the small town of Pogrodzie (formerly Neukirchen) I passed from East to West Prussia, as the borders stood prior to the Treaty of Versailles; after much of West Prussia became the Polish Corridor, the remaining portions, centred on Elbląg, were absorbed into the East Prussian exclave. The slanting late-afternoon sun intensified the russets and greens of the landscape as the road led through conifer plantations and open farmland. On the outskirts of Elbląg, the fields were increasingly punctuated by residential and light industrial buildings. Towards the centre of this sizeable town, the tarmac gave way to cobbles and the vehicle bumped and rattled alongside narrow, ancient-looking trams. Amid the busy roads and housing blocks, the gilding on an onion dome caught the sun, drawing my eye to a brand-new Russian Orthodox church. Behind the beautifully restored façade of a 16th-century merchant's house on the main square, the accommodation I had booked turned out to be a sleek modern business hotel. By now it was raining heavily, so I decided to take shelter for the night.

Elbląg was the site of a major trading emporium on the Amber Route, the Viking settlement of Truso. Its existence is recorded in just one written source, a late 9th-century account of a voyage by the Anglo-Saxon sailor and merchant Wulfstan, which was included in Alfred the Great's translation of Paulus Orosius' *Histories*. By the following century, Truso had declined, eclipsed by Gdańsk. In the early 13th century, the Teutonic Knights built a castle on the banks of the River Elbling, and a settlement swiftly grew up immediately to the north. An early member of the Hanseatic League, Elbląg soon had extensive trading connections throughout the Baltic and beyond. Old engravings and photographs depict a typical North European medieval port, with tightly packed gabled houses and tall church spires. Almost all of this was destroyed in the fighting that swept through the region at the end of the Second World War.

All that remains of the castle is its former maltings, a long, barn-like structure that in 1535 became Poland's first public grammar school, and which now houses the Elbląg Museum of Archaeology and History. The building has been restored in a joint venture with the Friedland Gate Museum in Kaliningrad as part of an EU-funded cross-border programme to commemorate the common heritage of the two cities. On a video screen, elderly Germans who fled in 1945–46 recalled their childhoods in Elbling before the war, while old photographs and street signs showed what the town used to look like: its factories, dockside cranes, streets lined with shops and 19th-century apartment buildings.

A cousin of mine was mayor of Elbling just before the First World War. The life of Wolfgang Jaenicke in many ways embodies the history of Germany in the 20th century. His mother Bettina, née Asch, was a grand-daughter of Albert Bauer, my great-great-great grandfather. She had converted to Christianity and married Karl Jaenicke, a mayor of Breslau. After fighting in the First World War – he was thrice decorated – Wolfgang served on the committee implementing the transfer of German territory to Poland stipulated by the Treaty of Versailles. A member of the liberal German State Party, he was elected president of the Potsdam regional government, but resigned when the Nazis came to power, and was sent as envoy to China. Recalled to Germany in 1936, he lived quietly in Bavaria, where he survived despite being half-Jewish and enduring a brutal interrogation by the SS. After the war he was appointed Commissioner for Refugees in the Bavarian state government, and in 1954 became Germany's first ambassador to Pakistan, before ending his career as ambassador to the Holy See.

The museum's vaulted undercroft evoked a much earlier

era with an exhibition called Skarby Gótow ('Treasures of the Goths'), including amber finds from the area, alongside trade goods such as Roman fibulae of silver and bronze. The curators had cleverly explained the function of the ancient objects by placing their modern equivalents – a comb, a disposable plastic razor – beside them. It also displayed the preserved timbers of an ancient roadway similar to the Sweet Track in the Somerset Levels. These once carried a branch of the Amber Route across a bog at Bagart, in the valley of the Dzierzgoń river (the Sorge in German) just south of Elbląg. The track was first discovered in the 1890s by the German archaeologist Hugo Wilhelm Conwentz (1855–1922), the author of many studies on amber. In 1879, he was appointed head of the newly established West Prussian Provincial Museum in Gdańsk, a post he held for 30 years. A pioneer of the conservation movement, he campaigned tirelessly for the establishment of a body to protect the region's environment, leading to the creation in 1906 of the Prussian State Agency for Natural Monument Care. The track underwent further investigation in 1994–95 by Przemyslaw Urbanczyk of the Polish Institute of Archaeology and Ethnology, who used Carbon-14 dating and dendrochronology to establish that construction began in the 1st century BC, and that the road was in continuous use until at least the 3rd century AD – at the height of the Baltic amber trade with Rome.

Despite the fall of the Roman Empire and the mass migrations that accompanied it, traffic along the Amber Route continued, albeit intermittently. Around AD 523, Cassiodorus, a Roman senator in the service of Theodoric, the Ostrogothic king of Italy, recorded a letter from his ruler to the Aesti thanking them for a gift of amber. By the 8th century, the port of Truso had grown up on the banks of the Elbling and, as the exhibits in the museum made clear, amber was among the principal commodities that changed hands there.

Antiquarians had been searching for its exact location

since the late 16th century, when Richard Hakluyt reprinted Wulfstan's account of his voyage in *The Principal Navigations, Voyages, Traffiques and Discoveries of the English Nation*. The exact site was eventually discovered in 1982 by Marek Jagodzinski, on the shore of Lake Drużno to the south of the present-day city. More than 25 years of excavations revealed a number of rectangular homesteads aligned along regular streets, and traces of flat-bottomed boats in the harbour. Many artefacts came to light, including numerous pieces of raw and partly worked amber, along with finished items such as beads and pendants, demonstrating that the material was processed at the site. Nearly 500 Arab silver coins, mostly cut into smaller fragments, were also found, as were a number of weights. Pottery and items of jewellery gave evidence of a trade network extending as far as Western Europe.

In the closing years of the 17th century, Glückel of Hameln, the widow of a Jewish merchant, recalled how a young relative had arrived at their house in Hamburg from Danzig, carrying 'his entire wherewithal, perhaps twenty or thirty Reichsthalers' worth of amber, which he left to my husband to hold or sell'. A century earlier, Georg Braun and Franz Hogenberg included a panorama of Danzig in their *Civitates Orbis Terrarum*, a compendium of city maps and bird's-eye views published in six stout folios between 1572 and 1617. Their view, taken from Gradowa Hill, which rises west of the town centre near the present railway station, shows a skyline bristling with steeples and dominated by the huge square tower of St Mary's, then the largest brick church on the planet. To its right rises the spire of the Town Hall.

   In the accompanying text, Braun, a canon of Cologne Cathedral, praised the port's 'most excellent docks and warehouses' and 'the abundance and variety of its trade with the whole of the west and the north'. He also noted that:

Taking a small boat, naked men go out to collect the *succinum*, which foreigners call amber, that is driven on to the shore by the waves. Soft at first, it soon hardens in the air, and may be shaped into a variety of forms with a lathe and a chisel. It is dark or light, the light fetching more money. It is said that if it is set on fire, its scent will kill poisons. Sometimes ants, gnats and other insects are to be seen in it, not by art, but by the working of nature, or by accidental inclusion. It is even thrown up on to the shore of the mainland by storms.

In 1652, the papal legate Giacomo Fantuzzi wrote in his *Diary of a European Journey* that, 'In Danzig, both white and yellow amber is processed ingeniously; the latter is much more precious, as it is used for minute figurines which are made so skilfully that they seem to be alive... Only those who have paid amber tax are allowed to collect it. In Gdańsk, amber is very expensive...'

Much of Gdańsk's Old Town has been painstakingly re-constructed after its devastation in the Second World War, and walking along Ulica Długi (Long Street) today, it is not hard to picture the Danzig where Glückel's young relation traded in amber. At the point where the street broadens out into Długi Targ (Long Square) stands the Town Hall, looking much as it did in Braun and Hogenberg's panorama. Construction began in 1379, when Danzig was controlled by the Teutonic Knights. In 1457, after the region rebelled against the Order, the city became subject to the Kingdom of Poland, while retaining autonomous rights. Trade flourished, and the Town Hall was enlarged, but it was only after a disastrous fire in the mid-16th century that it assumed its present form, a blend of Gothic and Renaissance, with an 83-metre clock tower topped by a gilt statue of the Polish King Zygmunt II Vasa (1548–72).

The Old Town is surrounded by gatehouses, and at the western end of Ulica Dług, beside the busy ring road, stands the Brama Wyzynna (Upland Gate), a Baroque triumphal arch of 1568, renovated in pompous Prussian style in 1886. In front of it, the 16th-century Prison Tower now houses the city's Amber Museum. In his essay 'Unpacking My Library', Walter Benjamin recalled that in the early years of the 20th century, the building was occupied by the antiquarian bookseller Hans Rhaue; and it was from the top of this tower that Oskar Mazerath, in Günter Grass's great Danzig novel *The Tin Drum*, first practised his window-shattering vocal technique.

You enter up a narrow, winding set of stairs, beneath beams that still bear the graffiti inscribed by prisoners. Beneath the low, vaulted ceiling are displays of clear and cloudy amber, great lumps the size of coconuts – one, with a tawny, pitted surface, from the Vistula lagoon, and another from Ukraine. One large, fractured piece is dark brown outside and sulphur yellow within. There is amber from afar afield as Spain, Morocco, Indonesia and Sakkhalin in Russia's Far East. One alcove houses a microscope carousel; push the button and a series of inclusions – plant fragments, a whole leaf, mosquitoes and other insects – revolve under the lens. The star of the show, however, is a whole lizard encased in a lump of amber, found on a beach near Gdańsk in 1997 by the amber hunter Gabriela Gierłowska and purchased for the museum by the L. Kronenberg Bank Foundation.

Archaeological finds from across northern Poland testify to the fact that people began fashioning raw amber into jewellery as early as the Stone Age. Perhaps the most striking was a large Mesolithic carving of a horse, dating from around 4500 BC, from Strzelce Krajeńskie, south of Szczecin: a stocky animal like a dray horse, its head bent, made of opaque, light yellow amber. A Neolithic circular amulet came from Olsztyn, and a conical one with incised decorations from Sandomierz. A large iron fibula dating from around 1000 BC, from Piekary Wielkie, near Wrocław, is decorated with an amber cabochon.

On the next floor, the Middle Ages are largely represented by the inevitable rosaries, but the Teutonic Knights' loss of West Prussia in the 1450s gave an unexpected boost to the art of amber carving. With their monopoly broken, guilds of amber workers – which the Knights had fiercely suppressed – sprang up in Danzig and elsewhere. The Reformation reduced demand for rosary beads, encouraging craftsmen to diversify, producing intricate *objets d'art* for collectors and experimenting with new techniques. Among the pieces on display are a 16th-century statuette of the Virgin Mary and child from Danzig, 17th-century caskets, an 18th-century inkstand, a selection of cigar holders and pipes with amber mouthpieces, and a magnificent cabinet by the Danzig craftsman Johann Georg Zernebach, dated 1724, with two rows of drawers either side of an arched recess containing an ivory statuette; on top, also in ivory, sits an infant riding a dolphin. Somewhat out of place amid these delicate Baroque curios is a hideous Soviet-era urn atop a tree-stump plinth, which was presented to Stalin in 1952.

The top floor is devoted to the products of the Staatliches Bernstein-Manufaktur at Königsberg – jewellery, boxes, locks, barometers and smoking accessories from the inter-war years. A selection of modern pieces, including an Orthodox icon in amber, testify to a revival of religious art since 1990. Here too is the Bursztynowy Słowik, the amber statuette of a nightingale presented at the Sopot International Song Festival each year; a video screen replayed the unlikely pairing of Lech Wałęsa and Elton John at the festival in 2006.

East of the Town Hall, Ulica Długa opened out into a large square, Długi Targ, much longer than it is broad. Across the square, Jack's American Bar faced the Russian Kitchen – *Kuchnia Rosyiska* – to see which would blink first. Amid the relaxed cosmopolitan crowds, between fine Hanseatic houses painted in pastel greens, blues and ochres, I found it hard to imagine that 70 years ago, all this lay in ruins. Surveying the square from a café table, I found myself reflecting once again on the restoration of historic buildings. Done well, with the right materials and an understanding of the techniques of the time, is restoration after catastrophic damage any more a falsification than the incremental repairs made over centuries to make good the ravages of time or everyday wear and tear? Like Washington's axe, many celebrated historic buildings must now contain very little of their original fabric. And why does it matter? Why, for example, do we deplore the destruction by groups such as Daesh and the Taliban of historic monuments that the armies of the Prophet left unscathed almost as much as their crimes against living humans? Partly, I think, because they are part of humanity's shared heritage and a measure of where we have come from and what has shaped us. The Nazis and the Soviets were selective in their destruction: they wished to distort the historical record in favour of their respective ideologies. Modern fundamentalists wish to obliterate the historical record entirely in a conscious assault on the very notion of a rational historical understanding.

The next day, I set off for the State Archives in search of a fragment of my own history. My great-grandfather, Adolf Schüler, was born in Bütow (now Bytow) in 1850, but after the early deaths of his parents Aron and Mina, he was taken to Berent, a small town some fifty kilometres west of Danzig, now called Kościerzyna. There, my grandfather recalled, he became apprenticed as a printer to a widow, Sara Cohn, and eventually took over the business, running the town newspaper, the *Berenter Zeitung*. The print shop had only medium-sized presses, one of which was a museum piece even then. There was another small, hand-operated press, while the remaining machines were treadle-operated.

When I first embarked on a career in journalism and publishing, many years ago, I was unaware of any precedent in the family. It was only much later, thanks to my cousin Irene Newhouse, that I discovered that I had printer's ink in my veins, so I was keen to learn more about my great-grandfather and his newspaper. Since Berent was part of the Danzig district, it was likely that any records would be held here. The archives were located to the north of the city centre, on Waly Piastowskie, a busy arterial road near the main railway and bus stations, and a stark steel monument to the shipyard workers killed in an uprising in 1970. Beyond it rose the cranes of the Lenin Shipyard where, a decade later, the strikes began that would lead to the formation of the Solidarity movement.

The Archiwum Panstowe Gdańsku was located in a dignified, step-gabled 19th-century building with a large modern annexe. Inside, the calm, studious atmosphere and ranks of microfiche readers informed me that I had come to the right place. The two staff members on duty spoke neither English nor German, but summoned a colleague who could. She explained that she would check to see if they had anything on Kościerzyna. After a while, she returned with several ring binders filled with computer printouts: a catalogue of their Kościerzyna archives. While many entries were in Polish, those for the period I was interested in were in German.

As I scanned the entries, a picture emerged of 19th-century life in this small town, which was only connected to the railway in 1884: council elections; an 1831 report by the security police on unrest in Warsaw; Polish agitation in the 1860s; proceedings against Polish and Russian immigrants; registers of beggars and vagabonds; the transport of prisoners; the creation of a voluntary fire brigade in 1888; the upkeep of the mill pond and cattle market; the introduction of a dog tax; prostitution; the construction of an electricity works in 1901 ... As the archive closed at 2pm, it was too late to call up any documents, and I was advised to come back the next morning.

On my way back, I looked into the Church of St Bridget. The 14th-century church was burned out in the Second World War, and during the 1980s its cavernous, austerely reconstructed interior became a sanctuary for the leaders of Solidarity. To commemorate the church's role in the movement, work began in 2001 on a huge altar made entirely of amber. The altar was not yet complete, but its central panel was on display: a relief carving of the Virgin Mary, wrapped in a milk-white amber gown and crowned with a bright coronet of golden amber.

This use of amber here, in the Sopot Song Festival and elsewhere as a symbol of Poland's struggle for freedom reflected conflicting national claims to the material. Nero commandeered it to lend sparkle to his gladiatorial games. The Teutonic Knights exercised a ruthless monopoly on the trade, while their successors, the Prussian kings, made it their signature diplomatic present to fellow rulers. After Prussia transformed itself into the Second German Empire in 1871, the new state also claimed amber as its own. The Stantien und Becker works were nationalised in 1899, and at the Paris Exposition Universelle the following year, the Prussian Ministry of Trade and Industry mounted an enormous display of amber in the German pavilion. After the Treaty of Versailles assigned parts of the Amber Coast to Poland, severing amber-rich East Prussia from the rest of Germany, claims that the substance was intrinsically German became more shrill. In a trade magazine in 1933, Christian Schwahn, a prolific writer on jewellery, waxed poetical to exhort his readers to wear this 'German stone from German soil' because they loved the Fatherland. And in 1938, the museum curator Alfred Rohde, whom we last met wandering the ruins of Königsberg castle, published a book entitled *Bernstein, ein deutscher Werkstoff* ('Amber, a German Material').

Since 1989, amber has been intensively marketed as a Polish product and an example of Polish craftsmanship. The Amberif trade show has been held in Gdańsk each year since 1994; the World Amber Council was established here in 2006; and amber was one of 15 industries identified by the Polish Ministry of Economy in 2011 for a special export programme. Yet the quantities found in Poland are insufficient to meet the demands of the country's jewellers, so ironically much of the raw material is imported from the Russian mine in Kaliningrad.

That evening, I walked north along the riverfront as locals took their evening stroll. The carillon of the Town Hall was joined by tolling church bells. A sea mist crept over the city. Trains of jackdaws swept restlessly across the rooftops, piercing the night air with their rusty squawks. Smaller and more dapper than their ragged rook cousins, they can be distinguished by their grey collars and white-rimmed eyes. Their name in Polish is *kawka* – *kavka* in Czech – an onomatopoeic rendering of the sound they make. Franz Kafka, punning on his surname, chose the bird as his personal emblem.

The next morning, I returned to the archive to find several thick, dusty volumes labelled in old German black-letter type waiting for me. I started leafing through the synagogue records and there, after a few pages, he was: 'Buchdrücker Schüler' – 'Book-printer Schüler'. He first appeared in 1879–80, and was listed regularly thereafter until 1898, when the family moved to Breslau. I turned to the census returns. Out of a population of around 6,500, roughly half were German and half were Polish. There were fewer than 300 Kashubians – a Slavic people who had settled in the region before the Poles. In *The Tin Drum* – whose author was of partly Kashubian descent – Oskar's grandmother Anna Koljaicek describes them as 'not German enough for the Germans, not Polish enough for the Poles'. The Jewish community was small, consisting of little more than

65 families, of whom the leading names were Blumenthal, Caspari, Pinkus, Cohn, Flatow and Baradowski. Caspari and Arendt were town councillors.

With stereotypical efficiency, the Prussian authorities conducted censuses every five years. In 1880, my great-grand-father was listed as a single man living at 23 Langgaße; by 1885 he was at 6 Langgaße, and the household now included two males and three females. By then, he had married Cäcilie Fraenkel, whom he had met in Breslau; their daughter Frieda was born in 1883. The second male cannot have been my grandfather, who was not born until 1888, but was perhaps a visiting relative; the second female was presumably a house-keeper. By 1890, the family had moved to 19 Markt (the town's main square), and in 1895 they were at Number 6, Markt.

Between the returns were copies of local newspapers announcing the census. The broadsheet *Berenter Zeitung*, which my great-grandfather published, developed from a newsletter called the *Berenter Anzeiger* – an 1890 edition says the paper had been going for six years as the *Zeitung* and 21 as the *Anzeiger*. The *Anzeiger* was printed by A. Schüler from 1883; by 1885, it states *Redaktion, Druck und Verlag von A. Schüler in Berent* – edited, printed and published by A. Schüler in Berent. Later that year, he expanded the paper into a broad-sheet and renamed it the *Berenter Zeitung*, redesigning the masthead to incorporate a picture of a bear – a pun on Berent and the German *Bär*. The paper came from Berlin with national and international news ready-printed on pages 2 and 3. On the blank side, Adolf printed local news on page 1 and advertise-ments on page 4. To produce the broadsheet, he bought a large rapid press powered by a drive gear, which was turned by hand, as electricity had not yet reached Berent. Nor had gas: the print shop was lit by oil lamps and heated by a coal-fired tile stove. In addition to the newspaper, he also printed books, leaflets and pamphlets, including the annual programme of the local junior school and a county bulletin issued by the government in 1896.

When I had finished at the archive, I crossed the road to the bus station, where I boarded a coach to Kościerzyna. The journey took just over an hour, along country roads through low, rolling hills, lakes glistening between stands of birch and spruce, ponds crusted with ice and lined with reeds and bulrushes. Kościerzyna was a smallish market town, now swollen by a belt of arterial roads flanked by supermarkets and business parks. The historic centre was bounded by an oval street that once marked the town ramparts, and dominated by two large redbrick churches. The Protestant church, built at the end of the 19th century, was in the north-German neo-Gothic style, while the Catholic one, constructed during the First World War, was south-German neo-Baroque, with an onion-domed cupola.

The broad main square had remained largely unchanged since the 19th century – the fighting that destroyed Bytow to the west bypassed Kościerzyna. In the middle of its northern side was the small redbrick town hall, now a museum. If the plan of the square I had obtained from a German genealogy magazine was accurate, the house numbers had not changed since the 19th century. From the northwest corner, Ulica Długa ran towards the Protestant church. This was Langgaße (the Polish and German names mean the same: Long Street).

As I stood on the corner, it became clear that during the two decades he spent in Berent, my great-grandfather never moved more than a few hundred metres. Yet his moves traced his rise through the echelons of small-town society, from half way down Langgaße to the corner of the main square, and then on to the square itself. Number 19, his first dwelling on the Markt, stood in the south-east corner, a large three-storey building that would have contained several apartments. His next place of residence, Number 6, was diagonally opposite, to the left of the Town Hall; its ground floor was now a milk bar. According to my grandfather, Adolf Schüler was an active, energetic man who belonged to the local choir, the gymnastic club and the newly-created volunteer fire brigade, and eventually became a member of the town council.

In 1920, as a consequence of the Treaty of Versailles, Berent, along with the rest of West Prussia, was awarded to Poland, and the German population – and most of the Jewish community – left for areas still under German rule. Kościerzyna today was a quiet town, with little going on; apart from a deserted pizzeria on the main square, I couldn't find a pub or café open at five on a midweek afternoon. In the bus back to Gdańsk, only one other passenger travelled the whole way, the rest getting off at the intervening villages.

The eastern end of Długi Targ is occupied by the Brama Zielona: the Green Gate. Neither green nor a gate, this ornately gabled palace was built in the Flemish style in 1564 over four arches opening on to the River Motława. A few hundred yards to the north, along a waterfront lined with tugs, river cruisers and barges, stood the redbrick St Mary's Gate. Together with the tall, 16th-century merchant's house that adjoined it, the gate was now home to the Gdańsk Archaeological Museum. On the grass verge facing the river sat four anthropomorphic figures carved from granite, each three or four feet high. Known as 'babas', these figures were found in Iława district and were created by the Old Prussians some time before the 13th century as monuments to their gods or heroes. Many were destroyed by the Teutonic Knights in their merciless assault on paganism; others survived as field boundaries, or were incorporated into later buildings.

One whole floor of the museum was given over to a permanent exhibition called 'A Millennium of Amber'. Like its counterpart in the Prison Tower, it presented a chronological survey from the natural deposits to the intricate works of art produced by Gdańsk craftsmen from the 16th to the 18th centuries. Among the raw amber, one huge opaque nugget with brain-like nodules stood out, along with some egg-sized teardrops that appeared to have frozen as they slid down the trunk of a tree, while other pieces still bore the imprint of bark. Backlit cases illuminated golden lumps of amber containing plant fragments, moths, caddis flies, ants and beetles. The prehistoric artefacts included a Mesolithic horse, similar to the one in the Prison Tower, from Dobiegniew, a carving of a bear, found at Slupsk, and a series of square amber beads that formed a prehistoric warrior's ornament, from Zabie near Lake Lanskie. There were also amber-working tools, including flint blades and a bone burin.

A wall-mounted map showing the Amber Route snaking its way from the Baltic to Italy presided over Roman-era finds from the Gdańsk area, including some large amber beads with concentric circles carved into them; a silver torc and three silver fibulae; a Roman bronze cauldron; and 10 sestertii dating from the reign of Hadrian (AD 117–138) to that of Marcus Aurelius (161–180). There was also an amber worker's hoard, found at Swiłcza, dating from the late 4th to 5th century, containing a gold pendant, two large gilded silver fibulae, and two smaller ones, along with various other silver ornaments, and ten Roman denarii bearing portraits of Hadrian, Faustina, Marcus Aurelius and Commodus, and therefore already antique when the hoard was assembled.

The continuance of the amber trade during the Migration Era was attested by finds of raw amber from a hill fort at Sopot dating from c.500–980. The later medieval period, from the 10th to the 13th centuries, was represented by both raw amber and unfinished rings, beads, crosses, and a fragment of a wooden drill used for making beads. All from Gdańsk, they were tangible evidence of the city's long tradition of amber working. Perhaps most touching, however, was the skeleton of a young woman from an 11th-century barrow grave found at Uniradzc, bedecked with amber ornaments, a necklace and a hairpiece.

On my last night in Gdańsk, I found myself attending a wake. I'd gone for a drink in an atmospheric, low-ceilinged bar on Ulica Piwna. It was getting late and the place was almost empty, but the young, bearded barman reassured me that they'd be open for a while yet, because the owner was coming in later. After about half an hour, a petite, elegant woman in her forties arrived at the head of a small group of people and invited me to join them. Anna had been living in Dublin for the past 11 years, where, after a series of jobs in restaurants and bars, she now worked for a Canadian investment bank. Her son had just completed his masters at Trinity. Her mother, brother and cousins were with her, having come from her father's funeral in a small town some fifty kilometres away. He had died suddenly in Leeds, she told me, where he had been working as a decorator; they had had to cremate him over there and bring the ashes home.

The Polish half of the Vistula Spit is wider, more densely wooded and less otherworldly than its Curonian counterpart, and dotted with hotels, campsites and holiday homes. In the summer, a ferry runs from Elbląg to the resort of Krynica Morska on the Spit; during the rest of the year, it must be reached from Gdańsk. It's one of the best places in the world to pick up amber, and a street in Krynica Morska is even named Ulica Bursztynowa – Amber Road. A few kilometres along the shore at the village of Jantar, the finals of the World Amber Hunting Championship have been held each summer since 1998. The competition attracts hundreds of participants from as far afield as Spain, who search for amber both along the tideline and by wading into the sea with dip-nets. The two-day event is accompanied by exhibitions and talks on amber, the Baltic ecosystem and the history of amber extraction and processing.

At the landward end of the Spit, I came to an unexceptional little town called Sztutowo, with its corner shop selling fags, mags and booze, ladies' hairdresser, neat block paving underfoot, and flyers advertising Zumba classes and rewards for the recovery of lost dogs. Only the little church and the redbrick post office were coeval with the horror with which the place is now irrevocably associated. Just a kilometre up the road, amid tranquil woodland, stood a stark concrete monument to the people – estimated at between 65,000 and 85,000 – murdered at the Stutthof concentration camp between 1939 and 1945. Beside the road ran a narrow-gauge railway; built to carry holidaymakers from Danzig to Krynica Morska, it was later turned to a more sinister purpose. The camp was established in August 1939, *before* the German invasion of Poland, by Nazis from Danzig as a place to imprison their opponents. In January 1942, Stutthof became an official concentration camp, and developed a chain of sub-camps.

To the right of the entrance stood a pretty gabled villa, built by inmates to house the commandant and his family. The Lithuanian writer Balys Sruoga, who was incarcerated here, recalled the eerie mundanity of Commandant Paul-Werner Hoppe's domestic life: 'In front of his family Hoppe acted absolutely normally... His wife was a homely kind. She pretended that she had no slightest idea of what was going on at the camp.' The homely Frau Hoppe was the daughter of the commandant of Dachau. Interned by the British in 1945, her husband managed to escape to Switzerland. On his return to Germany, he was sentenced to nine years' imprisonment, and released in 1966. 'All this never happened,' he is quoted as saying. 'It's all lies.' Sruoga died in 1947, his health broken in the camp; Obersturmbannführer Hoppe died peacefully in Germany in 1974.

Further up the entrance track stood the guards' redbrick barracks. A smaller building housed the guard dogs – German Shepherds and Rottweilers – the lightest of which weighed more than one of the starving prisoners. Beyond, a stark black watchtower stood guard over barbed-wire fences. The huts within were gone – broken up for firewood in the lean years after the war – but their concrete platforms were still visible. On my way out, I looked back at the commandant's villa, and noticed for the first time the well-kept garden, the satellite dish attached to the balcony, and the light burning in the net-curtained sitting room. I wondered who could live there – and *how* they could.

At Stegna, I got off the bus and walked a kilometre or so through the quiet village into thick forest. The air was rich with the scent of pine and woodsmoke. Last year's leaves, crisp and brown, still clung to the young oaks. I could hear the distant buzz of a chainsaw; then, close by, the rattle of a woodpecker. Suddenly, I came to a steep incline: the sea dune. I climbed a staircase formed by the roots of the pines and, as I crested the top, there it was, a few hundred metres away: the silver glitter of the Baltic. A long, wide beach of white sand curved away into the distance.

A group of four people, dressed warmly against the wind, were walking slowly along the beach, scanning the tideline for amber. At first I could see nothing, but then, as my eyes grew accustomed to the task, I found a small, golden grain. Soon afterwards, I found another, and then another. Strewn along the entire tideline amid the shells, seaweed and driftwood were hundreds of tiny, glittering pieces of amber. Before long, I had collected around two dozen. It seemed greedy to take any more, so I retraced my steps, stopping only for a couple of slightly larger pieces of a beautiful deep red.

Descending the pine-root stairs was trickier than going up. When I reached the bottom, the path stretched straight ahead between dense woodland, like the primeval forest of Grimm's fairy tales; an archetype from deep in the collective unconscious. The track was one of many running south from the Amber Coast, all the way to Rome.

CHAPTER 7

SLAV AND TEUTON

Up to this point, my journey had hugged the coast; if not always within sight or sound of the sea, I had never been so far from it that I could not catch its iodine tang when the wind blew from that direction. Now I was about to follow the Amber Route inland. It appears to have headed along the Vistula until the first big bend, downstream from Torún. From there, J. M. de Navarro traced a route running across the region south of Poznań to reach the Odra near Głogów, from where it headed upstream to Wrocław.

In 1980, the Polish historian Jerzy Wielowiejski charted another trail of finds running further east, through the ancient settlements of Biskupin, Konin and Kalisz, before rejoining De Navarro's route at Wrocław. There is archaeological evidence to support both theories, and both routes may have been in operation either simultaneously or at different periods. In the event, I chose to follow the latter; not only did Wielowiejski have the benefit of more recent archaeological evidence, but his route would take me through areas where some of my forebears once lived.

From Gdańsk, I took a train south to Malbork, where I found the stronghold of the Teutonic Knights in a scruffy park hemmed in by housing blocks. Above its towering walls of red brick loomed a battlemented tower and the apse of the great cathedral of St Mary. For centuries, the tall lancet recess at its eastern end held a colossal statue of the Virgin that was visible for miles across the surrounding plains, but since the artillery battle that raged here for two months at the end of the Second World War, it had stood as empty as the niches that once contained the Buddhas of Bamiyan.

The Order of the House of St Mary of the Germans in Jerusalem, to give its official title, was a brotherhood of crusading monks, like the Templars and Hospitallers, founded in 1190 to fight the Saracens in the Holy Land. In addition to the usual monastic vows of poverty, obedience and chastity, they also vowed to fight the 'enemies of Christ', and devised theological justifications for the waging of holy war. 'I have read that Jeremiah gave the sword to Judas,' wrote Nicolaus von Jeroschin, chaplain to the Order, in his *History of Prussia*, 'and said to him: "See, now take this holy sword as a gift from God, so that you cannot fail to subdue the enemies of the people of Israel."'

In 1291, however, the Egyptian Mamluks captured Acre, the Crusaders' last stronghold on the Levantine mainland. This left the papacy and monarchs of Europe with a problem: what to do with the Military Orders? Immensely rich, with land-holdings across the continent, influential (the brethren were largely the younger sons of nobility), and armed to the teeth, these self-governing fraternities of seasoned warriors were too dangerous to be left idle on European soil. The Templars were accused of heresy and violently suppressed in 1307 (giving rise to a thousand conspiracy theories); the Hospitallers were dispatched to defend the island of Rhodes from the Turks; while in 1309 the Teutonic Knights, after kicking their heels in Venice for a few years, transferred their operations to Prussia, where they had been conducting a papally sanctioned war against the pagan Prussians and Lithuanians since 1225. As their new headquarters, they chose Malbork, then known as Marienburg, or the castle of Mary; its strategic location on the River Nogat enabled the Knights to control the main trade arteries – including the Amber Route – from the Baltic to the Polish interior.

I passed through the sleek modern visitor centre into the Outer Bailey, which once housed the castle's workshops, armouries and storehouses, across a drawbridge and under a portcullis to the Middle Castle. This was the seat of their secular power, from where the Teutonic state was administered. To the right stood the Great Refectory, and behind it the Grand Master's palace, a soaring, steep-roofed hall in red brick, with granite pillars, capitals and quoins. This was no austere monastic retreat, but a courtly palace in which the Knights, as rulers of a powerful state, could entertain visiting potentates with banquets and tournaments.

At the far end of the courtyard stood bronze statues of four Grand Masters of the Order: Hermann von Salza (1209–39), Siegfried von Feuchtwangen (1303–11), Winrich von Kniprode (1352–82), and Albrecht von Hohenzollern (1511–25). They once formed part of a monument to Frederick the Great unveiled in 1877. The positioning of the figures at the four corners of a plinth supporting a statue – now lost – of the Prussian monarch was intended to depict the Teutonic Order as the precursor of the German state. The inclusion of the last Grand Master, Albrecht von Hohenzollern (despite the fact that he had no connection with Marienburg, which the Knights abandoned half a century before he was elected) is explained by the fact that he was the ancestor of Frederick, and thus of the reigning Kaiser, Wilhelm I.

From the Middle Castle, I crossed another drawbridge over a deep dry moat to the High Castle, the innermost and oldest sanctum, where 60 brethren knights – the number of warriors who guarded King Solomon – slept, ate and prayed. From its courtyard, I climbed the stairs to a first-floor cloister, its archways filled with delicate Gothic tracery. Leading off the cloister, the grand Gothic portal of the cathedral, known as the Golden Gate, retained much of its original polychrome ceramic decoration depicting the Knights as continuing the battle of the angelic host against the armies of Satan. The cathedral was off limits, as restoration was not yet complete, but a heavily carved wooden door creaked open to admit me to the incense and wax-polish scented chapter house. Beneath graceful rib vaults that sprang from three central columns, wooden benches lined the walls, with a throne for the Grand Master at the centre. Here the brethren would meet once a week to confess their transgressions and accept punishment. Some original frescoes were still visible in the vaulting, depicting the Virgin Mary, Jesus and the Archangel Michael, and the encaustic floor tiles were richly decorated with eagles, dragons, wild boar, flowers and geometric figures.

The eastern range of the Middle Castle was occupied by the castle museum. I struggled to view an exhibition of armour and weaponry amid a large and mulish tour group led by a self-important guide, before I discovered the amber galleries in the undercroft. I had seen the magnificent collections at Palanga, Kaliningrad and Gdańsk, but the exhibition at Malbork was unparalleled. When the museum was set up in 1961, the curators decided to assemble a historically representative collection, but it was not an easy task. Because of their fragility, Baroque amber artefacts of the 17th and 18th centuries are scarce, and rarely come on to the market. Gradually, however, through purchases at auction, private donations, archaeological finds and transfers from other museums, they managed to assemble more than 2,000 objects, many of the highest quality and importance.

The most impressive of the prehistoric ornaments was a series of round and cylindrical beads produced by the Neolithic Rzucewo culture that operated large-scale amber workshops in the Vistula Delta around 2000 BC, while a necklace found in a grave at Weilbark dated from the Roman era. The highlight, however, was the Renaissance and Baroque collection. Two items testified to the popularity of amber jewellery among people of wealth and status at the beginning of the 17th century: a necklace of cylindrical beads of semi-opaque amber engraved with garlands, made for a high-ranking citizen of Gdańsk, and a string of ten big, bright, faceted beads from a necklace that belonged to Dorothea-Sybilla Hohenzollern, Duchess of Brzeg and daughter of Johan Georg, Elector of Brandenburg and Duke of Prussia.

By the 17th century, Gdańsk craftsmen had devised ways of making larger, more elaborate pieces, many of them destined for the *Wunderkammern* of monarchs and aristocrats. A casket from the Gdańsk workshop of Michael Redlin, dating from around 1680, was composed of contrasting panels of clear and opaque amber, with a seated figure of Ceres on the lid. An elaborate amber altar made in Gdańsk in 1687 rose in tiers supported by serpentine columns and decorated with medallions. A central ivory relief depicted the Last Supper, and above an ivory crucifixion on the uppermost level floated an amber figure of the resurrected Christ. A late 17th-century casket said to have belonged to King Stanisław Leszczynski used the *eglomisé* technique also seen in the St Petersburg Amber Room, where an image was engraved in intaglio on the reverse of a thin sheet of transparent amber, backed with gold leaf to reflect the light.

The most spectacular of these pieces was a late 17th-century chest by Christoph Maucher. A riot of Baroque extravagance, it was festooned with scrollwork, putti, seashells and acanthus leaves in many shades of amber, surrounding a full-relief statuette of Venus. Already an experienced ivory carver when he arrived in Gdańsk from southern Germany around 1670, Maucher was never a member of the guilds, who fiercely opposed any attempts by the city council to employ him, and he eventually left Gdańsk in 1705.

The latest and most poignant of these objects was a portable cabinet made for Stanisław August Poniatowski, the last king of Poland, in Gdańsk in the 1770s. Its central recess, flanked by two tiers of miniature drawers, contained a 17th-century amber statuette of the Virgin Mary. The cabinet appears to have been created as a thanksgiving after the king narrowly escaped kidnap by Polish nobles in 1771; several of the panels carried inscriptions such as 'Life from death' and 'I will return'. This aristocratic feuding left Poland at the mercy of its neighbours, and by 1795 the country had been partitioned and Stanisław was forced to abdicate. By a twist of fate, the cabinet found its way to Scotland. After the former king died penniless in St Petersburg in 1798, it was purchased by an ancestor of the present Lord Carmont, finally returning to Poland in 1979, when Lady Barbara Carmont donated it to the museum.

I crossed the wooden footbridge over the Nogat to get a better view of the castle from the opposite bank. From here, I could take in the whole complex: the long walls with their twin-turreted River Gate, the ornate façade of the Grand Master's palace perched on a moraine over the river, the High Castle with its steep-gabled roofs, and away to the right, the Dansker, a free-standing tower connected to the main castle by a bridge, which functioned as both a latrine and a defensive outpost. Under the leaden sky, a mist was beginning to form on the wide, reed-fringed river. It was bitterly cold, so it was a relief to return to the castle and take refuge in the cosy restaurant deep within its vaults, where a log fire was crackling in an inglenook.

There was a grim postscript to the history of Malbork. In October 2008, construction workers digging the foundations of a new hotel uncovered some 70 skeletons in a mass grave. Over the following months, a total of 2116 corpses came to light. The bodies of men, women and children had been buried naked, without shoes, clothes, or personal effects.

They were presumed to be German citizens of Marienburg – 1840 of whom were classified as missing after the end of the war – along with refugees fleeing the advancing Red Army from the east. As several dozen had been shot through the head, it was speculated that all the victims had been massacred by the Soviets. The local prosecutor launched an investigation, which concluded, however, that the majority showed no signs of violence, and had probably died from cold, hunger or typhus. Because the bodies with gunshot wounds were all found in the uppermost layer, they were presumed to be German PoWs ordered by the Russians to bury their compatriots to prevent the spread of disease. Their task completed, they were shot and thrown into the grave with them. On 14th August 2009, all the remains were reinterred in a German military cemetery at Stare Czarnowo, not far from the present border, in a ceremony of reconciliation attended by both Poles and Germans.

From Malbork, a sleek, modern train carried me south through a landscape of gently rolling hills and silvery lakes, past Prabuty, a hilltop town crowned by a medieval redbrick cathedral, another stronghold of the Teutonic Knights. I had to change at Iława, a small town amid the Masurian Lakes, once known as Deutsch Eylau. Here, I boarded a much older compartment train with very hard seats, which carried me south-west across the plains bounded by the great bend formed by the Vistula as it swung east from Bydgoszcz to Toruń, the next waystation on the Amber Route.

By the time the train pulled in to Toruń, it was growing dark. The station was undergoing renovation, its old booking hall a shell stranded between platforms with no direct access to the street. I dragged my luggage across the tracks to the rear exit and caught a taxi into town. The drive took me over a wide bridge across the Vistula and beneath the floodlit walls of the medieval town, studded with gates and bastions, the towers and spires of the city's churches pricking the night sky above them.

Under a thin drizzle, the taxi deposited me on the cobbles of the New Town Square (the New Town being only marginally less venerable than the old), beneath the double tower of St James's Church. A bespectacled priest in a cappello romano and soutane emerged from the church gates, unfurled his umbrella and glid past, the very image of G. K. Chesterton's Father Brown. The Hotel Legenda, where I had booked a room, was a handsome old blue-washed house on the east side of the square, with beamed ceilings, welcoming staff, and a cosy restaurant serving homely and filling Polish cuisine (but atrocious corner-shop wines). By now, the drizzle had turned into a downpour, so I decided to spend the evening reading up on the history of the town.

Toruń – Thorn in German – was one of the first settlements of the Teutonic Knights in Prussia. Invited into Poland by Duke Conrad of Masovia around 1231 to assist in his war against the Prussians, the Knights established their frontier on the Vistula, building a small castle on a hill by the river. 'They called the castle Vogelsang [birdsong]', the 14th-century chronicler Nikolaus von Jeroschin records, 'and here the brothers began the long war, establishing themselves without hesitation with just a few ill-equipped armed men against the heathen horde (which was innumerable). In their many tribulations they did not sing the song of the nightingale but songs like the songs of grief the swan sings as it dies . . .'

'History to the defeated,' wrote W. H. Auden, 'May say Alas but cannot help or pardon'; nor does it record the songs of grief sung by the pagan Prussians massacred by the Knights or converted to Christianity at sword-point, their very name appropriated by their Germanic conquerors. By inviting the Teutonic Order into his territory, Duke Conrad unwittingly unleashed a terrifying enemy who rapidly conquered the entire

south-east coast of the Baltic, cutting off Poland from the
sea. To consolidate their hold on the region, they introduced
German settlers, thus initiating an ethnic conflict that would
rage for seven centuries and at times threatened the very existence of the Polish nation.

In 1233, Hermann Balk, the Knights' Master in Prussia,
granted a charter for the founding of the civilian town of Toruń.
In 1236, after repeated flooding, the townspeople moved their
settlement to its present location, and some time afterwards the
Knights abandoned Vogelsang and built a new castle beside the
town. Toruń flourished, joining the Hanseatic League in 1280
and developing trade links with the Flemish mercantile cities
of Bruges, Ghent and Ypres. By the 15th century it had become
one of the main exporters of Polish grain. 'With its beautiful
buildings and roofs made of gleaming fired brick,' wrote the
Polish chronicler Jan Długosz in 1546, 'no other place can
compare with its location, beauty and splendid lustre.'

The next morning was bright and clear, so I strolled up the
pedestrianised Ulica Szeroka that connected the New and
Old Town squares. One of the few historic towns in Poland
not to have been badly damaged in the Second World War,
Toruń remained a magnificent north European townscape of
tall, step-gabled merchants' houses, soaring Gothic spires,
redbrick granaries and grandiloquent Renaissance archways.
Yet despite its architectural splendour, modern Toruń was less
cosmopolitan than Gdańsk; a university town with a population of just under a quarter of a million and a computer
industry based in a new technology park outside the centre.
Its streets were lined not by cafés and souvenir shops but with
greengrocers, pharmacies, two bookshops, a hardware store
and a charmingly old-fashioned haberdashery, its window a
rainbow of bright ribbons.

Rounding the gentle curve of Szeroka, I came unexpect-
edly on a family connection: a plaque commemorating Zvi

Hirsch Kalischer (1795–1874). Though born in Leszno, this early proponent of Zionism spent most of his life in Toruń, where he served as acting rabbi, his fiercely ascetic nature not permitting him to accept a salaried position. He was a friend and mentor to Heinrich Graetz, author of the first comprehensive history of the Jewish people, who became principal of the Jewish Orthodox school in Breslau from 1845. There Graetz came into conflict with my great-great-grandfather David Honigmann. Kalischer and Graetz were Orthodox Jews of almost mystical intensity, seeing the industrial world of the 19th century as a cesspit of depravity, and the diaspora as an extension of the Babylonian captivity. Honigmann, one of the founders of Reform Judaism and general secretary to the Upper Silesian Railway, was an assimilationist and a moderniser. A bitter battle of words ensued in public lectures and in print.

The Old Town was dominated by the Church of St John. Built in the second half of the 14th century in the North German Gothic style, it was elevated to cathedral status in 1994. Its stumpy tower, never completed to its intended height, terminated at the level of the nave roof, adding to the foursquare appearance of the building. Almost in the centre of the main square stood the Town Hall, a tall brick building with a clock tower at one corner. The four sides enclosed a flagstone quadrangle, in which a giant creeper, each of its intertwined stems as thick as a man's arm, grew to the roof. The hall was built in the late 14th century, when the medieval city was approaching the peak of its prosperity; in the early 17th century, its severe Gothic verticality was embellished with gables, corner turrets and stone facings in the Dutch Mannerist style. The building now housed the district museum, the highlights of which were some extraordinary 14th- and 15th-century stained glass from Chełmno, and some very good religious sculpture, including a powerful, anonymous *Ecce Homo* of c.1100 and a sinuous, swooning *Mary of the Sorrows*. Upstairs, in the Grand Hall, hung the only contemporary likeness of the city's most famous son, Copernicus, along with superb portraits of many other local worthies by followers of Dürer and Cranach.

Outside the Town Hall stood a large bronze 19th-century statue of Copernicus holding an armillary sphere. A couple of streets to the south was the merchant's house where he is believed to have been born; although there is no firm evidence for the claim, his parents did own the house at the time. Born in 1473, the astronomer passed his first 18 years in Toruń before studying at Kraków and Bologna. Although he spent the rest of his life at Frombork, he always identified himself as Nicolaus Copernicus Torunensis. Poles and Germans have both claimed him as their own. He was a subject of the Polish kingdom, and remained loyal to the Catholic Church throughout his life. All his published writings are in Latin, though a few of his private letters are in German, and that was probably the language he spoke every day. In many ways, the controversy is an anachronistic product of 20th-century nationalism, projected backward on to a place and a time in which concepts of nationality were fluid; he was, above all, a member of the Europe-wide community of Renaissance humanists.

To the south of the town centre, on a bluff overlooking the Vistula, stood the remains of the Knights' castle. Although much smaller than Malbork, manned by just a commander and 12 brother Knights, it must have been intimidating, its sheer walls of brick and stone commanding both the river and the town. The main building was erected in the 13th century, towards the end of which a tall octagonal tower was constructed in the courtyard.

By the turn of the 15th century, however, the Knights' fortunes were on the wane. When the Polish King Louis died without a male heir in 1382, he was succeeded by his eight-year-old daughter Jadwiga. Four years later, the Polish nobles offered her in marriage to the Lithuanian ruler Jogalia, on condition he converted to Christianity. This he did, taking his people – the last pagans in Europe – into the Catholic fold. At once, the Knights' justification for waging holy war, and papal backing for it, evaporated. Furthermore, the marriage of Jadwiga to Władisław Jagiełło, as he was now known, began a powerful dynasty that would rule a united Poland-Lithuania for two centuries. The Knights now faced a formidable adversary.

The blow fell on 15th July 1410 – the Feast of the Apostles – when Jagiełło, resplendent in silver armour, led an army of Poles, Lithuanians, Hungarians, Czechs and Russians against the Teutonic Knights at Grunwald, some 120 kilometres northeast of Toruń. By the end of the day, the once invincible Knights had been crushed: Grand Master Ulrich von Jungingen lay dead on the field of battle, along with almost half his 27,000-strong army. Many more were drowned in the lakes and marshes as they fled. The defeat went down in German history as a national catastrophe, which was not avenged until their victory over the Russians at nearby Tannenberg in August 1914.

At the First Peace of Thorn, concluded the following February, the Knights were forced to pay substantial reparations in exchange for a release of prisoners, but managed to retain most of their territory – for the time being. In 1454, however, the townspeople drove the Knights from the city and demolished the castle, turning the site into a rubbish dump. The ensuing war ended with the Second Peace of Thorn in 1464, under which the Knights were forced to withdraw to East Prussia, abandoning Malbork and transferring their capital to Königsberg. Toruń, along with the rest of West Prussia, was now Polish.

Only some of the outer walls and the lower storeys of the Gdańsker remained, the latter connected to the main castle by a covered bridge over a stream. The foundations of the rest were excavated in the 1950s, including the octagonal keep and, ranged around it, the chapter house, chapel and refectory, linked by a cloister. Below these, the undercroft, crypt and dungeon survived, and were used to exhibit fragments of stone tracery and tiles found during the excavations. Beside the Gdańsker stood a 13th-century mill that once provided the Knights with flour. Enlarged in the 19th century, the building was now an appealing boutique hotel and restaurant, where I stopped for a beer and watched the prismatic sparkle of the millrace through a long window.

As I set about planning my onward journey, it became clear that I would have difficulty visiting several places associated with the Amber Route and my family history by public transport. Though the distances were not great, services were infrequent and indirect, so I bowed to the inevitable and hired a car in Torún, arranging to return it in Wrocław. As I bowled through the outskirts of Inowrocław, a flurry of sleet turned into a full-blown snowstorm, the flakes driven horizontally by the wind. A series of satnav-guided detours sent me up farm tracks before I eventually arrived at Biskupin, one of the most important ancient settlements in northern Europe.

As I approached the archaeological park on foot, a stocky mastiff hurled its considerable weight against its chain, barking furiously. A custodian emerged, dressed in a quilted jacket and beanie hat, and insisted that the place was closed. I protested that it was not yet dusk, and that I had driven a long way and wouldn't have the opportunity to return, but he was implacable. Eventually I asked if there was anywhere that afforded a decent view from outside the fence, and he directed me off to one side of the entrance. Following a narrow-gauge railway line under a bridge, I came to a spot where, through reed beds, I could glimpse the watchtower and palisade of the reconstructed fort. With the late afternoon sun glancing between scudding clouds, it was an atmospheric sight, and I waded through the reeds, soaking my boots, to get a photograph.

The Iron Age settlement consisted of the fort, strategically located on a peninsula jutting into a lake, and the houses in the village that served it. Discovered by Polish archaeologists in 1933, it was soon acclaimed as the 'Polish Pompeii'. Because of the waterlogged conditions, much of the timber had survived. Dendrochronology has since shown that the oak was felled between 747 and 722 BC, although there was evidence of occupation as early as the Mesolithic and as late as the early Middle Ages. Its extensive trading connections were attested by bronze fibulae, silver-tin belt clasps, amber and glass beads, spinning whorls and iron knives.

The site rapidly became an arena for competing nationalisms. The Polish government hailed it as evidence of the achievements of prehistoric Slavs, but after the Germans occupied Poland in 1939, Biskupin was renamed Urstädt and attributed to ancient Germanic people. Since the time of the Kaisers, there had been a growing tendency among German archaeologists to interpret prehistoric remains as proof of a longstanding Teutonic presence in the contested lands of the East. Once the Nazis took power, this became the only permitted interpretation. A foundation for the study of prehistory – revealingly called *Ahnenerbe* (the legacy of our ancestors) – was set up under the supervision of the SS. The aim was clear: the function of archaeology in the Third Reich was to provide historical justification for its territorial claims. In 1940, excavations were resumed by the *Ahnenerbe*, and continued until 1942. When the Germans were forced to retreat, they flooded the site with the intention of obliterating all evidence of it, though ironically the inundation actually helped to preserve the ancient timbers.

As I squelched my way back to the car park, the custodian beckoned; for some reason, he had relented, and let me in. Within a stockaded rampart, thirteen parallel rows of buildings were packed together, separated by corduroy roads. The 105 houses were estimated to have sheltered a population of between 700 and 1,000. The survival of organic materials provided evidence of a broad-based economy in which agriculture, farming and fishing were supplemented by metalworking, leatherworking, pottery, weaving, horn and bone carving. The wooden huts, clustered around a central clearing, were timber-framed, in some cases infilled with wattle and daub, of which traces survived. Among the reconstructed huts, live horses and cattle were tethered.

I first heard about Biskupin in November 1998, at the Wigmore Hall in London. At an evening of music and readings to commemorate the 60th anniversary of Kristallnacht. Juliet Stevenson read from the opening chapter of Anne Michaels' 1996 novel *Fugitive Pieces*: 'For centuries, only fish wandered Biskupin's wooden sidewalks...' The book tells of the site's destruction, and of seven-year-old Jakob, rescued by a Greek archaeologist after his parents are murdered by the Nazis. It is a sombre, poetic meditation on the nature of identity, human resilience, and the long shadow such events cast down the generations.

As you approach Konin from the north, the first sight of the town is the chimneys of the electricity generating plant on its outskirts. This industrial town, capital of a coal-mining county, was ringed by spoil heaps and approached along wide avenues lined by Khrushchev-era blocks of flats. A settlement first arose here at a ford on the River Warta; Ptolemy named it *Setidava* or *Getidava*, and it appears to have been an emporium used by merchants travelling along the Amber Route. On the dunes to the west of the town centre, a burial ground dated back to the Przeworsk culture of the 2nd and 3rd centuries AD. The medieval city was originally located a few kilometres to the south, but after it was sacked by the Teutonic Knights in 1331, it moved to its present site, growing in importance in the centuries that followed. After the Second Partition of Poland in

1793, Konin came under Russian rule; during the Napoleonic Wars, it became part of the French-backed Duchy of Warsaw, but after the Emperor's defeat, the Congress of Vienna placed it back in the Russian sphere, where it remained until Poland regained its independence in 1918.

Skirting an aluminium works, I crossed a wide modern bridge over the Warta and found a parking place on one of those dusty streets lined with liquor shops and car parts dealers that one finds on the edges of towns around the world. From here it was a short walk to the main square, Plac Wolności, a cobbled expanse framed by sober 18th- and 19th-century houses. To my right, a graceful bridge led back across the river to the north bank; from the other end of the square, two narrow, shop-lined streets ran south. I followed the larger, Third of May Street, a few hundred metres to where it converged with the other around a little Baroque town hall with an octagonal turret. The street name commemorated the Polish constitution of 1791 and was adopted on the proclamation of the republic in 1919. Under Tsarist rule, this was Ulica Długa (Long Street); since 1939 it had been called Hermann Göring Straße, Red Army Street and, after the fall of Communism, Third of May once again.

The old centre had a dowdy, small-town feel; it was neither a busy commercial hub – that lay across the river – nor a tourist destination. A little further on, I came upon the church of St Bartholomew in the corner of a square park. In the churchyard stood the town's main claim to fame, and its connection with the Amber Route: a phallic Romanesque pillar. Set up by a local count in 1151, it was the oldest milestone in Europe outside the Roman Empire. The Latin inscription translated:

> 1151 years after Our Lord's Incarnation. To Kalisz from Kruszwica here is the midpoint of the road indicated by this formula of justice. Which was ordered to be raised by

count Piotr who carefully halved the road. To remember
him, may every traveller pray to gracious God.

From the church, I wandered back up Third of May to Plac
Zamkowy – Castle Square, though there was no trace of a
castle. Nor did this bland expanse of modern block paving and
municipal shrubbery give any clue that it was once the Tepper
Marik, or pot market – the beating heart of the Jewish *shtetl*.
The few surviving old buildings had been cement-rendered
into pastel uniformity with their modern neighbours, but in
the north-west corner, one stood out: a library with orientalist
triangular-topped windows. This was once the *bes-medresh*,
the Jewish house of religious study. Immediately beyond it,
on Mickiewicza Street, stood a graceful white synagogue with
Moorish-style windows. Built in 1829, it was vandalised by the
Nazis, and restored in the 1980s. Used as a library until 2008, it
had now been returned to the Jewish community. Of that once
substantial population, however, there was little trace.

On 1st September 1939, a few hours after the attack on
Westerplatte, German troops crossed Poland's western border.
The Polish army, hopelessly outnumbered, fell back towards
Warsaw. Bombers patrolled the skies above Konin, and the roads
filled with refugees from the west. German troops entered the
town on the 14th, and raised the swastika over the Town Hall. A
week later, in response to an alleged act of sabotage, the occupiers took a number of Jewish and Christian hostages. On 22nd
September – the Day of Atonement – two of them, a 30-year-
old Catholic restaurateur named Alexander Kurowski and the
70-year-old Jewish merchant Mordechai Słodki, having been
chosen by lot, were executed by firing squad in the north-east
corner of Plac Wolnosci. Shortly afterwards the Nazis began
deporting the city's Jews to ghettos and concentration camps
until, in November 1941, the SS took some 3,000 who remained
into the forests to the north of the city and murdered them there.

In the 1980s, Theo Richmond, a British documentary film-maker whose parents had emigrated from Konin in the early 20th century, set out to discover and commemorate the life of this vanished community, travelling throughout Britain, the United States and Israel to interview survivors and their children. The sights, the sounds, the very texture of Jewish life in the town are as vividly alive in the pages of his book *Konin: A Quest* as they are absent from its streets today.

From Konin, I drove the 55 kilometres south to Kalisz. Regarded as the oldest town in Poland, it may be the Calisia listed in Ptolemy's *Geographia*, which probably drew on reports of Roman merchants travelling the Amber Route. By the early Middle Ages, it was part of the Piast kingdom of Poland. The city's Jewish community dated back to the 12th century; in 1264 Duke Bolesław the Pious drew up the Kalisz Statute, guaranteeing them protection and the right to administer their own internal affairs. The city changed hands many times. Like Konin, it was annexed by Prussia in 1793, and after 1815 became part of Russian-ruled Congress Poland.

By the time I made my way through the industrial outskirts, it was almost dark. Having found a hotel, I had a late supper and fell gratefully into bed. The next morning, I walked into town past the Doric-porticoed turnpike arch and across two branches of the River Prosna, a tributary of the Warta, via the stone bridge originally named after Tsar Alexander I. The Rynek was dominated by a cream-stuccoed Town Hall which, despite its neo-Renaissance appearance, was built in the 1920s after the Germans destroyed much of the town in the opening days of the First World War. Over the narrow, winding streets behind the Rynek rose the vertiginous walls of the redbrick St Nicholas Cathedral, its spire bracketed by flying buttresses. A little further on, on Babina Street, I came upon a monu-ment shaped like a stone lectern, on which a bronze book lay open. It commemorated the destruction of several thousand volumes, many of irreplaceable antiquity, looted by the Nazis from Polish and Jewish libraries in the city between 1942 and 1944, and used to fill a canal here.

The Regional Museum was located a couple of blocks west of my hotel. The building was uncompromisingly Modernist, but far from the usual brutalist slab of concrete. With its tall upper windows jettied out at an angle of 45 degrees over the ground floor, it had rhythm and verve, and I wondered which Polish architect, working within the diktats of Communist planning, had created a building of such architectural flair. The exhibits were impressive: an array of Bronze Age axes, Iron Age pottery from Biskupin and elsewhere, spearheads, daggers. Roman and Migration-era fibulae and swords, and a Gothic silver belt buckle from the 5th century. The concentration of raw amber along with Roman coins and jewellery attested to an established trade with the Roman Empire, while a map showed the Amber Route passing through Kalisz en route from the Baltic to the Adriatic.

As I drove south through flat farmland and forest, winter fought a last-ditch battle against the advancing spring with a fusillade of snow and hailstorms. By the time I arrived at Kępno and parked in the large, eerily deserted Rynek, the weather had cleared. A town of some 15,000 in Wielopolska, close to the border with Silesia, Kępno was annexed by Prussia in 1793 as part of the Second Partition, and became known as Kempen (its Polish name is pronounced *Kempno*). It was here that my great-great- grandfather David Honigmann was born in 1821.

Kępno lies in the basin of the River Warta, in an area rich in prehistoric remains associated with the Amber Route. Six sites where amber was deposited as a votive offering have been found in the area, including one in Kępno itself. In the summer of 1865, a workman digging a road through a field near

Hennersdorf (now Woskowice Górne), some 20 kilometres to the south, found a number of prehistoric burials beneath the sandy soil. Urns containing ashes, bones and iron and bronze rings had been placed under a layer of boulders. One grave held approximately eight *Metzen* – an obsolete measurement corresponding to about twenty litres – of mostly small, unworked pieces of weathered amber.

The main square had been recently restored; the 19th-century neoclassical Ratusz in the centre and the Catholic church of St Martin looked spanking new, though paintwork and stucco still flaked from a few buildings in the corners and the small streets beyond. East of the Rynek, on Ulica Łazienkowa, I found the synagogue. Designed by two master masons from Brzeg in Lower Silesia, Friedrich Wilhelm Scheffler and Karl Friedrich Scheffler, to replace an earlier building destroyed by fire, it was a dignified early 19th-century temple with a tall neoclassical portico and pilasters, faced with rusticated stucco that was now falling away from the brickwork.

At the time, some 60 per cent of Kępno's 6,000 inhabitants were Jewish – the rest being Polish Catholics, with a smaller number of German Protestants – and the synagogue was the most imposing building in town. Swelled by a steady influx of refugees from persecution in Russian-occupied Poland, the community remained strictly Orthodox. Yiddish was spoken, the men wore beards, kaftans and fur-trimmed caps, the women covered their heads, and the secular ways of assimilated German Jews were looked on with suspicion. There were just two coaches a week from the Silesian capital Breslau (now Wrocław), so news from the outside world reached Kempen slowly.

According to Isidor Kastan's memoir of life in the town, published under the title 'Alt-Kempen: eine Kulturskizze aus der Mitte des vorigen Jahrhunderts' in the *Jahrbuch für jüdische Geschichte und Literatur* for 1923, there was emigration to

New York, St Louis and Chicago, and to Britain, where many Kempen Jews settled in London's Commercial Road and Petticoat Lane. Late in life, the English writers Christopher and Peter Hitchens discovered that their mother's great-grandfather was Nathan Blumenthal, who had emigrated from Kempen to Leicester in the 19th century.

A more local magnet was Breslau, 75 kilometres to the west, where some local young men went to seek a modern, secular education and 'dropped their traditional dress and sought to assimilate with all speed'. Among them was David Honigmann. The son of Loebel Schaje Honigmann, a grain merchant, and Hannah, née Astrich, David was one of five siblings, and was educated in the Cheder, the only Jewish school in town. In his memoir 'Aus einem Knabenleben von vor 50 Jahren', published in *Liebermanns Jahrbuch* in 1884, he recalls the school as dark and dingy, as it was cleaned only once a year before Passover. On winter evenings the children went home with lanterns and staffs. The education consisted of memorising Bible verses in Hebrew and Yiddish, the Commentaries, and the Talmud. No other subjects were taught.

Honigmann's parents hired a tutor, whom he identifies in his memoir only as H. This young man taught him grammar and logic, and used Moses Mendelssohn's 1783 translation of the Bible, something the more traditional Jews of Kempen regarded as blasphemous, but which enabled David to learn High German. When H left Kempen, David attended a non-denominational Christian school, and was taught French by a disabled veteran of Napoleon's army known as Monsieur Pierre. After his bar mitzvah when he was 13, David chose to attend school in Breslau, where he studied at the Gymnasium and went on to read law at the university, becoming friends with the city's charismatic rabbi Abraham Geiger, an ardent proponent of Reform Judaism.

It was on a return visit to Kempen in October 1841 that

Honigmann, recently graduated, met his adversary Heinrich Graetz. In his diary, Graetz recalls passing through 'through a road full of gawking Jews to the Hotel Schlesinger' on his way to a wedding. A lawyer called Wertheimer – known as 'the Mephisto of Kempen' – showed up. 'With him came a young bespectacled man, about 20, with an impertinent, disdainful expression, Honigmann, a high-school graduate, showing much spirit, but puffed up, a lap child of Geiger's. With what contempt, with what Geigerish irony, he spoke of Jews and Judaism . . .'

As a result of emigration, the Jewish community of Kempen slowly dwindled from more than 3,000 in 1855 to fewer than 750 in 1910, although its standard of living improved thanks to the funds sent back from England and the United States. When Kempen, along with the rest of the region, was transferred to Poland after the end of the First World War, most of the remaining Jews departed for Germany.

I found the synagogue a shell, its doors and windows boarded up. During the Nazi occupation, it was used as a stables and then as a storehouse, a function it continued to serve after the war. A fire destroyed much of the interior in 1973. Renovation work began in 1988, but ground to a halt a couple of years later. Since 1999 the building had been owned by the Jewish community of Wrocław, who repaired the roof and fitted new gutters and drainpipes to prevent it from becoming completely ruinous.

In 2007, workers renovating the market square uncovered a small reservoir lined with flat, heavy stones. Closer inspection revealed designs and Hebrew inscriptions. The local newspaper *Tygodnik Kępinski* reported that there were about 200 in all, probably looted by the Nazis from the Jewish cemetery in the nearby village of Bralin. After the war, the Russians used headstones, gravel and bones from the cemetery to pave the roads. Other tombstones were used to build two monuments, now demolished, to Communist heroes. As recently as 2007, a private home was reported to have a driveway paved with gravestones. After their rediscovery, the surviving memorials were stored in the grounds of the synagogue; I could see them, standing in piles or stacked against the walls, through the chain-link fence.

Visiting these small Polish towns was a dispiriting experience. Their neat historic centres seemed lifeless, their synagogues empty and falling into ruin, the few Polish shoppers lost in the expanses of their depopulated market squares. These places were as drowned as Biskupin.

CHAPTER 8

ISLAND CITY

On Tumski Island, the ancient heart of Wrocław, orange street-lights flared in the thin mist that shrouded the towering Gothic spires of the cathedral. Though not technically an island since 1810, when the northern branch of the River Odra was filled in, the area still had a sequestered, ecclesiastical atmosphere, its cobbled lanes deserted except for two priests in birettas and soutanes gliding silently through a Baroque doorway. This was where the city – among the oldest in Poland – grew up on one of the many sandy islets formed as the Odra diverged and converged around its confluence with the Ślęza, the Widawa and the Oława. It was here, where the river could be forded at low water, that the Amber Route crossed the east-west Salt Route that ran from the Russian steppes to Provence. Despite development and reclamation, Wrocław still spread over a dozen islands, connected by more than 100 bridges.

In the 4th century BC, people of the Lusatian culture surrounded one of the islands with wooden palisades to create a fortified settlement similar to that at Biskupin. The Lusatians were followed by the Przeworsk culture, who may have been a west Slavonic people, east Germanic ancestors of the Vandals, or possibly Celts, according to the competing claims of national-ist prehistorians. Whatever their ethnicity, they traded amber from the Baltic in exchange for luxury goods from Rome. The settlement became an emporium for raw amber: three ancient warehouses containing a total of three hundredweight of the substance have been found here.

By the time it became a bishopric in the 11th century, Wrotizla – as it was then known – was the chief city of Silesia and a part of the Piast kingdom of Poland. Under the various names it has borne at different stages of its history – Wrotizla, Vretslav, Presslaw, Breslau, Wrocław – it was the cockpit of almost every major European struggle, and endured just about every vicissitude that history could throw at it: plague, pogroms, attack by the Mongols, the Hussite wars, the struggles of the Reformation, the Thirty Years War, Prussian expansionism, the Napoleonic Wars, Nazism and Stalinism.

Wrocław's location at the crossroads of Europe, which made it one of the most important staging posts on the Amber Route, also gave it a unique place in the history of my family. During the 1981 census, the enumerator who called at my father's house was puzzled that, having given his place of birth as Poland, he expressed no personal interest in the events then unfolding in that country with the rise of Solidarity and the shipyard strikes. But the census requires you to give the country in which your birthplace now stands, not the one it was part of at the time of your birth; and in 1919, when my father was born, the city of Breslau, as it was then called, was one of the great cultural and industrial centres of eastern Germany.

At a family gathering a few years ago, an elderly cousin recalled being kept awake at night in the 1920s by the sound of ice cracking in the River Oder, which their apartment over-looked. Five generations of my family lived here in the 19th century and the first third of the 20th. Doctors, lawyers, journalists, furniture dealers, they were typical of the city's secular, assimilated Jewish middle class. Albert Bauer (1800–75) – whose portrait hangs in the study of our London home – was the patriarch. Born in Berlin, he owned, along with his brother Wilhelm, a furniture factory with retail outlets there and in

Breslau. Bauer was a founding member of Breslau's chamber of commerce, and both he and his wife Fanny Adler, the daughter of a Krakow senator, were prominent in the city's charitable concerns. Their one surviving son, Wilhelm, followed Albert into the business.

Of their four daughters, Jenny married Sigismund Asch, a young doctor who made his name as a radical firebrand in the revolutionary unrest of 1848. In November, as the militia moved to suppress a demonstration in the city's New Market, Asch urged the crowd to keep the peace, but also to 'stand immovably for their freedom and their rights'. The Bauer girls watched from the roof of their father's house, and Jenny, stirred by his rhetoric, decided that this was the man she would marry. Asch was sentenced to a year's imprisonment, but went on to become a city councillor and, by the time of his death in 1901, one of the most respected citizens of Breslau.

Another daughter, Lina, married the businessman Theodor Morgenstern and moved with him to Berlin, where she devoted herself to social reform and philanthropic causes. Born in 1830, she set up a *Pfennig-Verein* (Penny Union) to provide books and clothes for Breslau's disadvantaged schoolchildren when she was only 18, and went on to found the League of German Housewives and edit Germany's first women's newspaper. When the Austro-Prussian War of 1866 caused serious food shortages, she set up Germany's first soup kitchens. The youngest of the Bauer sisters, Anna, married David Honigmann who, with his friend the Rabbi Abraham Geiger, played an important role in the development of Reform Judaism. The couple were my great-great-grandparents.

After my grandparents died, I acquired a couple of picture books that had belonged to them: *Breslau – so wie es war* and *Die Schlesischer Bilderbibel* – post-war exercises in German nostalgia for the lost Heimat. The old photos were uncanny: the Baroque churches and cobbled streets, so reminiscent of

Prague or Krakow; the stolid burghers and Prince-Archbishops; the Jewish patrons of the arts, painted in their fussy drawing rooms or photographed in earnest conversation with Gustav Mahler or Richard Strauss; the sleek Jugendstil department stores and Bauhaus-style apartment blocks.

This was Mitteleuropa – a world that has disappeared forever. The rise of Nazism crushed the civic autonomy and cultural élan of the city, while those members of the Jewish community fortunate enough to escape were scattered across the globe. In the closing weeks of the war, Breslau was all but obliterated as the Wehrmacht made its last stand against the Red Army. After its surrender in May 1945, the city underwent a complete exchange of population. The remaining Germans were driven out and replaced by Poles, themselves expelled from the eastern areas annexed by the Soviet Union, and Breslau was henceforth known by its Polish name, Wrocław. Reflecting on this troubled history, I drifted into sleep as freight barges slid through the turbid waters of the Odra beneath my hotel window.

The next morning, I set out armed with a pre-war map of Breslau and a modern street plan, to locate the places where our ancestors lived and worked. Old blue and white trams clanked across Sand Island, past the forbidding walls of the Church of St Mary on the Sands, and over Piaskowsky Bridge into the Old Town. I picked my way along the grid of narrow streets, roughly following the line of the Amber Route from north to south. Compared to the old photographs, the city appeared a shadow of its former self; the Neumarkt, once a broad square that opened out between picturesque merchants' houses, was now little more than a parking lot flanked by brutalist concrete architecture.

But then I emerged on to the Rynek, the piazza that formed the heart of the Old Town. Known in German times as the Ring (for reasons no one can recall, since it is square), it was flanked on all sides by gabled buildings in the Flemish style, picturesquely adorned with Renaissance friezes and ornate Baroque doorways. Freshly painted in bright pastel colours, the old merchants' houses were now occupied by restaurants, bars, boutiques and jewellers' shops, including a large emporium selling amber jewellery. It was hard to imagine that, just 70 years ago, all this lay in ruins, and that much of what I was looking at was a painstaking restoration.

One of the great civic spaces of Europe, the Rynek was laid out in the 14th and 15th centuries, when the city was part of the Kingdom of Bohemia. Vretslav – as it was known in its Bohemian incarnation – was a flourishing place, with many churches, guildhalls and monasteries, and privileged trading rights. After the Bohemian throne passed to the Habsburgs in 1526, Silesia and its capital became part of the Austrian empire. By 1561, Presslaw was larger than Vienna, and its main square had largely assumed its current appearance. Its centrepiece was the Ratusz, or Rathaus, a magnificently gabled town hall; with its steeply pitched roof, filigree spires and pinnacles, lanterns, belfry and astronomical clock, it resembled nothing so much as a late Gothic gingerbread house. Mercifully, it came through the war relatively unscathed.

Entering through a door in the west façade, I passed under the vaults of the Burghers' Hall, which occupied most of the ground floor and for centuries performed the twin offices of covered market and public meeting place. A marble staircase took me up to the Great Hall, a soaring, airy space illuminated by a large oriel window. But the real interest for me lay beyond one of the stone portals at the far end. Here, under the magnificent Gothic vaults of the Princes' Hall (Sala Ksiazeca) stood a long octagonal table where the Stadtrat, or city council, used to meet. One of the first Jews to be elected to this assembly, David Honigmann served on it for nearly twenty-five years and was selected as representative for Breslau to the provincial government. Sigismund Asch also served on the council for many years, campaigning successfully to have the city's open sewers, a breeding ground for typhoid and cholera, filled in.

Albert Bauer lived immediately behind the Town Hall, on Sukiennice (formerly Elisabethstraße), a narrow street that runs along the back of it to emerge through an archway in the façade. His house was easily identifiable from the drawing that had come down through our family – a large building, seven windows wide and three storeys high, with an additional row of dormers in the roof, though the arched windows on the ground floor had been converted into rectangular shop fronts. These framed an ice-cream parlour and the Friends Bistro, while the upper floors were occupied by solicitors' offices. I had lunch at Friends, and amazed the young waiter by telling him that my great-great-grandmother was born in the building. The 20th century, never mind the 19th, was ancient history to him.

I continued down Ulica Swidnicka (the former Schweidnitzerstraße), the main north-south axis, in search of the Bauer department store. As I compared maps, it was apparent that the layout of the town remained much the same, though the street names had changed. A little way south of the Rynek, however, a wide road had been driven through the old town in the 1970s. I hurried through a dreary concrete under-pass and continued down Swidnicka, as the street gathered the remnants of its dignity about itself once more.

Breslau developed rapidly under Prussian rule, and by the time of German unification in 1871 it was the third largest metropolis in the empire, after Berlin and Hamburg. It was a bustling, confident place, its prosperity built on engineering, chemicals and the manufacture of railway carriages. Schweidnitzerstraße was its Regent Street, and the grandiose 19th-century buildings testified to its worldliness, swagger and sophistication. No city of such pretensions could be without an opera house, and the neoclassical building on ul. Swidnicka was built between 1837 and 1841 by Carl Ferdinand Langhans, the son of Carl Gotthard

Langhans, architect of the Brandenburg Gate. The city's opera company, however, was already a century old by then, having staged early performances of Mozart's *Don Giovanni*, *The Marriage of Figaro*, *Così fan tutte* and *The Magic Flute*. Between 1804 and 1806, its director was the young Carl Maria von Weber, the creator of German Romantic opera. Opposite, the Art Nouveau Hotel Monopol still exuded a faded, *fin de siècle* elegance. In its heyday, it played host to such a diverse figures as Marlene Dietrich, Paul Robeson, Pablo Picasso . . . and Adolf Hitler.

At the southern end of Swidnicka, you come to the moat that surrounds the old town. Originally an arm of the Odra, this natural defence was canalised in the 16th century and fortified. Much of it survives as an ornamental canal, bordered by a tree-lined park, which preserves the star-shaped outline of the fortifications. Like many other cities, Breslau lost its defensive walls when the development of high explosives and long-range artillery rendered them obsolete, and they became an obstacle to urban expansion.

The area west of Schweidnitzerstraße was once the Jewish quarter. In the Middle Ages, the city had a sizeable Jewish community, until the heretic-hunting prelate John of Capistrano arrived in 1453 to stamp out the Hussites. Finding few of them in town, he incited the people against the Jews instead, all of whom were killed or driven out. From then on, Jews were not permitted to reside in the city until the Imperial Edict of Toleration of 1713, and only really began to return after the city came under Prussian rule in 1741.

By the 19th century, Breslau's Jewish community was at the forefront of its cultural and civic life. It was, for the most part, highly acculturated and liberal in outlook; its energetic rabbi, Abraham Geiger, was one of the founding fathers of Reform Judaism. Clean-shaven and sporting the shoulder-length hair of a radical, Geiger looked nothing like a traditional rabbi.

Troubled by the fact that many better educated and enterprising German Jews were abandoning the faith – Heinrich Heine had cynically described his conversion as the 'entry ticket to European culture' – Geiger and his followers determined to develop an enlightened, outward-looking Judaism that would not hinder its adherents from participating in modern society. At two synods held in Frankfurt (1845) and Breslau (1846), the reformers set out to distinguish the eternal ethical principles of Judaism from outdated rabbinical practice. Their proposals were controversial. In addition to encouraging the printing of the Torah and other holy texts in German, they even contemplated abolishing the dietary laws and circumcision. These latter proposals did not win approval, but even so, a large body of Orthodox Jews separated from the reformers, a schism that persists to this day.

In one significant respect, Geiger succeeded: by the end of the 19th century, Breslau's Jews were not only prominent in the economic life of the city but also held important posts in the civic administration, the law, and the university. But his belief that, by conforming to the outward norms of gentile society, Jews would no longer find themselves subject to persecution, would prove a tragic mistake.

Just beyond the moat, I found myself at a busy crossing, intersected by tramlines and overhead wires. The building on the opposite corner, Ulica Swidnicka 37, was recognisably a department store, though to judge by its late 19th-century style, it must have been put up by Bauer's heirs, replacing the original building. An 1868 advertisement describes the firm as 'Bauer Bros, by appointment to His Royal Majesty the Crown Prince of Prussia. Manufacturers of Furniture, Parquet, Mirrors and Upholstery and dealers in antiques. Construction work and refits of palaces and other buildings carried out carefully and economically in the latest styles.'

Just behind Bauer's store, on Anger Straße (now Ulica

Łąkowa), stood the great Moorish-Byzantine New Synagogue. The Honigmanns worshipped here, and David Honigmann wrote and published a 'Table Song' for the banquet to celebrate its dedication on 29th September 1872. There was nothing left to mark its existence but a small plaque. On Reichskristallnacht, 9th November 1938, that 'spontaneous' uprising of the German people against the Jews, a division of Wehrmacht sappers dynamited the building, reducing it to rubble.

One old synagogue survived, however. Back on the northern side of the moat, hidden away in a courtyard behind some flats on Ulica Włodkowica, stood the White Stork Synagogue (*Zum weißem Storch*). This graceful neoclassical building, adorned with Corinthian pilasters and a relief carving of the bird that gave it its name, was built in 1829 to designs by the younger Langhans. It was the main place of worship for Breslau's Jews until the construction of the New Synagogue, and it was here that Geiger conducted the marriage of Lina Bauer and Theodor Morgenstern in 1854. The Nazis used it as a transit station for Jews en route to the camps, and to store their looted belongings. After the war, it was taken into state ownership and fell into disrepair. Although the city's Jewish community requested the return of the building in 1966, it was not until 1995, after protracted negotiations and legal action, that the Polish government agreed.

In 2005, the Stork Synagogue was placed in the care of a foundation set up by the Norwegian-Jewish musician and performance artist Bente Kahan. When I visited Wrocław that year, restoration had only just begun, and the building was little more than a battered shell shrouded by scaffolding. Now it was magnificent, an elegant, cream-stuccoed neoclassical temple. With its sweeping, arched galleries, the interior – used for cultural and educational events as well as worship – was a Biedermeier gem. The present community consisted mostly of Polish Jews displaced from Ukraine after the Second World

War, and numbered little more than 3,000; many had only recently rediscovered their faith, having been brought up in ignorance of their religious heritage by parents fearful of Communist persecution.

There was little else to see of the old Jewish quarter, so I followed the moat round to the north-west until I reached the river. On the opposite bank, the spires of Cathedral Island were illuminated by the late afternoon sun, struggling weakly through an overcast sky. To my right stretched the long, elegant façade of the university's Collegium Maximum, its Baroque cupola reflected in the river. One of the great academic institutions of Europe, the university was founded in 1702 by the Austrian Emperor Leopold I as a Jesuit theological seminary. The Leopoldina, as it was known, became a fully fledged university in 1811, gradually expanding to fill the adjoining palaces and ecclesiastical buildings.

An imposing stone staircase led up to the main ceremonial hall, the Aula Leopoldina. Under the ornate Baroque ceiling and flanked by portraits of the university's founders, my grandfather, Alfred Schüler, my great-grandfather Baruch Spitz and my great-great-grandfather David Honigmann all received their degrees. University life at the time was dominated by student fraternities devoted to drinking, wild pranks and duelling, the main object of which was to acquire a scar – a *Schmiß* – which was considered a badge of honour and the mark of the educated elite. When Brahms wrote his *Academic Festival Overture* for the university in 1881, he scandalised the more strait-laced academics by including the student drinking song *Gaudeamus Igitur* in its finale.

Baruch Spitz, sent to study in Breslau by his father, completed his medical degree here in 1879. Of the student fraternities, the aristocratic, reactionary Corps were off-limits to him as a Jew; he might have joined the more liberal, middle-class Burschenschaften, but he was a studious young man, and opted instead for the Academic Medical Association, through which he came into contact with the Honigmann family, whose youngest son, Franz, was also a doctor. In 1885 he married David and Anna Honigmann's daughter Elise.

By the end of the 19th century, the University of Breslau's reputation for science and medicine was second to none. Among those who taught or studied here were the Nobel Prize-winning physicist Max Born, the immunologist Paul Ehrlich, Alois Alzheimer, who first identified the form of dementia named after him, and Robert Bunsen, inventor of the gas burner. It was here too that Clara Immerwahr (1870–1915) became the first woman to be awarded a science doctorate by a German university. Her story is a curious and tragic one. In 1901 she married her fellow chemist Fritz Haber, the baptised son of a Jewish merchant in Breslau. Young and idealistic, they were determined to use their scientific knowledge for the betterment of mankind. The Haber process, a method of synthesising ammonia from hydrogen and nitrogen, opened the way for the manufacture of nitrogen fertilisers, saving millions from starvation throughout the world.

But Haber's work had a darker side. On the outbreak of the First World War, he put his laboratory at the service of the war effort, conducting experiments on animals with chlorine and ammonia. Disturbed by this development, Immerwahr became alienated from her husband. In April 1915, Haber personally directed the first chlorine gas attack at Langemarck on the Ypres salient. The new weapon claimed several thousand Allied lives – mostly French, Algerian and Canadian troops – and was hailed as a great success. Haber was promoted to captain and held a dinner party to celebrate. After a savage row, Clara took his service revolver, stepped into the garden and shot herself through the heart. Haber left for the Eastern Front the next day, without waiting for her funeral.

In 1918 his work in developing nitrate fertilisers was

rewarded by the Nobel Prize for chemistry – an award that provoked bitter controversy, for the Allies considered him a war criminal and dubbed him 'Dr Death'. He spent the post-war years pursuing a doomed scheme to extract gold from seawater to pay off Germany's war reparations, only to be driven into exile by the Nazis. He took up a post at Cambridge, but died of a heart attack soon afterwards, 'broken, muddled ... in a mental and moral vacuum', according to his friend, the Zionist leader Chaim Weizmann. His death did at least spare him a further, unbearable irony: another of his discoveries, Zyklon B, which he had developed as an insecticide, was later used to exterminate many of his own family.

With the Nazis in power, the university was systematically purged of Jewish, Polish and dissident academics. The archaeology department, which had contributed so much to the understanding of the Amber Route, was turned into a propaganda arm of the Reich. The President of the German Academy spelled it out in a speech in November 1941: 'The Reich University in Posen, together with the old eastern universities in Königsberg and Breslau, shall form a consolidated Eastwall of German spirit which shall ever watch and prevent any Slav inroads.'

While preparing for this journey, I spent a few days in the Sackler Library in Oxford studying archaeological reports of finds along the Amber Route. In the spring of 1906, a metre-wide pit filled to a depth of two metres with about 10 hundredweight of unworked amber mixed with fine sand was found in the southern suburb of Hartlieb, now known as Partynice and then, as now, famous for its racecourse. Thirty years later, roadbuilders came across more amber nearby. Archaeologists were called in, and uncovered two further pits, about a metre across and two metres deep, that between them contained a further 17.5 hundredweight of amber. Most of the pieces were hazelnut-to walnut-sized, but some were as large as a fist, and they had been sorted by size, with the largest at the bottom. Around the pits was a series of post-holes, suggesting that they were covered by some sort of wooden shed. The structures, and the amber in them, were dated to the 1st century BC. As the area is rich in Roman artefacts, the site is thought to have been a trading centre where merchants travelling from the north and south would meet to exchange their wares.

The discovery is described in a book by Christian Pescheck, published in 1939 by the Institute for Prehistory at the University of Breslau under the aegis of Professors Hans Seger and Martin Jahn, and entitled *Die Frühwandalishe Kultur in Mittelschlesien*. The title – 'Early Vandal Culture in Middle Silesia' – is laden with political overtones. Seger had been teaching in Breslau since 1907, and assisted J. M. de Navarro in his research, but Jahn occupied one of eight new chairs of prehistory set up by the SS *Ahnenerbe*. A note acknowledged the assistance of the 'Reichsminister für Wissenschaft, Erziehung and Volksbildung'. This was Bernhard Rust, Hitler's education minister, who was responsible for Nazification of the German education system and the purging of Jewish scholars such as Einstein and Haber. After the war, with the faculty replaced by Polish scholars from the Ossolineum at Lvov, Wrocław University once again became a major centre for the study of the Amber Route, publishing important articles on the subject by Jerzy Wielowieyski and others.

The next morning, I set off on a long walk into the southern outskirts of the city, to see where my grandparents lived and my father spent the first four years of his life. Beyond the city moat was Plac Kosciusko, formerly Tauentzien Platz, where my great-grandfather Baruch Spitz had his surgery, now completely rebuilt in the formal classical moderne of the post-war Communist era. Baruch and Elise lived a short distance away on Gartenstraße, near the railway station. My grandmother vividly recalled life here at the turn of the 20th century. It was a 'decent but not luxurious private house', and at that period had no gas, let alone electricity; every night she would take a candle to guide her grandmother – whom Baruch had brought from Kempen after the death of his father – to her room at the end of a long corridor. It cannot have been an easy coexistence. Hannah Spitz was the embodiment of the ultra-orthodox Jewish community David Honigmann had fled. While Hannah held rigidly to the ways of the past, the family into which her son had married was secular, assimilated and at ease with the modern world. They went to the synagogue only on high holidays, attended school on Saturdays and even exchanged Christmas presents – clandestinely – with their other grandmother Anna Honigmann.

Though the household was kosher, it was not strict enough for Hannah, and she insisted on cooking all her own food. Though voices were never raised in argument, the old woman cast a pall of disapproval over the house. She kept to her room day and night, reading aloud in a tearful voice from the Bible and other religious texts. 'Whether she grieved the general fate of the Jews or her own – the death of her husband or because she thought we were on a sinful path and God will not like it – who will tell?' my grandmother wondered.

A little way along Gartenstraße, at Number 36, lived my other Breslau great-grandparents, Adolf and Cäcilie Schüler, who came here from Berent in 1898. The move was Cäcilie's idea; born in Breslau, where her father was secretary of the Jewish Association, she had not enjoyed small-town life. But for her husband, the move was a disaster. In Berent, my grandfather recalled, he was someone; in Breslau he was a nobody *('In Berent war er "wer", in Breslau war er nichts')*. From being the publisher of the local newspaper and a prominent member of the Jewish community, he became just one jobbing printer among many, turning out letterheads, visiting cards and invoice forms in a fiercely competitive market. Not surprisingly, the marriage suffered; as he paced the room railing against the downturn in his fortunes, his wife sat silent and embittered at the way her life had turned out.

Beyond Plac Kosciusko extended 19th century suburbs, their surviving Wilhelmine buildings interspersed with postwar housing blocks. Eventually I reached Ulica Zaporoska, formerly Hohenzollernstraße, a broad, long street of Communist-era estates. There was no trace of my grandparents' apartment – the area saw some of the fiercest fighting during the last days of the war.

From here, it was a shortish walk to the Jewish Cemetery on Ślężna Street (formerly Lohestraße), where the Bauers and the Honigmanns were buried. Behind its high walls, under birch and sycamore trees, amid ivy, ferns and Virginia creeper, the cemetery survived in remarkably good condition. Somehow, the Nazis never got round to vandalising it; what damage there was had resulted from fighting in the last months of the war and decades of neglect afterwards. It was only in 1975 that it was taken over by the city authorities as a 'Museum of Cemetery Arts'. It was now well cared for, thanks largely to the efforts of Maciej Łagiewski, director of the city museum, and many graves had been painstakingly restored.

Many of the tombstones showed spread hands for descendants of the tribe of Aaron, a water jug for the Levites, or a deer for the Naphthali. Alongside traditional Jewish *masebhas* – a square column with a triangular top – were grand mausolea in the neoclassical, Romanesque or Moorish styles, while the more modish had opted for tombs in Art Nouveau and Secession styles. There was even an Iron Cross in a wreath for a Jewish soldier who died for his German fatherland in the First World War.

Geiger conducted the first burial here in 1856, and the gravestones formed a pantheon of Breslau's Jewish society. Sigismund and Jenny Asch are here, under a red granite obelisk, as is David Honigmann's antagonist Heinrich Graetz (1817–91), the botanist Ferdinand Cohn (1828–98), the parents of both Fritz Haber and Clara Immerwahr, and the parents of Edith Stein, who became a Catholic nun and was was murdered in Auschwitz and canonised by Pope John Paul II in 1987.

The most visited tomb was that of Ferdinand Lassalle, founder of Germany's Social Democratic Party. The son of Heymann Lassal, a Breslau silk merchant, he turned his back on the family business to take up the cause of workers' rights, Frenchified his name and became a political journalist. Heine wrote of him as 'a young man of remarkable intellectual gifts . . . he combines an energy of will and a capacity for action which astonish me.' Lassalle became friends with Marx and Engels, but his belief in the pursuit of socialism through democratic rather than revolutionary means led them to quarrel. Even while Marx – in his London exile – was scrounging money from Lassalle, Engels referred to their benefactor as a 'greasy Breslau Jew *(den schmierigen Breslauer Jud)*, using all sorts of pomades and rouges to pretty himself up and force himself into the distinguished world.' David Honigmann, an old university friend of Lassalle, inclined to a similar view, though he was less coarse in his expression of it: 'Nature had not made this modern Olympian out of real marble,' he recalled later, 'but from the synthetic material that passes for marble in our salons.'

The circumstances of Lassalle's death at the age of 39 attracted as much attention as his career. In 1864, after the party he founded had rejected his autocratic leadership, he travelled to Geneva, where he became engaged to an old flame, Hélène von Dönniges. Her father, a Bavarian diplomat, scandalised at the idea of her marrying a Jew and a socialist to boot, persuaded Hélène to break off the engagement and marry a rival suitor, the Romanian Count Janko von Racowitza. Lassalle challenged the count to a duel. Neither man, it seems, had any intention of killing the other. The count, an inexperienced marksman, aimed at the ground – and missed. Mortally wounded, Lassalle died three days later, and his body was brought back to Breslau for burial beside his parents.

'It could only happen to Lassalle,' Engels wrote to Marx a few weeks later. 'What was fatal was that he didn't just throw the creature on the hotel bed and give her a good seeing to. It wasn't his beautiful mind she wanted, but his Jewish rod.'

Yet it was Lassalle who had the last laugh. In 1863, he had founded the *Allgemeiner Deutscher Arbeiterverein* (General German Workers' Association), which later became the Social Democratic Party (SPD) – a movement that outlived the collapse of communism, and is now the oldest political party in Germany, while its sister organisations remain a significant force in the politics of many European nations.

My earlier reflections on the authenticity of historic restoration took a personal turn when I located the tomb of Albert and Fanny Bauer, immediately opposite the shiny black marble gravestone of David and Anna Honigmann. When I last visited, I had found the Bauer monument in a sadly dilapidated state, the white marble slabs that bore the inscriptions having been stolen during the decades when the cemetery was neglected, revealing the bare brickwork behind. Now, however, they had been replaced with gleaming new panels on which the names were inscribed in gold. I later discovered that the restoration had been carried out by my cousin Dagmar Nick, working with Maciej Łagiewski.

I stood back and tried to visualise the scene that took place here on a November day more than 140 years before. Fanny Bauer died on 3rd November 1874, and was buried the following Friday. The entire family assembled from near and far. Cäcilie and her husband Jakob Adler came from Vienna, Wilhelm and his wife Helene, and Lina and Theodor Morgenstern from Berlin, to join Albert Bauer, the Aschs and the Honigmanns, with all the grandchildren, at the house in Neue Schweidnitzerstraße. The cortège set out from there at half past two in the afternoon for the cemetery.

Albert was inconsolable and, despite the care of his daughters, outlived his wife by just seven months, dying on 5th June 1875 at the age of 74. Anna continued her mother's philanthropic activities in Breslau, supporting bodies such as the Girls' Union, the Vocational School for Jewish Girls, and the Nurses' Home. Her husband David Honigmann died in 1885, around the time their daughter Elise married Baruch Spitz.

In June 1905, the three surviving Bauer sisters (Cäcilie had died in Vienna in 1903) gathered in Breslau for probably the last time to celebrate Anna's 70th birthday. Lina came by train from Berlin, and stayed overnight with her sister Jenny. The two went round to Anna's apartment the next morning, where they found their sister in a drawing room full of flowers, surrounded by her children and grandchildren, who serenaded her with songs and poems. Then delegations from the many charitable institutions Anna had supported filed in to pay their respects, and a district judge paid tribute to her philanthropic work.

The old generation was passing – Jenny died in 1907, Anna in November 1909, and Lina the following month – and their world was passing too. The civic optimism of the Wilhelmine era was shattered by the First World War and the economic depression and political violence that followed. During the war, Franz Honigmann became the chief surgeon of the military hospital in Breslau, and was plunged into four years of grim and unremitting work treating casualties from the Eastern Front. He invested all his savings in war bonds and, with the collapse of the German Empire, lost everything.

As the Treaty of Versailles awarded large tracts of eastern Germany to Poland, Breslau filled with refugees. My grandfather, newly qualified as a solicitor, had difficulty finding work because of the influx of more experienced lawyers from the lost territories. As an eastern city and headquarters of the VI Army Corps, Breslau was especially susceptible to the 'stab-in-the-back' myth – the idea that Germany's armies, victorious in the field, had been betrayed by politicians, socialists and the Jews. The Freikorps – bands of right-wing war veterans – patrolled the streets, and a mob destroyed the Polish and French consulates. In March 1920, a reactionary agitator called Wolfgang Kapp, backed by senior army generals, launched a putsch to overthrow the Weimar Republic. Breslau fell into the hands of the insurgents, and before a general workers' strike brought about the collapse of the coup, the Freikorps had murdered the 25-year-old Bernhard Schottländer, who had reacted against his privileged upbringing by becoming a left-wing activist and publisher of a socialist newspaper, the *Schlesische Arbeiter-Zeitung*.

It seems my grandparents witnessed the turmoil in the city. In one of their photo albums is a sepia print, made from a cracked glass negative, labelled *'die Folgen des 18.3.1920'* – 'the results of 18th March 1920'. Taken from an upper floor on Schweidnitzerstraße, it shows a domed corner building between the opera house and the church of St Dorothy. Now the Hotel Monopol, it was then shared between two Jewish-owned businesses, the Berlin publisher Rudolf Mosse and the umbrella seller Baruch & Loewy. Its façade is riddled with bullet holes and its windows are smashed.

After the Nazis took power in January 1933, the civic authorities pursued an aggressive policy of 'Germanification'. The town council was sacked *en masse* and replaced with Nazi appointees. Jewish shops were boycotted, and Polish students beaten up. A decree of 7th April demolished at a stroke the hard-won emancipation of the 19th century by banning Jews from holding office in the civil service, the universities, the judiciary and the medical profession. The same month, the

SA raided a number of bookshops in the city and confiscated works by Thomas Mann, Stefan Zweig and Emile Zola – all writers my grandparents had on their shelves.

After the enactment of the Nuremberg Laws on 15th September 1935, Jews were deprived of German citizenship, and were not permitted to marry, or have sexual relations with, non-Jews. By the end of 1938, Breslau's Polish community had completely disappeared, while two-thirds of the city's Jews had left. The gradual but relentless constriction of their lives was chronicled in a diary kept by Willy Cohn. Day by day, he noted the systematic revocation of civil rights and humiliations suffered as their once expansive world shrank to a few streets around the Stork Synagogue. After the city's parks were declared off limits to Jews, Cohn would bring his children to the cemetery here on Lohestraße to enjoy the green space while he communed with his ancestors.

When my grandparents left Germany for Barcelona in 1936, Elise went with them, but two years later, when the Spanish Civil War forced them to move to Italy, she insisted on returning to Breslau. After a decree of 12th November 1938 demanded that Jewish-owned businesses be transferred into 'German' ownership, Adolf Schüler was forced to sell his print shop, though he continued to work there. By 1940, Elise Spitz was living in a Jewish old peoples' home at 36a Kirschallee. Willy Cohn visited her there on 2nd November that year. She gave him a number of papers relating to her father, David Honigmann, and a bundle of letters from Abraham Geiger, before explaining her family's odyssey from Barcelona to Italy, back to Barcelona 'to pick their belongings from the ruins', and thence to the USA. 'A Jewish fate for our times,' Cohn noted in his diary. 'At least one family is safe.'

A year later, Cohn, his wife and two youngest daughters were deported to Kaunas in Lithuania and shot dead on arrival. His diary remained hidden throughout the war, and was eventually published in 2012. Elise Spitz and Adolf Schüler were both deported from Breslau on 30th August 1942, on transport IX/2, and arrived at Theresienstadt the next day. Among the 1,000 other people on the same transport were Elise's brother Franz Honigmann and his wife Kaethe. By the end of the year, all four were dead.

After leaving a small stone on each grave, I walked back into town, taking shelter from the rain in the Museum of Architecture. Housed in the bombed-out shell of a 16th-century monastery, this was another of Łagiewski's achievements. Yet despite an illuminating model of the ancient Amber Route settlement, I found the place dispiriting, a graveyard of quoins, corbels and gargoyles from the city's shattered buildings. If history, as Gibbon wrote, is 'little more than the register of the crimes, follies and misfortunes of mankind', Wrocław has had more than its share of it.

Breslau is gone. Just a few buildings and the cemetery offer a tantalising glimpse of what was. My grandmother Hedwig took a tough-minded view of the matter: 'Though I feel very sorry that Breslau ... and all the familiar Silesian places that formed our special Homeland is lost, I can't join in the indignation and outcry for "justice", i.e. taking it back. In every war the defeated country has to pay, and especially with loss of land.'

CHAPTER 9

THE MORAVIAN GATE

Wrocław Głowny station was crowded with people heading home for Easter. The little yellow train to Kłodzko rapidly filled with students and older working men, but I managed to find a seat in the last carriage, next to the guard's van. A whistle blew, and the train pulled out past sidings full of freight trucks, grey concrete housing and light industrial units. After crossing the river Ślęza, the track wheeled south, past the racecourse at Partynice – where the Iron Age amber pits were found – and out into wide, flat fields of reddish earth with light snow lying in the furrows.

The land began a gentle rise, and we entered a forest of pine and silver birch, the occasional oak still clad in last year's dry, brown leaves. The line followed the Amber Route through the Sudety Mountains into the ancient County of Glatz. Known as Kłodzko to the Poles and Kladsko to the Czechs, this lozenge-shaped peninsula of Polish territory projecting into the Czech Republic is an oddity of European geopolitics. Once a semi-autonomous fiefdom of Bohemia, it was absorbed along with the rest of that kingdom into the Austrian Empire in 1526. After Frederick the Great conquered it in 1740, the region was annexed by Prussia, and on German unification in 1871 it became part of the Reich.

On passing his jurisprudence exams in Breslau, my grandfather Alfred Schüler spent a year as a referendar – the apprentice stage of the Prussian judiciary – at the local court in Neurode (now Nowa Ruda) in the west of the county, before returning to his home city to take his assessor's exam, which would qualify him as a judge. After the First World War, newly independent Czechoslovakia claimed the region, but was over-ruled by the Treaty of Versailles; at the end of the Second, the Potsdam Conference awarded it to Poland.

Straining against the rising gradient, the train let out a whistle like a plaintive dog. The sun hung low on the western horizon, and the avenues of poplars that lined the roads cast long, diagonal shadows across the fields. A gibbous moon hung above a bank of grey cumulus, beneath which the horizon showed pearly pink. The rotating arms of a row of wind turbines gesticulated over the brow of a hill. As the train emerged from a pine forest, the town of Kłodzko rose from the River Nyasa (Neisse) like a miniature Prague.

I hauled my luggage up steep, cobbled streets into the Old Town; with its churches floodlit, it was dramatic and pictur-esque, but eerily deserted. In the main square, dominated by the dark bulk of the 19th-century Town Hall, a few youngsters hung around looking bored. I asked a young man for directions to my hotel. It was not far. When I picked up my bag to silence the clatter of the wheels on the cobbles, he offered to carry it. I refused politely, and we struck up a conversation. I remarked that it was a beautiful town. 'Yes,' he replied, 'but there's not much here for young people to do.' Dusk had only just fallen, yet everywhere was closed. Two smartly dressed elderly ladies emerged from a *kawarnia* in the side of the Town Hall as the owner pulled down the shutters. The Town Hall clock was an hour slow: summer time had begun almost a week before.

Thanking my young friend for his help, I checked into my hotel before returning to the square, where I found a solitary bar open on the first floor of the Town Hall building. The place was decorated to resemble an archetypal English pub, with hunting prints and a Scotch whisky map on the walls. A Timothy Taylor mat lay on the bar, and above it were hung old vinyl album covers, including a Russian LP by Элтóн джóн. I was the only customer, and after a couple of beers, I headed back down the hill to my hotel.

In the morning I called at the tourist office to enquire about trains to Olomouc, in the Czech Republic. The only train that day left at 2.49pm, and took five hours by a circuitous route involving several changes. Conscious of time, I climbed the steep path to the massive, star-shaped fortress that loomed over the town. Constructed by the Austrians, it was enlarged by Frederick the Great, who had casemates and tunnels bored into the mountain with explosives in order to lodge an occupation force of 3,000. It was here that my great-great-great uncle Sigismund Asch was incarcerated for a year for *lèse majesté* and incitement to riot. As I walked through the echoing vaults crusted with flaking lime wash, I imagined him looking out of the barred windows at the tantalising view of distant, snow-covered mountains.

Descending the castle rock, I moved swiftly to the town museum, which was housed in a 17th-century Jesuit seminary. A stern elderly lady led me through a labyrinth of tunnels to an octagonal vaulted chamber that housed a display of vellum manuscripts, while Renaissance polyphony played softly in the background. She then beckoned me upstairs to view a display of antique pewter and silverware, a beautiful concert hall with a grand piano, and an elegant 18th-century salon. I would have appreciated all this much more were I not becoming increasingly concerned about catching my train.

My guide ushered me into a room devoted to the products of the local glass industry over the centuries, and then – switching on the lights as she went – into a room full of clocks, another regional speciality. There were carriage clocks, wall-mounted clocks, grandfather clocks, china-faced kitchen clocks, and cuckoo clocks. She pulled up the weights on one of the cuckoo clocks and flicked the pendulum into motion. Its loud ticking joined that of all the others like a chorus of cicadas. Again, she beckoned me into a further room. More clocks, all showing the minutes ticking away. She gestured for me to follow her into yet another room, but this time did not turn on the light. The floor was paved with mirror tiles, which left me disoriented until my eyes adjusted to the gloom and I saw that they reflected a wooden ceiling covered in... clocks. I had walked into a Salvador Dalí painting. It was then that I realised I would not be on the 2.49 to Olomouc.

It was, to be honest, a relief. I needed to catch my breath and update my notes, and it gave me time to explore this unusual town. According to the chronicler Cosmas of Prague, there was a fortified settlement here as early as 981. The medieval bridge that spanned the River Kłodzko was lined with statues like the Charles Bridge in Prague. Beyond it stood the Baroque Franciscan church; above the river loomed the sturdy medieval bulk of the parish church of Our Lady. Nearby, an inconspicuous steel door gave entry to the catacombs, a network of tunnels restored after a flood in 2007. I made my way through the labyrinth of crumbling brick, fitted out with gruesome waxwork tableaux of plague and torture. I emerged, to my surprise, on the other side of the old town, beneath the castle. That night I had supper in a pub in an old watermill opposite the hotel, and realised that the millrace was the source of the rushing sound that had filled my room when I opened the window.

I woke the next morning to find that it had snowed in the night, and took a taxi to the station. I could buy a ticket only as far as the border; from there, I would have to pay the conductor for the Czech part of the journey. The railway followed the River Scinawka to Bystrzyca Kłodzka, where the landscape became more mountainous and the houses started to take on the appearance of Alpine chalets amid stands of tall pines. At noon, the train crossed into the Czech Republic at Lichkov. There were no border formalities, but I needed to buy a new ticket, and a kindly Ukrainian woman came to my assistance. The snow lay thicker on this side of the frontier. We followed a rushing river swollen with meltwater along its steep-sided valley, as the line descended the Sudety mountains into the Moravian Gate, a pass of strategic and economic importance that leads from Silesia into Moravia and, ultimately, to Vienna. I had also passed from the historic kingdom of Prussia into the former territory of its rival for leadership of the German-speaking world, the Habsburg Empire, a swath of Central Europe extending from the Netherlands to Tuscany, from Burgundy to Ukraine, ruled for six centuries by an eccentric dynasty of autocrats, mystics, warriors and melancholics.

At Ustí nad Orlicí, I had to change for a connecting train to Česká Třebová. It was the intercity to Brno, where my Ukrainian friend was bound, so she shepherded me aboard with motherly concern. She introduced herself as Nadine, and told me she was from Tarnopol. She was travelling for the Jehovah's Witnesses, and clutched a carrier bag full of copies of *The Watchtower*. She seemed at ease in all the Slavic languages, but as my grasp of them was as rudimentary as her German, we struggled to make ourselves understood. I was sorry we were not able to communicate more effectively, as I would have liked to learn more about her experiences. We tend to mock the Jehovah's Witnesses in Britain, but they were cruelly persecuted in the Soviet Union, and it must have required great courage to uphold her faith.

We parted company at Česká Třebová, where I boarded an express from Prague, which brought me to Olomouc within the hour. The city stands on the River Morava, which drains into the Danube. I had crossed the watershed from the catchment area of the Odra and the Vistula, which flow north into the Baltic, to where the rivers flow south and east into the Black

Sea; hydrographically, this was the mid-point of my journey.

I walked the kilometre into town along Cosmonauts' Avenue, a broad, straight road lined by gleaming office buildings, which was designated an 'amber trail' on the town map. Crossing a modern bridge over the wide, green Morava, I turned into a cobbled street and made my way uphill to the historic centre. This stunning assemblage of churches, palaces, statues and fountains clustered around two connecting squares. In the centre of Horní Náměstí (Upper Square) stood the Town Hall, its astronomical clock refashioned in the Socialist Realist style with a mosaic showing a worker and a chemist. Beyond it rose a grandiloquent column on which a brace of gilded angels bore the BVM aloft to a triumphant Holy Trinity. The edifice was constructed on such a monumental scale that its base contained a chapel. The smaller, quieter Dolní Náměstí (Lower Square) was dominated by an only slightly less imposing Baroque corkscrew in honour of the Virgin Mary.

Olomouc had an urbane if sedate cultural life centred around the Moravian Theatre and the Philharmonic Society on Horní Náměstí. At one corner of the square, the Café Mahler exuded Central European elegance; the composer conducted a season at the theatre here in 1883. Around the two squares, the arcades of the ancient merchants' houses were occupied by fashionable bars and boutiques. In a small street off Dolní Náměstí, I found a quiet pension decorated, somewhat incongruously, in a cool Moroccan style, all white arches, blue tiles and wicker chairs, with rooms ranged around a shady courtyard. Deciding to base myself in this agreeable city for a few days, I checked in.

The next day was Easter Sunday, and bells were ringing from the many churches. A few snowflakes tumbled to the cobbles through the bright, cold air. In front of the Town Hall, a large crowd had gathered to listen to a band playing Moravian folk music, their lusty male voices raised over cimbalom and skirling violins. Most of the al fresco audience were Czech.

At the corner of the Upper Square stood a 1725 equestrian statue of Julius Caesar by Johann Georg Schauberger. The legend that Caesar founded the city, and that its name derives from Iuliomontium (Mount Julius), is probably spurious, but there is archaeological evidence of a Roman fort on St Michael's hillock, where St Michael's church now stands – a rare outpost north of the Danube. The allegorical figures reclining beneath the Roman's steed represented the rivers Morava and Danube, symbolising the loyalty of the Czech and Austrian lands to the Holy Roman Emperor – regarded as Caesar's heir – in Vienna.

First mentioned by Cosmas in 1055, Olomouc was the capital of Moravia until it was captured by the Swedes in the Thirty Years War and ceded that position to Brno. It was in Olomouc – Olmütz to the Austrians – that the eighteen-year-old Franz Joseph was proclaimed emperor in 1848 after his uncle Ferdinand had been persuaded to abdicate in response to that year's uprisings. During Franz Joseph's long reign, to assuage nationalist sentiment, the system known as the dual monarchy was devised, whereby he was emperor in Austria and king of Hungary; 66 years after attaining the throne, the aged monarch would respond to the assassination of his heir Franz Ferdinand by starting the war that destroyed his empire and set in train the catastrophic events of the 20th century.

On Palachovo Square, a couple of blocks south of the town centre, I found a plaque marking the site of the synagogue. Consecrated in 1897, the Byzantine-style temple by the Viennese architect Jacob Gartner was one of the largest and finest in Czechoslovakia. On the night of 15th–16th March 1939, it was burned to the ground by local fascists, who refused to allow the fire brigade to extinguish the flames. Looters pillaged what remained of the ornaments and furnishings until the ruins were bulldozed in 1941. It was long thought that all trace of the synagogue had disappeared until, in the early years of the

21st century, eight stained-glass windows were found hidden in a private house. Around the same time, ten carved wooden benches out of the original hundred were discovered in a village church near Prostejov. One of the windows bore the name of the first Olomouc rabbi, Dr Berthold Oppenheim, who served the community for 47 years until his temple was destroyed. He was murdered in Treblinka in 1942. The windows and three of the benches are now displayed at the synagogue in Loštice.

At breakfast the next morning, I met a middle-aged African-American man who asked if I knew whether he could get some scrambled eggs, and we struck up a conversation. I explained that I was a writer, and he told me that he was a musician, a bass guitarist, and had just come from playing at a festival in Ostrava, a large industrial town in the east of the Czech Republic that reminded him of Detroit. When he introduced himself as Fernando, I realised who he was: Fernando Saunders, who played bass on several of Lou Reed's albums, starting with *The Blue Mask* in 1980. His long, melodic bass lines added much to the texture of that darkly brilliant album, and to Marianne Faithfull's melancholy, jazz-tinged *Strange Weather*. He had, he told me, been touring solo 'since Lou passed'. He need not have worried about his eggs – the staff remembered his preferences from a previous visit, and while we were talking a young man brought his breakfast. He gave me a copy of his latest CD, *Happiness*, on which Reed sings with him on the Velvet Underground's 'Jesus', and Suzanne Vega joins him on his own song 'Feel Like Crying', while the Czech musicians Karel Holas and Peter Krajniak contribute to the album's sophisticated, eclectic arrangements.

I wandered uphill to where the tall, twin-spired Gothic cathedral of St Wenceslas stood on a bluff overlooking the Morava, its antiquity somewhat obscured by a harshly mechanical late 19th-century restoration. A little further along Republic Square, opposite the university, the Regional

Museum occupied the 18th-century Convent of the Poor
Clares. Alongside exhibits on the region's geology and
environment, it presented a chronological survey of Czech
history from the arrival of the Slavs in the 6th century. The
displays included rings, beads and earrings in gold, silver and
bronze, mostly from the 9th century, although there was no
sign of any amber. Perhaps the most impressive exhibit was a
sword dating from the late 10th or early 11th century. Found
in 1889 in a courtyard between the convent and the university, it was forged of Damasc steel and bore the name of its
maker: +V...FBEH, or Ulberth. Its broad blade of braided
steel evoked the world of *Beowulf* and the *Nibelungenlied*; I
could imagine the smith Ulberth pulling the weapon from the
glowing forge, quenching it in a cloud of steam, and handing
it to a mail-clad warrior, who tests its balance and peers down
the edge to judge its sharpness.

I made my way back past the Church of the Virgin Mary,
with its Baroque candy-twist columns, and through the
arcaded passages near the university, where I was struck by
the graffiti that seemed to embody the anarchic streak that
runs through Czech culture. In stencilled images, Salvador
Dalí rubbed shoulders with Mr Spock, while Harold Lloyd
dangled precariously from a clock in the famous scene from
Safety Last! 'Liebe is eine universelle Sprache,' proclaimed one
idealist, while a quotation from a song by U2, 'You can't return
to where you've never left', seemed to carry a personal message
for me: tempting as it was to linger in this pleasant city, I would
soon have to move on.

On my way back to the pension, I called at a branch of
Rossman to buy toothpaste and mouthwash. The latter turned
out to be manufactured by Odol, the firm my grandfather
worked for in the 1930s. After the Nazis came to power, they
transferred him to their Barcelona office, placing him and
his family out of harm's way. During my childhood, a bottle

of Odol would appear in the bathroom whenever my grand-parents came to visit.

Because the Amber Route followed several alternative paths through Moravia and into Austria, I needed to make a couple of side trips from Olomouc. The first was to Hranice na Moravě, some 35 kilometres to the east. Big, fluffy cumulus clouds drifted through a bright blue sky as the train carried me through fallow fields and bare woods misted by the green of the first hazel buds. Hranice stood on a small rise in the valley of the river Bečva, surrounded by wooded hills. I walked the kilometre into town past blocks of flats and light industrial plants. First mentioned in a document dating from 1169, this small town has a convincing claim to be the geographic centre of Europe. Stick a compass into the map at Hranice, draw a circle with a radius of 1,500 kilometres, and it will pass through or near Barcelona, Paris, London, Edinburgh, St Petersburg, Moscow and Istanbul.

The open space beneath the cream-painted castle was called Pernštejn Náměstí – a Czech spelling of the German Bernstein – or Amber Square. The town's feudal lords were called Pernštein, so the square may have been named after them, or perhaps it referred to the commodity that could have been traded here. Beyond the castle stretched the cobbled expanse of the main square, dominated by the church of St John the Baptist, a tall, narrow 18th-century building painted dusty pink and cream.

On a narrow street leading into the square stood a low, arcaded building, one of the few remnants of the town's Jewish quarter. The arch nearest the square led to a narrow stair running down to the river. Beside it, towering over the small tributary of the Bečva that bounded the old town, stood the synagogue. The tall gable end was pierced by arched windows, and on the gable, the Ten Commandments were inscribed in Hebrew. There had been a synagogue here since the 17th century, though its present Moorish-Byzantine façade dated from the 19th. Not far away, on Zborovska Street, stood the Jewish cemetery. It was partly demolished by the communist city authorities, and what remained was saved in the nick of time by the Velvet Revolution of 1989. Sigmund Freud's brother Julius and Franz Kafka's cousin Oscar, who shot himself after he failed to get into Hranice's presitigious military college, were buried here, under ivy-festooned ash trees beside the little river Lydina.

I made my way down to the military academy, an austere neoclassical barracks that extended for half a kilometre along the road to Olomouc opposite the Bečva. Founded in the 19th century when the town was called Mährisch Weisskirchen, it was an elite institution dedicated to forging the officer class of the Austro-Hungarian Empire. Its alumni included the poet Rainer Maria Rilke, the film director Erich von Stroheim, and Robert Musil, who chillingly evoked its culture of violence and repressed homoeroticism in his novella *The Confusions of Young Törless*. In his diary, Musil described the place as 'the Devil's arsehole'; in the novella, it is identified only as 'a celebrated boarding school' in the town of W, 'a small station on the long railroad to Russia'.

The town's other claim to fame – the Hranice Chasm – proved harder to find amid the suburban streets on the southern edge of town. Eventually, a bohemian-looking gent with a neatly trimmed grey beard and gold earring directed me up a steep road between high hedgerows. Past a camper van park, I came to the entrance to a nature reserve just as a fierce snowstorm whipped up. The hill was wooded with beech, pine, sessile oak, and hornbeam just coming into bud. Amid the leaf litter, the first wood anemones were raising their heads. The path wound upward until I found myself on a rocky outcrop topped by a faintly ludicrous statue of St John Nepomuk kneeling on a small cloud, which itself had a face. Below me, the rock fell a sheer

70 metres to a deep pool. The abyss was formed when the roof of an underground cavern collapsed, and the lake at the bottom was believed to be almost 300 metres deep, the deepest in the Czech Republic. It was no longer permitted to climb down for safety reasons, but the summit afforded an exhilarating view of the town and the river valley, through which the amber traders made their way between the mountains to either side.

The chasm became notorious when Hugo Schenk, a serial killer who preyed on housemaids, threw the body of one of his victims into its depths in 1883. He was hanged in Vienna the following year. Two decades after publishing *Young Törless*, Musil embarked on his novel *The Man Without Qualities,* left unfinished at his death in 1942. Central to this mesmerising panorama of Viennese society on the brink of the First World War is the troubling figure of Moosbrugger, a sex murderer awaiting sentence in prison. Musil modelled Moosbrugger on the real-life Christian Voight, who was condemned to death for murdering a prostitute, Josefine Peer, in Vienna in 1910, a sentence subsequently commuted to life imprisonment on the grounds of insanity. But when the writer enrolled at the military academy in 1894, Schenk's crime was little more than a decade old and still infamous, so it is hard to avoid the suspicion that the idea of Moosbrugger was first planted here.

Some 40 kilometres southwest of Olomouc stood one of the most important sites on the Amber Route: the Celtic oppidum, or fortified settlement, of Staré Hradisko, where large quantities of amber have been found. A bus took me there in little over an hour, between low, rolling hills, ploughed fields and pasture, past roadside shrines and onion-domed churches. The road wound up a hillside and into Malé Hradisko, a neat village of a few thousand souls, clustered on a slope around a tiny, cream-painted church of St Mary. Affixed to the bus shelter was a plaintive appeal for the return of a lost golden labrador called Kora. The name of the village meant Little Hradisko. The name of the Celtic settlement translates as Old Hradisko. There was, to my knowledge, no Great Hradisko. A few tractors and trucks loaded with logs rumbled through, and a man puttered up the hill on a motor-assisted bicycle; otherwise, there were few people around.

The oppidum was about a kilometre east of the village, up a rutted farm track. Spreading over some 40 hectares of pasture, its earthen ramparts were clearly visible. Once surmounted by high wooden walls, they were now crowned with oak and blackthorn. The many huts that once packed the enclosure are thought to have supported a population of up to 5,000. The summit, crowned with a stand of pine, offered a commanding view of the surrounding hills and valleys.

On its hill overlooking the Morava basin, the oppidum controlled an important branch of the Amber Route. A typical Celtic settlement of the late Iron Age La Tène culture, it was occupied from the middle of the 2nd century BC until the 1st century AD, when Germanic peoples invaded Moravia. The presence of amber here has been known for a long time. As early as 1519, local land tables refer to the place as 'Weihrauchberg' – 'Incense Hill'. In 1552, Ján Dubravius, bishop of Olomouc, wrote in his *Historia Bohemica* that myrrh was found here alongside ancient coins, while the Moravian theologian and educator J. A. Comenius, on his 1627 map of Moravia, named the oppidum *Hradisceo, ubi myrrha effoditur* ('Hradisko, where myrrh is dug up').

The site was extensively excavated between the 1960s and the 1980s, revealing the construction of the city walls, posts, and doors, and a stone-paved road that ran through the middle of the settlement. One large enclosure was found to contain rich furnishings and traces of craft activities. Many imported goods, including wine amphorae from Marseille, millefiori glass, bronze utensils, and numerous Roman coins, testified to the settlement's far-reaching trading connections.

Throughout the settlement, substantial quantities of amber, both raw and worked, were found, which chemical analysis showed to be of Baltic origin. The many unfinished pieces shed light on the manufacturing process. The raw material was first cut into its basic shape, either a disc, a cylinder or a truncated cone. Then the beads were drilled; this appears to have been a tricky operation, judging by the number of unfinished pieces that had broken before the hole was complete.

The next stop was Mikulov, a hilltop fortress town that grew up along the Amber Route and for centuries guarded the border between Moravia and Austria, just as Kłodzko controlled the mountain pass from Silesia. What was once a main north–south route, however, became a cul-de-sac with the descent of the Iron Curtain. There was still no direct connection from Olomouc, so I caught the train to Břeclav, the main crossing into Austria, where I had just three minutes to rush into the booking hall, check which platform I needed, and find the train that would take me the last 20 kilometres.

It was late afternoon when the little train trundled into Mikulov. I caught a bus part of the way into town, and then hauled my luggage up the cobbled slope. Mikulov – Nikolsburg in German – was another hilltop town built around a castle; the main square, actually a long, narrow triangle beneath the castle walls, was simply called 'Náměstí', i.e. 'square'. Dominated by the colourful Renaissance tower of the church of St Wenceslas and a 16th-century corner house decorated with bold monochrome sgraffito, it was lined with cafés, restaurants and wine shops; this was wine-growing country, just a stone's throw from Austria's Weinviertel.

Over it all stood the castle, a square, cream-coloured Baroque edifice with corner turrets and an octagonal tower topped by an onion-shaped cupola. I continued along Husova Street, once the heart of the Jewish quarter, and all that remained after the rest was demolished in the 1960s and 70s. The one surviving synagogue was a stout redbrick building, with a ground-floor arcade and steep pitched roof, hard by the castle rock. The foundations dated back to 1550, though the building assumed its present appearance in 1720 after a fire destroyed both the castle and the ghetto. The community had been here since the 14th century, when the town was settled by Jews expelled from Vienna, and was once the largest in Moravia. Mikulov was the seat of the regional rabbi; the celebrated Judah Loew ben Bezalel, who is said to have created the Golem in Prague, officiated here from 1553 to 1573. By the 18th century, Jews made up almost half the town's population, but after the 1781 Austrian 'Decree of Toleration', many moved to Vienna or Brno. By 1939 there were fewer than 500 living in Mikulov, of whom more than 300 were murdered in the Holocaust.

As I rounded a corner by a house once occupied by Alfons Mucha, a drunk shambled up the hill, a bottle in each hand, singing and shouting as a man repairing his car looked on disdainfully. Completing my circuit of the old town, I returned to my pension to plan the next few days of my journey, which would take me into Austria. When I emerged in search of food, I found the square, so lively a couple of hours earlier, deserted, and most of the restaurants and cafés closed. Eventually, I located somewhere open, a cavernous and over-lit cellar. The other diners – more accurately drinkers – were all Czech, and smoked furiously. By the time I left at 10, the town had completely shut down for the night. Olomouc would still have been buzzing. From somewhere near the sombre façade of St Anne's church – converted into a mausoleum for the local nobility after it was gutted by fire in the late 18th century – a dog howled inconsolably.

I slept badly and woke early. In the breakfast room, a notice read, 'Prohibition of salvaging fruit and vegetables from the restaurant!' Above the town rose a strange sugar-loaf hill.

Grizzled rocks broke through its scant grass cover, pines clung precariously to its sides. On its summit sat a strange assortment of geometrical shapes: a dome, a square tower with a pointed roof, and two objects like sentry-boxes. Then I realised that these were the component parts of a church, its lower storeys obscured by the brow of the hill. This was the Svatý Kopeček, the Holy Hill, with its church of St Sebastian – patron saint of plague sufferers – and free-standing bell-tower. The sentry-boxes marching to the summit housed the Stations of the Cross.

I climbed a roughly cobbled path to the Jewish Cemetery. A sign on the gate read ominously: 'The Jewish Cemetery is observed by police CCTV cameras.' The steeply sloping site clung high on a hillside, commanding views of the mountains and valleys. Hawthorn was coming into flower; dog violets spangled the grass; a red admiral sunned itself on the bark of an ash. The graves were of all ages and styles: simple stone markers of the 17th and 18th centuries, their Hebrew inscriptions weathered to illegibility, leaning at angles and almost sunk into the ground, the grand monuments of the 19th century, and the shiny marble slabs of the 20th, the most recent dated 1942. To judge by the stones placed on them, many had recently been visited. At the far end stood a war memorial, the individual plaques set into a semi-circular wall, with a monument in the centre:

ZUR ERINNERUNG
AN DIE IM WELTKRIEG

1914–1918

GEFALLENEN KRIEGER UNSERER HEIMAT

'Ach, wie sind die Helden gefallen!'

Gewidmet von der Israelistischen Kultusgemeinde
Nikolsburg

The quotation, in Hebrew and German, was from the second book of Samuel: 'How are the mighty fallen!' They fell mostly on the Eastern Front, in Serbia and in Italy. Moritz Jung, an academic painter, was killed at Höhe Malinowa in the Carpathians on 10th March 1915; Erich Pisk, a law student and only son of the town doctor, fell in battle at Kirlibaba in Romania on 8th December 1916; Richard Mährischl, another law student, died in a mobile field hospital in Russian Poland on 6th December 1914; while Wilhelm Teltsch died of wounds at Mährisch Weisskirchen – Hranice – on 26th August 1916, having been brought back there from the front. A separate plaque, added later, commemorated 21 Hungarian Jewish prisoners murdered in a nearby clay pit by Nazis in April 1945.

From the cemetery, I climbed further up the hill, which became a wind-blasted limestone outcrop covered in moss and lichen, interspersed by gnarled hawthorns; at the top stood an ancient watchtower known as the Goat Tower. From this dizzying perch, I had a breathtaking view down on to the terracotta roofs of the town and across the valley of the Djye (the Thaya in German) – a tributary of the Morava – to the mountains of Austria: the Trappenhügel in the foreground and, in the hazy distance behind it, the Mitterberg, the Schweinbarther Berg, and the Heidberg. Somewhere far below, a cock crowed.

The day was turning warm and sunny. I made my way back down the steep path and sat under the Doric arcade of the Café Dolce Vita, drinking a latte and watching the comings and goings in the square, before taking a walk. Beside the synagogue, an old stairway led up to the castle grounds, from where I had another panoramic view into Austria. Hearing the distinctive chip-chip-chip of a bird of prey, I looked up to see two kestrels take flight from an embrasure high in an ancient bastion, their shadows racing across the cobbled courtyard, before they swooped back to their roost. Then they emerged again and set off for another circuit, and another, patrolling the rooftops.

Back at the railway station, I had a long wait. Doves cooed and sparrows chattered around the rural halt. I was impressed by the nonchalance with which people wandered across the track to chat with their friends, until it became clear that the risk of a train coming along was minimal. By the time I reached Břeclav, it was getting late. I checked into an unpretentious but comfortable modern hotel beside the river. Its clientele were mostly sportspeople in town for various tournaments; from the bar, a large plate-glass window looked directly on to a squash court. Located on the River Dyje some 85 kilometres from Vienna, Břeclav is the main railway crossing from the Czech Republic into Austria. Formerly known as Lundenburg, it was an ordinary town of hardware shops, supermarkets and Chinese takeaways, with a locomotive works and a brewery. I liked the place. It lay on low ground, so the castle stood not on a rugged outcrop but in a scruffy park. The building was in a poor state of repair, its Renaissance first-floor arcade roofed with corrugated iron. Nearby, some riverside warehouses were crumbing into dereliction. Ducks squabbled along the river-bank. As the sun set behind the castle, a bat flitted through the purple twilight. Soon it was joined by another, and they pirouetted across the castle square, swooping and diving for insects. A great black stork glid overhead, its spare, seemingly effortless wingbeats contrasting with the bats' frenetic motion. A blackbird hopped on to a low wall and burst into song.

The next morning was bright and sunny as I boarded the Vienna-bound train. The sleek, modern double-decker trundled slowly across an iron bridge over the Dyje, past freight trucks stacked with logs and sawn timber. A small flock of lambs gambolled in an enclosure. A bonfire smouldered. As the train pulled into the tiny halt at Bernhardsthal, my mobile phone chimed, and a text message announced, 'Welcome to

Austria'. I had almost imperceptibly crossed what was once the impenetrable Iron Curtain. To the left, beyond a series of lakes fringed by wooden hunting shelters on stilts, lay the Morava – the March in German – and the Slovak border.

The train sped through fallow fields, past trucks of beet and a large processing plant, into Hohenau-an-der-March, where I got out. The area to the north and east of Vienna is the Weinviertel, or wine district, of Lower Austria. Several strands of the Amber Route ran through here, the easternmost following the course of the Morava. An organisation called the Österreichische Bernsteinstraße had brought together some thirty museums in the region, with a red-haired cartoon girl called Betty Bernstein as a mascot. Most of these museums, I discovered, had little to do with amber, but focused on local history, wine, food and folklore. Hohenau was only a staging point on my route – I was planning to use local buses to visit a few villages associated with the Amber Route – but I found its smug prosperity dispiriting after Poland and the Czech Republic.

After a change of bus at Dobermannsdorf, I arrived at Palterndorf. At first sight, despite a fine parish church and a 15th-century plague column by the bus stop, the village looked uninspiring; its neat cottages were all faced with the same bland concrete render, the bottom two feet or so clad, hideously, with what looked like bathroom tiles. The occasional house that – in an uncharacteristic departure from Austrian *Gemütlichkeit* – had been allowed to fall into disrepair revealed stone and brick walls of considerable antiquity. The history and character of the others had been obscured by an application of architectural Botox.

Further up Kellergaße and Florianisplatz, however, the buildings became more irregular, their sloping walls and exposed timbers revealing the village's medieval origins. As I turned into Turmstraße, there it was: the 13th-century watchtower built by the Teutonic Knights. Visitors had to enter through the adjoining pub, but when I got there the door was firmly locked. Then a boy of about 11 pulled up on a bicycle and knocked on the door. A woman in her thirties, who appeared to be his mother, opened it, and agreed to let me see the tower. She handed me a key and showed me the way, allowing me to let myself in.

Gutted in the Second World War, the tower was restored in 2005. Sturdy wooden steps led up through successive storeys, which housed tableaux about the Knights, including their control of the amber trade. One of the upper floors was used for temporary exhibitions of modern art, while the topmost was a glazed observation platform offering commanding views of the surrounding country. Two starlings had found their way in, and were beating frantically against the glass. After letting myself out of the tower, I drank a beer in the pub, and told the landlady about the birds. Walking away up Kellergaße, I looked back at the watchtower, and could see the silhouette of the boy moving around in the observation gallery. Then a window opened, and a bird flew free.

CHAPTER 10

MOZART'S REQUIEM

It was a warm evening, and people were strolling on the broad boulevards of the Ring and chatting at café tables. The train had arrived at Floridsdorf towards dusk, the lines from the north having been rerouted to this suburban station after the war and never reinstated. In February 1934, this northern suburb was the scene of a violent standoff between the right-wing government of Engelbert Dollfuss and the Social Democrats; the housing blocks such as the Karl-Marx-Hof that the party had built here were a centre of resistance. After four days of fighting left 300 dead and thousands injured, the workers were shelled into submission. The Social Democratic Party was banned, its leader Otto Bauer fled, and other prominent insurrectionists were executed. Dollfuss himself was assassinated by Austrian Nazis in July. Among those who took part in the uprising were Litzi Kohlmann and Kim Philby, who married in Vienna on 24th February and left for England shortly afterwards.

After checking into my hotel on Annagaße in the Innere Stadt, I decided to go to one of my favourite haunts, Café Hawelka on Dorotheergaße, to write up my notes. As I was about to leave, I checked my pockets for my notebook and found it was missing. I searched my clothes, my luggage, the room, with no success. Did I leave it on the train? Then I remembered – I had taken it out in the taxi when the driver asked for the name of the hotel, which I had written in the back. I must have left it in the cab.

It contained all the notes I had made since arriving at Gdańsk, and I would sooner have lost my wallet or my passport.

I had kept up a punishing schedule over the previous weeks, rarely stopping more than a night or two in any one place between the Baltic and the Danube. Through sheer fatigue, I had succumbed to the perennial travel writer's disaster. I thought of Patrick Leigh Fermor's lost notebooks – the one stolen with his rucksack in Munich, and the one left with his lover Balasha Cantacuzene in Romania and only recovered twenty-five years later. I tried to take comfort from his ability to recall events after so many years, and from the advice of my friend, the brilliant and sadly missed travel writer Michael Jacobs, who once told me that he never kept a notebook while travelling, but wrote everything from memory on his return. But I failed to convince myself. This was the bleakest moment of my journey. I asked at the hotel reception, and they told me they would contact the taxi authorities and try to trace the driver. I did not entertain much hope, but set out for the Hawelka as planned, where I wrote up the day's events on whatever scraps of paper I could find.

Vienna, Brecht observed, is 'a city built around a few coffee-houses where the population sits together and reads papers'. Viennese cafés are a joy, civilised places where you can enjoy a coffee or a glass of beer, read a newspaper or a book, or even play an afternoon-long game of chess without being hurried by the staff or assailed by the piped music that pollutes almost every public space in Britain. They are places where solitude is accepted as normal; people have written novels or run businesses from their regular table. The typical denizens of the Viennese café, according to the satirist Alfred Polgar, are people 'who want to be alone but need companionship for it'.

Arthur Schnitzler, Hugo von Hoffmannsthal, Hugo Wolf and Arnold Schoenberg frequented the Café Griensteidl on Michaelerplatz. Gustav Mahler favoured the Imperial, near the Staatsoper, as did Sigmund Freud. The café was the defining institution not just of Vienna but of the whole Austro-Hungarian Empire, and can still be found throughout its former lands, from Budapest to Sarajevo. Joseph Roth believed it was part of the glue that held the empire together. 'The one coffeehouse in Zlotogrod,' he wrote of a remote town in Galicia, 'looked very much like the Café Wimmerl in the Josefstadt where I was accustomed to meet my friends in the afternoon ... The chessboard, the dominoes, the smoke-stained walls, the gas lamps, the cake-trolley in the corner by the lavatories, the blue-aproned waitress ... all of this was home, stronger than any mere Fatherland.'

No café in Vienna pleases me as much as the Hawelka, so I was glad – insofar as I could feel glad about anything in my notebookless state – to find the place gloriously impervious to 'improvement'. The dark, dilapidated interior was archetypal. You entered through the *Windfang,* a glazed lobby intended to prevent draughts, which also functioned as a transition zone between the outer and inner worlds, allowing the customer to survey the clientele to see if there was anyone they wanted to meet – or avoid. Inside, beneath a maroon ceiling, the dark wood panelling and peeling wallpaper were adorned with tattered film, theatre and concert posters. From an old iron stove, a rickety flue ran up one wall and turned a sharp right angle to exit through another. The round, marble-topped tables were surrounded by bentwood chairs, with mauve-and-white striped banquettes against the walls. The woodwork was a stratigraphy of overpainted chips and drips. The seedy lavatories were approached through a heavy velvet curtain at the back. On the doors, several letters had dropped off so that, instead of HERREN and DAMEN, they read ERR and AMEN.

On a banquette in the corner, a middle-aged gay couple were ignoring one another with the comfort of long familiarity, one texting on his mobile while the other pored over the crossword in *Der Standart*. A couple sat at one of the tables playing cards, while at the back an old biddy silently headbanged to Bon Jovi on her headset. A man in tattered jeans came in and asked if there was any work available, to be turned away politely by the waiter. Amid all this, a young Englishman in highly polished brown shoes looked simultaneously impressed and bemused.

I awoke the next morning to the news that the taxi driver had been found, and would bring my notebook to the hotel after he began his evening shift. Much cheered, I headed for the Hofburg, the palace complex that occupies most of the southwest quarter of the Innere Stadt. The heart of the imperial city was the Michaelerplatz, a surprisingly small circus bounded on one side by the curved facade of the Hofburg and the other by the Baroque church of St Michael. Horse-drawn fiakers clattered over the cobbles, their bowler-hatted drivers ferrying tourists around the sights. In the middle, a trench had been excavated to expose the remains of several Roman buildings, one with underfloor heating and wall paintings, overlaid by the 17th-century wall of the imperial pleasure garden and a 19th-century drain, each brick stamped with the imperial crest. This was the centre of Roman Vindobona, a garrison town established early in the 1st century AD after the suppression of a revolt in Pannonia, where the Amber Route crossed the Danube and entered Roman territory. The nerve-centre of Habsburg power was built directly on top of the remains of the earlier empire.

Inside the Hofburg, an eerie stillness prevailed. For Ulrich, the protagonist of Musil's *The Man Without Qualities*, it was 'an island lying there, grey, secluded, and armed, with the city's swift life heedlessly rushing past.' Beneath the sepulchral lighting of the Schatzkammer, I peered at the glimmering imperial regalia. The most ancient and charismatic was the octagonal crown of the Holy Roman Empire, its gold arches set with sapphires, emeralds, amethysts and pearls. Charlemagne is anachronistically shown wearing it in Dürer's idealised portrait that hangs nearby, though the crown actually dates from the 10th century. It was worn until 1806, when Napoleon dissolved the Holy Roman Empire and Francis II restyled himself Francis I of Austria, relinquishing his (by then theoretical) claim to rule over the states of northern Germany. Ever since, the crown had been exhibited here 'until there is again a Holy Roman Emperor of the German Nation'. After that, Francis used the crown of the melancholic Rudolf II, whose court at Prague became an academy of artists, astronomers and occultists, and the sceptre of his hard-headed brother Matthias, who deposed him in 1612. On the wall, Francis could be seen wearing the one and grasping the other in a brooding portrait by Friedrich von Amerling.

Here too was the imperial amber collection, of which the most spectacular example was a north German altar dating from around 1640; its five tiers of classical columns were surmounted by a crucifix, and the whole thing was covered in sheets of amber using the then relatively new inlaying technique later employed in the Amber Room. Amid the gem-studded crucifixes and reliquaries was a macabre curiosity: a *Sinnbild der Vergänglichkeit* (symbol of transience) created in Vienna by Daniel Neuberger in 1660 to commemorate the death of Ferdinand III. In this small relief made of wax, wood and sand, the emperor lies on his bier, an hourglass by his side, while nine skeletons merrily perform a dance of death around him.

Most bizarre, perhaps, were the 'inalienable treasures': a narwhal tusk once thought to be a unicorn's horn, and a beautiful 4th-century agate bowl looted from Constantinople during the Fourth Crusade and believed to be the Holy Grail. Other relics included a spear, supposedly the one that pierced Christ's side, and a fragment of the 'True Cross'. I felt oppressed by the ponderous futility of it all; only Andrea

Appiani's portrait of the upstart Napoleon as King of Italy brought life and energy to this melancholy display of power drenched in cloying religiosity.

By 1900, the 'Royal and Imperial Capital and Residence City of Vienna', as it was officially known, was not only a mausoleum of Habsburg pomp, but a maelstrom of modernism ablaze with neon advertising, gridlocked with motor cars and fizzing with dangerous new ideas. This was the Vienna of Freud, Mahler, Schoenberg, Klimt, Schiele, Schnitzler, Schrödinger and Schumpeter – the crucible in which much of modern art, architecture, science, psychology and economic theory was forged. It was also the city where, between 1908 and 1913, an unsuccessful artist would nurse his resentments, soak up the anti-Semitic rhetoric of the mayor Karl Lueger, and begin to formulate the incoherent ideology that would bring about the deaths of millions.

That evening, the cab driver brought my notebook to the hotel. Relieved of anxiety, I went to hear a string quartet perform at the Annakirche, a few doors up the street. The church was the most florid Austrian Baroque, all pink and blue marble, gilded capitals, and gilt angels perched on every ledge, cornice and pediment. The young musicians gave superb performances of one of Mozart's later quartets, and one of Beethoven's first. The 'Spring' quartet, K387, with its energetic fugal finale, is dated Vienna, 31st December 1782, while the fourth of Beethoven's Opus 18 set, written in 1799, is a majestic, muscular work in which the composer's mature voice is clearly emerging. Afterwards, I returned to the Hawelka, where I happily wrote up the day's events in my recovered notebook.

The next morning I headed for the Kunsthistorisches Museum on Vienna's Ring. On Braun and Hogenberg's 1617 panorama, the Innere Stadt is surrounded by zigzag defensive walls. By the mid 19th century, however, these fortifications, which had withstood two Ottoman sieges in 1528 and 1683, were militarily obsolete – they had failed to stop Napoleon from taking the city in 1805 – and had become an obstruction to the expanding suburbs. In 1857, Franz Joseph ordered their demolition, and over the following decades this wide boulevard ring was constructed in their place, lined with monumental buildings in the historicist style: the State Opera, the Kunsthistorisches Museum, the Museum of Natural History, the Burgtheater and the parliament. Like Haussmann's epic building projects in Paris, they were designed to create a fitting capital for an empire; and as with Haussmann's *folie de grandeur*, the empire they were intended to glorify barely outlived their completion.

The Kunsthistorisches Museum occupied an imposing neo-Renaissance pile that faced its identical twin, the Natural History Museum, across a grassy square. I made my way through the Kunstkammer, where the imperial collections of medieval and Renaissance art were piled in dazzling profusion. Centre stage was Benvenuto Cellini's solid gold salt cellar representing the sea and the earth in the form of Neptune, his trident stiffly erect, and Tellus, coyly fingering her nipple. In stark contrast to its brazen Renaissance sensuality was Gregor Erhart's *Allegory of Vanities*, a painted limewood carving made in Augsburg around 1500. As you approach, you see a naked young man and woman, slender and graceful; turn to the other side, however, and the woman is depicted in scrawny, snaggle-toothed old age. Its sour moralising had more than a hint of misogyny; the male figure, significantly, was not shown in his decrepitude. I was more taken by some small boxwood figures of a naked man, woman and child. The work of an anonymous German woodcarver around 1550, they were astonishingly realistic and curiously touching, a reminder of human vulnerability amid the glamour and power of the marble and bronze gods, goddesses and emperors that surrounded them.

As I entered the hall of Greek and Roman antiquities, I came face to face with its collection of portrait busts. Each was displayed at eye-level and eerily spotlit from above, so that I had the unsettling feeling that I was looking directly at a crowd of long-dead Romans, from emperors to anonymous children, and that they were looking back at me. They were ranged around the only full-length statue, that of Marcus Aurelius, who stood stoically amid the shades of his subjects. In the further galleries, the finds from two burials caught my eye. One, dating from the early 4th century AD, was found at Cejkov in eastern Slovakia in 1855, and contained gold necklaces, Roman glass playing counters, a silver denarius of Antoninus Pius (already an antique by the time of the burial) and several grooved amber pendants. The other was discovered at Untersiebenbrunn in Lower Austria in 1910. Dating from the early 5th century, it was the grave of a young woman of high status between 20 and 24 years old. Among the magnificent gold and garnet jewellery, rings, torques, and two giant silver-gilt fibulae, were several big, round amber beads, evidence of the continuance of the Amber Route into the Migration Era.

I made my way back up Kärntnersraße, which was thronged as usual with shoppers ogling the luxury goods in the windows, towards the Stephansdom. Near the cathedral, I came across a shop selling amber jewellery and smoking accessories. Though there is little evidence of it today, Vienna was once a a major amber-processing centre producing cigar and cigarette holders, mouthpieces for meerschaum pipes, cigarette boxes, cases, snuff-mouthpieces for oriental water-pipes, Muslim prayer beads and jewellery exported as far afield as China. From 1860, a large proportion of the amber produced by Stantien und Becker, subsequently the state amber works of Prussia, was processed in Vienna.

I walked into Stephansplatz, and made my way around the cathedral. The long, narrow street that ran from the north-east corner of the square was called Schülerstraße, so naturally I was drawn to investigate (it was actually named after the cathedral school that used to be here). A plaque recorded that Mozart lived in an apartment on the street for a while. A little way down, I came upon the Gulaschmuseum – not actually a museum but a charmingly old-fashioned restaurant. The lengthy menu was about as compendious an exhibition of this species of cuisine as you're ever likely to find, featuring beef, venison, goose, chicken, fish, wild mushroom and even horse-meat goulash, all served with huge potato dumplings.

On Singerstraße, in the lee of the cathedral, a small, in-conspicuous chapel housed the *Schatzkammer des deutschen Ordens*: the treasury of the Teutonic Knights. After the con-version of Prussia to a secular duchy, some of the Knights refused to accept the new dispensation, and continued their activities within the Holy Roman Empire. When Napoleon abolished the Empire, the Knights moved to Vienna, taking many of their treasures with them. The *Schatzkammer* was located on an upper floor; from one corner, a small oriel looked into the chapel, with its lofty Gothic vaults. Here were treasures amassed by the Knights over centuries: the 15th-century insignia of the Order, the Chain of Swords; suits of armour; magnificent reli-quaries, chalices, crosses, goblets, and glass. On a fantastically ornate silver gilt table clock inlaid with turquoise, garnet and amber, the Reaper marked the hours with his scythe. Portraits of the Grand Masters looked down from the walls: Hermann von Salza (1209–39); Archduke Maximilian (1594–1618); and the last of the line, Archduke Eugen of Austria (1863–1954), testifying to the strange afterlife of the Order.

From Michaelerplatz, the street known as Kohlmarkt ran north – along the course of the Roman road once followed by amber traders – to Hoher Markt, a long square standing on what was once the forum of the legionary fortress. A small modern museum incorporated the remains of two officers' houses, complete with underfloor heating. In AD 97, the garrison was enlarged to form a permanent legionary head-quarters, and a fortress was built, on the classic playing-card plan, to the north of the civilian settlement on the bank of the Danube. Troops from all over the empire were stationed here: from Spain, North Africa, the near East, and even from Lincoln and Colchester.

The upper floors displayed carved stone excavated in the city: a magnificent marble torso found in 1849; a votive altar dedi-cated to Apollo by the centurion P. Aelius Lucius in the 2nd or 3rd century AD, and unearthed in 1951; and a relief of the god Mithras found in the Botanic Gardens. Smaller artefacts such as pottery, cooking utensils, jewellery and glassware testified to the domestic life of the town. After the Germanic peoples known as the Marcomanni and Quadi invaded the region in 395, however, the settlement was gradually abandoned; there were no archaeological traces of any activity after 430.

From the museum, I walked north up Judengaße, where two stone pillars marked the entrance to Vienna's medieval Jewish quarter; a chain was drawn across them to close the area at night. Around the corner in Seitenstettengasse, the graceful Biedermeier City Temple still stood. Built in 1825, it was the only synagogue in Vienna to survive the de-struction of Kristallnacht. It was here, in March 1885, that Lina Morgenstern's elder sister Cäcilie launched a charitable foundation in memory of her late husband, to provide assist-ance to the Jewish poor.

Cäcilie had married her maternal uncle Joseph Adler in Krakow in 1847 (avunculate marriage was legal and not uncommon in those days; indeed it is still permitted in Austria today). The couple moved to Vienna, where Cäcilie founded the city's first *Volksküche*, or soup kitchen. In 1883 she joined the board of the Jewish Institute for the Blind, located on Hohe Warte, just north of the city centre. To raise money, she came up with the idea of distributing collecting boxes to homes and businesses. These proved such a success that the idea was soon copied by charities in other cities.

My grandmother Hedwig remembered meeting Cäcilie in Vienna about a year before the latter's death in 1903, when she herself was 12; she recalled her great-aunt as a tall, slender, distinguished-looking woman. In a personal capacity, Cäcilie helped many needy individuals, and after her husband's death in 1883, impoverished relatives began to take advantage of her generosity. The most demanding was the husband of one of her nieces, an unemployed ophthalmologist named Klein. When she asked her sister Jenny for advice, her husband Sigismund Asch intervened in a characteristically robust manner. Having bankrupted one family, he wrote to Cäcilie, the feckless Klein must not be allowed to bankrupt another. There were plenty of vacancies for ophthalmologists in the provinces, and if he was too proud to live in the sticks, tough. The only assistance he should be given was a one-way ticket to America or a revolver to blow his brains out.

A couple of blocks to the west, I came to Judenplatz, a typical old Viennese square lined with Baroque houses, in one of which Mozart wrote *Così Fan Tutte*. Its charm, however, was disturbed by an unsettling intrusion: an enigmatic white concrete cube. Rachel Whiteread's *Nameless Library* is a calm and understated memorial to the Austrian victims of the Holocaust. The four-metre-high monolith represents a library turned inside out, its shelves of books facing inwards. The double panelled doors, cast in negative, are closed and have no handles. Engraved around the plinth is a litany of the places where the Jews of Austria were murdered: Auschwitz, Belzec, Bergen-Belsen, Brcko, Buchenwald, Chelmno, Lodz, Lublin, Majdanek, Maly Trostinec, Mauthausen, Minsk . . . The monument is disturbing in its reticence, offering no consolation or catharsis; it simply denotes an absence.

The idea of a memorial to the 65,000 Austrian Jews killed by the Nazis was first suggested by the veteran Nazi-hunter Simon Wiesenthal in 1994. In January 1996, Whiteread, a British sculptor then still in her thirties, won the competition to create the monument. Much of her previous work, including the Turner prize-winning *House*, had consisted of interiors, cast in plaster and concrete and turned outwards, that spoke eloquently of memory and loss. The monument was intended to be unveiled on 9th November 1996, the 58th anniversary of Kristallnacht, but the project became mired in bureaucratic obfuscation and thinly veiled hostility. There were even complaints that it would reduce parking space and have a detrimental effect on local businesses. When the city authorities tried to get it moved elsewhere, Whiteread threatened to sue.

Opposition came from an unlikely combination of the extreme right, still in denial about Austria's complicity with the Nazis, cultural conservatives who did not want the charm of old Vienna disfigured by a reminder of its shameful history, and a section of the city's small Jewish community. The opposition of the latter was based on the very reason the site was chosen in the first place: beneath the square lay the remains of a medieval synagogue.

After years of wrangling, a compromise was reached: the memorial, finally unveiled in October 2000, stood above ground, while beneath it, the foundations of the synagogue could be viewed in a subterranean visitor centre. I entered through a discreet doorway in the corner of the square, and descended the clanking metal stairs to this memorial of an earlier Holocaust. The stone foundations survived to a height of about five feet; in the middle stood the footing of the hexagonal *bima*, or pulpit. Projecting from the east wall were the foundations of the Ark of the Law. Built in 1240, the synagogue was extended some time before 1294 to form a two-naved Gothic hall. The vaulted ceiling was supported by two columns, the foundations of which could still be seen. The main part of the building was the men's shul; the women's section was separated by a wall pierced with narrow openings through which they could see the *bima* and the Ark.

The museum contained an exhibition on the religious, cultural and social life of the Viennese Jews in the Middle Ages, when the city was a spiritual centre of Jewish scholarship. By 1360, the community numbered around 800, making it one of the largest in Europe. In 1420, however, The Holy Roman Emperor Albrecht II ordered the expulsion of the Jews from Vienna; the following year, some 200 who remained were burnt at the stake, and the synagogue was razed.

'Vienna?' Whiteread told an interviewer after her monument was unveiled. 'I absolutely hate it ... The opulence, the lack of black faces, the fact that you can lift up the corner of any carpet in Vienna, and you're going to find something fairly nasty underneath.' This was, after all, the capital of a nation that elected the former UN General Secretary Kurt Waldheim as its president *after* his involvement in war crimes in Yugoslavia had been exposed, while the entry into a coalition government of Jörg Haider's far right Freedom Party (FPÖ) in 2000 led to the imposition of sanctions by the European Union. A stretch of the Ring is still named after Karl Lueger, while a square in the city centre honours the former Austrofascist politician Julius Raab.

Germans have long since been forced to confront their complicity in the crimes of the Nazis, and it has formed the subject of much German literature from Günter Grass's *The Tin Drum* and Christa Wolf's *A Model Childhood* to Bernhard Schlink's *The Reader*. At the Moscow Conference in October 1943, in contrast, the United States, the Soviet Union and Britain declared that Austria was 'the first free country to fall a victim to Hitlerite aggression'; after 1945, this delusion was fostered by the Western powers because they feared that Austria might join the Soviet bloc. 'Austria,' as the writer Elfriede Jelinek said in her Nobel Prize acceptance speech in 2004, 'is built on the lie that it was the first country to fall to Hitler.'

Discovering that the Wienbibliothek had digitised Vienna's 19th-century street directories, I spent a morning checking them online to see where Cäcilie Adler lived. I found a woman of that name at 8 Wasagaße, in the ninth district, from 1885 onwards, but could not be certain it was her until I had worked my way through to 1900, when she was listed more fully as *Adler, Cäcilie, Curatorin d. Blinden-Inst. auf der hohen Warte. IX Wasag. 8.*'

The ninth district, or Alsergrund, lay just to the north of the Ring. Incorporated into the city in 1862, it was built up with stolid, respectable apartment blocks of five or six storeys to accommodate the city's burgeoning middle classes. Freud had his apartment and consulting rooms there, at 19 Berggaße; Herzl, Schnitzler and Schoenberg all lived nearby. I took a tram out to Berggaße, a sloping street leading down from the Anatomical Institute to the Danube Canal. The father of psychoanalysis moved here in 1891 when the building was still relatively new, and conducted his practice at the flat until 1938, when a visit from the Gestapo persuaded him to relocate to London. Informed that he would be granted an exit visa on condition he sign a statement that he had been treated 'with all the respect and consideration' due to his scientific reputation, he added the ironic postscript, 'I can heartily recommend the Gestapo to anyone' (*'Ich kann die Gestapo jedermann auf das Beste empfehlen'*).

It is strange to climb the stairs to the first-floor apartment as his patients must have done. The waiting room contained its original furnishings, books, and a selection of Freud's collection of Egyptian and other antiquities. His consulting room, however, was now an exhibition space with little atmosphere, as his couch and all the other contents were at his last house in Hampstead, North London.

Freud's ideas on psychoanalysis arose out of discussions with his colleague Josef Breuer, in particular the case of a patient referred to in their joint publication *Studies in Hysteria* by the pseudonym Anna O. While nursing her dying father in 1880, this well-educated young Jewish woman had become paralysed on the right side, and suffered hallucinations, fainting fits, aphasia and deafness. Breuer visited her almost daily at her home on Liechtensteinstraße, just around the corner, and reported back to Freud. Finding no physical cause for her symptoms, he became convinced that they were psychosomatic. After he encouraged her to talk about her frustrations – she was a lively, intelligent young woman who felt suffocated by the role she was expected to fulfil as a respectable Orthodox girl – her condition began to improve.

Anna herself referred to the process humorously as 'chimney sweeping' or – in a term still used to describe psychoanalysis – the 'talking cure'. Freud would later describe her treatment as 'a great therapeutic success', but her recovery was not immediate. She suffered numerous relapses, and on several occasions was admitted to sanatoria such as the Bellevue on Lake Constance. In his novel *The Radetzky March,* Joseph Roth, in typically caustic vein, described this institution as a place where 'spoiled lunatics from rich homes receive onerous and cautious treatment.'

In 1953, in his biography of Sigmund Freud, Ernest Jones revealed that Anna O. was in fact Bertha Pappenheim, to the outrage of her friends and family. Their reaction was due in part to her subsequent career as an energetic, capable and highly respected feminist, whose international repute earned her an obituary in the *New York Times*. Having emerged from her ordeal with her dark hair turned silver at 29, Bertha began volunteering in soup kitchens for immigrants from Eastern Europe and at a Frankfurt orphanage for Jewish girls. Under the pen name Paul Berthold, she published a book of fairy tales called *In der Troedelbude* ('In the Junk Shop'), which originated in the stories Breuer had encouraged her to invent as part of her therapy. In 1898 she published an article 'On the education of young women in the upper classes' in which she denounced the restrictions that had contributed to her break-down, and the following year translated Mary Wollstonecraft's *A Vindication of the Rights of Woman* into German.

In 1904 she founded the *Jüdischer Frauenbund* (League of Jewish Women), which became the largest Jewish women's organisation in Germany, with some 50,000 members. One subject of particular concern to her was the trafficking of Jewish girls from the impoverished regions of eastern Poland. Lured by false promises of marriage or a job as a maid in a respectable household, they were then sold into prostitu-tion. After her mother's death in 1905, she began to travel to Galicia, Greece, Constantinople, Jerusalem and Alexandria to rescue girls forced into prostitution. In 1907 she opened a refuge near Frankfurt where victims of trafficking could live with their children in a caring, cultured environment, and learn a trade. By 1928, the centre had 158 residents. Her efforts met with fierce hostility from Orthodox rabbis and the Jewish press, based partly on fears that drawing attention to the issue might fuel anti-semitism, but also on her outspoken criticism of patriarchal attitudes.

Bertha's mother's maiden name was Goldschmidt, and with the help of her brother Wilhelm and her cousin Stefan Meyer, she established their kinship to Glückel of Hameln, whose memoirs she translated from Yiddish into modern German and had privately printed in 1910. She even had her portrait painted as Glückel in 17th-century costume. Bertha Pappenheim never saw any contradiction between the three strands of her identity as a feminist, a Jew and a German. When the Nazis came to power in 1933, she was slow to recognise the seriousness of the situation; she remained strongly opposed to the Zionist policy of emigration to Palestine until the enactment of the Nuremberg race laws in September 1935 forced her to change her mind. She did not live to see the worst, dying of stomach cancer in May 1936 at the age of 77. Many of the women in her refuges were subsequently murdered in concentration camps.

One grey, overcast afternoon, I took a desultory walk through the frigid grandeur of the Hofburg and the Burgpark. The real object of my wanderings, however, was the Kapuzinergruft, the catacombs where the Habsburg emperors were interred. My curiosity about the place had been aroused not by any guidebook but a novel: Joseph Roth's *Die Kapuzinergruft*, translated into English by Michael Hofmann as *The Emperor's Tomb*.

As a young journalist, Roth – who styled himself 'Red Joseph', a pun on his surname – was a fierce critic of the monarchy. After its downfall, however, he became nostalgic for the ramshackle empire, whose indulgence, if not the same as tolerance, bore sufficient resemblance to it to allow some room to breathe, in contrast to the strident nationalisms that took its place. His novels evoke the sweeping expanse and diversity of the old empire, from the lavish court ceremonial and giddy waltzes of Vienna to the harsh peasant existence of its remote, frog-infested marshlands. The longest of them, *The Radetzky March*, is a sumptuous elegy for the dual monarchy, tracing its decline through three generations of the Von Trotta family. Towards the end of his life, in exile in Paris and drinking heavily, Roth appended a short, sour sequel, *Die Kapuzinergruft*, in which a minor scion of the Trotta family, unpropitiously named Franz Ferdinand, returns from the war to an empire that has imploded, leaving a small, landlocked republic, and his beloved

Vienna transformed into a rackety milieu of cheap rooming houses, black marketeering, jazz clubs and fashionable lesbianism. Unable to come to terms with this post-war world, he seeks solace at the tomb of the emperor Franz Joseph, whose reign began in the revolutionary upheavals of 1848 and ended with his death at the age of 85 in the middle of the Great War that brought the empire to a catastrophic close.

Twilight was gathering, the shop lights were coming on, and office workers were beginning to make their way home by the time I stumbled across the vaults on Neuer Markt. The catacombs lay not beneath some imposing Baroque edifice but under the unassuming, terracotta-coloured Church of St Mary of the Angels, tucked away in the corner of the long, narrow square. I must have walked past it several times without noticing. I was just in time; the crypt would be closing shortly. As I entered through a small door to the side of the church and descended the stairs, the dank air left a metallic taste on the tongue. I was the last visitor, and found myself alone, my footsteps echoing as I made my way between the ornate bronze coffins. The Habsburg rulers had been buried here since 1633 – or rather parts of them had. Until 1878, their bodies were dissected during the embalming process: their hearts were preserved in silver urns in the Augustinerkirche, the entrails placed in copper urns in the Ducal Crypt under St Stephen's Cathedral, and the rest of the body interred here.

Successive generations expanded the catacombs, burrowing further and further under the surrounding plots. In the 18th century, Maria Theresia had a new vault built under the monastery garden, with a dome to allow daylight to stream down on to the florid rococo catafalque she shared with her husband Franz Stefan. It was all sublimely macabre. The dark, heavy coffins were festooned with scrollwork, armorial crests, angels, crucifixes and imperial regalia. On the Baroque casket of Karl VI, a grinning skull sported the crown of the Holy

Roman Empire at a jaunty angle.

Here too was the hapless Maximilian, a surplus Archduke installed as emperor of Mexico by Napoleon III's armies in 1864, only to be dispatched by Benito Juarez's firing squad three years later. Franz Joseph's marble tomb occupied a Secession-style vault of its own, between those of his wife Sissi, stabbed to death by an Italian anarchist, and his son and heir Rudolph, who shot himself at his hunting lodge in a suicide pact with the mistress they wouldn't allow him to marry. A plaque on the wall commemorates the assassinated Franz Ferdinand and his wife (they are buried at his country estate) as 'the first victims of the First World War'.

Also absent was the last emperor, Karl, buried on Madeira where he was exiled by the British after trying to reclaim the throne of Hungary in 1921. Zweig, in *The World of Yesterday*, recalls his earlier departure from Austria in November 1918, a sad and lonely figure on a station platform. Karl's wife, Zita von Bourbon-Palma, lived on in exile in Belgium and the United States before retiring to a nunnery in Switzerland. Since the Habsburgs had never renounced their claim to the throne, the Austrian government insisted for decades that no member of the imperial family should be allowed to return. In 1982 they relented, and Zita was able to revisit her homeland for the first time in more than 60 years. On her death at the age of 95 in 1989, she was buried in the Kapuzinergruft with an anachronistic display of Habsburg pomp that would have warmed the heart of Joseph Roth. After a funeral service in St Stephen's to the strains of Mozart's *Requiem*, the coffin, draped in the imperial flag, was borne to the catacombs. In accordance with ancient ritual, the priest knocked three times on the door. Through a small aperture, a Capuchin monk asked who was there.

'Zita, Empress of Austria and Queen of Hungary,' the priest replied.

The monk answered, 'I do not know her.'

The priest knocked again, and once again the monk asked, 'Who is there?'

The priest responded, 'Zita, Queen of Lombardy, Duchess of Styria and Queen of Jerusalem.'

Again the monk answered, 'I do not know her.'

For the third time, the priest knocked, and the monk inquired, 'Who is there?'

This time, the priest said quietly, 'Our sister Zita, a sinning mortal.'

With that, the Capuchin permitted the funeral train to enter, and Zita was finally laid to rest among her forebears.

PART III

FORTRESS EUROPE

CARNUNTUM TO VENICE

Why are the streets and squares emptying so rapidly, everyone going home so lost in thought?

Because night has fallen and the barbarians have not come. And some who have just returned from the border say there are no barbarians any longer.

And now, what's going to happen to us without barbarians? They were, those people, a kind of solution.

C. P. Cavafy, 'Waiting for the Barbarians'

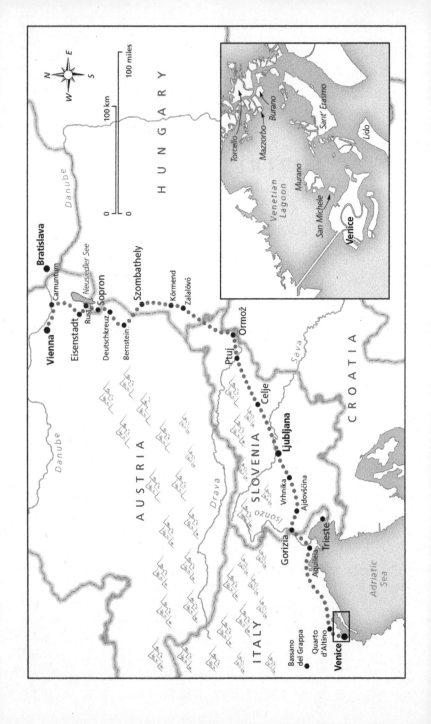

CHAPTER 11

BORDERLANDS

A cutting wind scythed across a plain stretching all the way from the Urals, turning the white poplars inside out like ragged umbrellas. Around me stretched fields of kohlrabi, birch coppices, wind turbines and huntsmen's hides on stilts. Ahead, in the middle distance, a battered stone arch loomed against a leaden sky. Beside it lay a huge chunk of collapsed masonry, its crumbling mortar studded with Roman tiles. Only the western part remained of the colossal four-sided arch, built between AD 354 and 361, possibly to commemorate the victories of Constantius II, though the foundations of the two fallen pillars had been partially rebuilt. The original stones were scarred by centuries-old graffiti. Tiles had been found here bearing the stamps of the 10th and 14th legions.

The scattered ruins of Carnuntum – two amphitheatres, streets, houses, a bath complex and this triumphal arch, known as the Heidentor ('Heathens' Tower') – extended for five kilometres between the villages of Petronell and Bad Deutsch-Altenburg, close to the southern bank of the Danube and nearer to Bratislava than Vienna. Standing beneath the Heidentor, I recalled the distance – more than 2,000 kilometres – I had travelled, and the lands I had crossed. A trader passing under this gateway with a bag of amber from Wrocław, to which it had been brought by pale, broad-cheekboned people from the fringe of the known world, would be entering an empire that stretched from Hadrian's Wall to the Libyan desert. On this windswept plain, the route became a physical – and in places visible – Roman road, which continued through Hungary and Slovenia to Aquileia at the head of the Adriatic. The road and the stations along it were clearly marked on the Peutinger Table, a medieval copy of a late Roman map, and in the Antonine Itinerary, a route list with place names and the distances between them that probably dates from the 2nd century AD.

It was in this garrison town that Marcus Aurelius wrote parts of his *Meditations* towards the end of the 2nd century AD, as the sun began to set on his empire. That most pacific of emperors spent years here, fighting a bitter war to defend Rome's northern frontier against the Quadi and the Marcomanni. The brutality of that conflict can be glimpsed amid the Stoic resolve of the *Meditations*: 'Have you ever seen a hand or a foot cut off, or a head sliced off, lying anywhere apart from the rest of the body?'

The first written reference to Carnuntum occurs in the *History* of Velleius Paterculus, in an account of the future emperor Tiberius's campaigns against the Marcomanni. As at Vienna, there was a military camp and a civil settlement. When the Roman Empire expanded to the Danube, the region was inhabited by the Boii, a Celtic tribe. The soldiers stationed at Carnuntum had to be fed by a civilian population, so settlers were introduced, probably from the provinces of Pannonia and Noricum. Around the middle of the 4th century, the city appears to have undergone some kind of catastrophic destruction, either by earthquake or invasion. By AD 375, the historian Ammianus Marcellinus, whom Gibbon considered 'an accurate and faithful guide, who composed the history of his own times without indulging the prejudices and passions which usually affect the mind of a contemporary', found the place *desertum nunc et squalens*: abandoned and in ruins.

At Bad Deutsch-Altenberg, I came to the Carnuntum Museum. This Jugendstil interpretation of a Roman villa stood before a beautiful park lined with mature horse chestnuts and fragrant with the scent of newly mown grass. The entrance was flanked by two columns topped by busts of Augustus and Marcus Aurelius. Between them stood a bronze statue of the Emperor Franz Joseph, who opened the museum in 1904. The implication – that the Austrian Kaiser was the heir of the Roman Caesars – was clear. Inside was an array of finds from the site, including small bronze statuettes of Juno, Jupiter, Minerva, Neptune and other gods and goddesses, bronze and silver fibulae, oil lamps, and an array of Roman coins ranging from the 1st century AD to the twilight of the empire. Among the gravestones of Carnuntum's cosmopolitan population were those of Marcus Mulvius, a banker, and of Publius Aemilius Verecundus, who died aged 75, and his son Publius; all three men hailed from Judaea, and were buried some time between AD 71 and 135.

The next day, under a hazel tree in Deutsch-Altenburg, I climbed aboard a bus crammed with schoolchildren and elderly women on their way to market. It trundled through the little town of Rohrau, the birthplace of Joseph Haydn, to Bruck an der Leitha, where I got out in the main square as the noonday bell was sounding from the tower of the huge Baroque church. Across the river at Bruckneudorf, in a field beside the busy Vienna to Budapest autobahn, a Roman villa had been excavated. The walls had been reconstructed to waist height, coloured modern paving showed where the mosaics, now in the State Museum at Eisenstadt, were found, and a section of hypocaust had been reconstructed.

There were several successive phases of building. The initial wooden structure, put up in the second half of the 1st century AD, was replaced by a wattle-and-daub house in the early 2nd. This was in turn replaced by a stone villa, which was enlarged around AD 170–180 to form a palace, possibly for a nobleman of the Boii, M. Cocceius Caupianus. His tombstone was found here, reused to cover a heating duct in yet another rebuild during the 4th century, when the rooms were paved with mosaic floors, probably as the residence of the provincial governor. The imperial court may even have stayed here during a campaign in AD 375. In the 5th century the villa was at least partly destroyed by a fire.

Swifts flipped and turned over fields of young wheat splashed with poppies and cornflowers. As the bus laboured up the wooded slopes of the region's only significant uplands, the Leithagebirge, I caught a glimpse, far to the west, of the white mass of the Schneeberg, the easternmost rampart of the Austrian Alps. The hills marked the beginning of Austria's easternmost and newest state, Burgenland. Until the collapse of the Habsburg Empire after the First World War, the largely German-speaking region was part of the Kingdom of Hungary; in 1921, in accordance with the Treaty of Saint-Germain-en-Laye, it became part of Austria. To this day, places in the former Deutsch West Ungarn have both German and Hungarian names.

As the bus crested the hill, a silver expanse of lake came into view, stretching far to the south. Some 36 kilometres from north to south and 12 kilometres from east to west, the mysterious Neusiedler See straddles the border with Hungary, where it is known as Lake Fertő. It is Central Europe's largest steppe lake – an endorheic basin that has no inflow or outflow such as a river, but collects water from rainfall and loses it by evaporation. In the middle of the 19th century it disappeared altogether for a few years. The lake now draws birdwatchers from all over the world, and has Europe's largest population of Silberreiher – the endangered great white egret.

Following the Roman road along its western shore, I came to the pretty village of Purbach – Fekete Varos in Hungarian. The

Herberge where I had booked a room was located at the end of a narrow street of ancient buildings, one of which had a stork's nest on its tall chimney. A plaque on a wall announced that the Amber Route passed through here. Aside from a little low-key tourism, the town was largely devoted to wine growing, agriculture, and fishing on the lake. It was ringed by towers – the Ruster Tor, to the west, the Turks' Tower to the north and the Bruckertor to the east – built between 1630 and 1634 to defend it from the Ottomans. A small museum devoted to local history featured a Bronze Age grave discovered in 1930, evidence of a Roman settlement, and a display on the Amber Route. On the landward side was a long, wide street with a tree-lined brook running up the middle. Named Kellerplatz, it was lined with old wine cellars with arched doorways under stone gable ends. Built around 1850, many now served as restaurants and pubs. At night, under a sky full of stars, I could hear the burbling of the stream as it flowed past the bottom of the street, and the croaking of frogs in the lake.

The next morning, I took a bus south through the small towns and villages along the lake. Many had set up maypoles, tall birch or fir trees stripped of all but their uppermost branches and decked with ribbons. The roadside was lined with posters for parties campaigning for the state legislature elections: the SPO, Greens and the Rot-Schwarz Allianz, the latter demanding work for Burgenlanders and stricter border controls. For several miles, the view was dominated by the yellow Baroque church of Donnerskirchen, its sturdy tower high on the Leithagebirge topped by a rust-red cupola. From the Bergkirche, as it was known, the market town spilled down the slope to the shore. The place was deserted, except for an elderly lady riding in a trailer towed by her husband's tractor.

Cresting the hills, the bus descended a hairpin zigzag to the regional capital Eisenstadt (Kismarton), depositing me in Domplatz beneath the sheer white walls of the cathedral.

The town centre was dominated by the yellow palace of the Esterházy family, who employed Haydn as court composer. I walked uphill to the Burgenland State Museum, where a well-presented collection of gravestones, mosaics and domestic utensils testified to the Romanised way of this frontier region. Lumps of iron ore – extracted here since the 2nd century AD – explained how the place got its name: Eisenstadt means 'Iron Town'. A relief excavated at Bruckneudorf in 1990 showed a wagon of the type that traversed the Roman road through the area, a point reinforced by a reproduction of the Peutinger Table and a map of the Amber Route. Goods recovered from roadside graves included gold and silver rings, earrings, and a bracelet of glass and amber beads. A beautifully carved catfish of opaque, tawny amber, about 12 centimetres across, was found in the grave of a high-status individual at Girm, some 25 kilometres to the south.

The gravestones testified to the cosmopolitan population of the region in Roman times: there were memorials to auxiliary soldiers and veterans from all over the empire; the indigenous Celtic population was represented by Bituriso, son of Cotisai; while Folnia, Iulianus and Putulla were identified as 'newcomers'. A tiny, delicate leaf of gold inscribed with the Hebrew prayer *Shema' Yisroel*, dating from the 3rd century AD, was found in a child's grave at Halbturn in 2008 – the earliest evidence of a Jewish presence in Austria.

This part of town was once the Jewish ghetto, and beside the museum stood a stone pillar with a heavy chain attached that would have been used to close the quarter at night. Next door, in a private house built around a cobbled courtyard with a large fig tree in the centre, was a synagogue set up in the late 17th century by Samson Wertheimer, *Hoffaktor* to the court of Esterházy. It was one of the few in Austria to have survived the Nazi era. The Jewish community left Eisenstadt in October 1938, but it was used once again by Jewish soldiers in the Red

Army from 1945 to 1955, when the town lay deep within the Russian sector of occupied Austria.

I followed a first-floor balcony to the synagogue, its walls painted with Gothic-Oriental decoration in the early 19th century. A spiral staircase led up to the exhibition rooms on the first floor. Alongside a portrait of Wertheimer was a collection of ritual implements gathered from the vanished synagogues of Austria, including a late 17th-century Torah curtain of silver embroidered lace, tefillin, and shofars made of rams' horns. A pair of silver rimmonim – the finials that decorate the rollers of the Torah scroll – from a synagogue in Mattersburg were topped with gilt Habsburg eagles. An eerie snapshot of a Purim carnival at Landsberg in 1946 showed celebrants impersonating Hitler and a concentration camp inmate. In a corridor, a framed issue of *Der Stürmer* from 1938 carried the chilling headline '*Juden unerwünscht*'.

Then I came to a bare room, painted black, its window blacked out. The slogan was repeated, between swastikas, on a banner strung across one wall. At the other end, a painting by the Israeli artist Oz Almog consisted of nine panels, each with a rose, and above it, in Hebrew, the name of a concentration camp: Auschwitz, Treblinka, Buchenwald ... In the centre of the bottom row, over a purple rose, was Theresienstadt, where two of my great-grandparents died.

From Eisenstadt, I took another bus to Rust, the most attractive of the little towns on the shore of the Neusiedler See. The road passed between flat fields and vineyards flanked by poplars. Between the village of St Margarethen and Rust was the Römersteinbruch, a quarry cut into the hillside by the Romans in the 1st century AD. Much of the sandstone from which Carnuntum was built was extracted here. Half the hillside had been chiselled smooth, creating an amphitheatre. Local people first put on a Passion Play here in 1926, and operas were also staged each summer.

The sandy heathland above the quarry was a nature reserve. As I made my way up to the summit, a small brown animal hurtled across my path and disappeared into a hole in the ground. I had never seen one before, and had no idea what it was – it was too elongated for a rat, too plump for a stoat, and had ears too small for a rabbit. I was soon enlightened: a noticeboard informed me that the reserve supported an important colony of European ground squirrel – known as *ziesel* in German, or *suslik* in Czech. They are found only in southern and central Europe, and their main predators, apart from domestic cats and dogs, are kestrels and buzzards. The reserve was also home to many bats, and the largest colony of jackdaws in Europe. From the top, I had a magnificent view down to Rust and across the Neusiedler See into Hungary and, to the west, over the Leithagebirge to the Alps. As I left, a buzzard circled overhead.

Rust was centred on a long, triangular cobbled Rathaus Platz, which sloped down towards the lakeshore. At its landward end brooded the ancient Fishers' Church, as darkly Gothic as a medieval woodcut; behind it rose the pink neo-Baroque tower of the Evangelical church. The square was lined by Baroque buildings, including the Rathaus itself in the corner, their chimneys crowned by storks' nests; from one, a big old stork warily eyed a stall selling eels, carp and catfish from the lake. On the far side of the square, a Gothic archway led down to the shore, where a long wooden jetty ran out through the reeds to the open water. Storks, herons and egrets speared fish in the shallows, while enormous dragonflies hovered like prehistoric raptors.

The Landesstraße running south from St Margarethen between the stumps of pollarded limes was a patched, uneven road with just one lane in either direction. After a couple of kilometres it crested a small rise, and I was on the border with Hungary.

At what was once the Iron Curtain, there was no fence, no checkpoint, and not a single guard; both Austria and Hungary were now members of the Schengen zone. To one side of the road stood a curious landmark consisting of a stone gateway in which a rusted iron door swung open. In a park on the Hungarian side, a dramatic sculpture in white stone depicted people breaking through a shattered gatehouse. These monuments commemorated one of the most significant events in recent European history.

In 1989, encouraged by Gorbachev's reforms, Hungary's Communist government agreed with the Austrian authorities to open the border here for three hours on 19th August, to allow delegations from each country to exchange greetings at a 'Pan European Picnic'. On the day, however, some 600 East Germans holidaying in Hungary arrived at the picnic and walked across the border into Austria. The next day, the Hungarian government, fearing a hardline backlash in Moscow, reimposed border controls. During the night of 21st–22nd August, Kurt-Werner Schulz, a 36-year-old architect from Weimar, was shot dead by a border guard while attempting to cross. 'I felt ashamed,' the Hungarian Prime Minister Miklós Németh said later. On 11th September, the border was reopened, and in the following weeks some 30,000 East Germans crossed to the West.

Despite this haemorrhage of its citizens, the hardline regime of Erich Honecker clung grimly to power, to the increasing embarrassment of a Soviet administration bent on *glasnost*. In September 1989, my uncle and aunt, who lived in the East German town of Ilmenau, visited Britain to celebrate my father's 70th birthday; the travel restrictions did not apply to retired people, whose defection would save the state the cost of their pension. We sat around our kitchen table in London, discussing the rapidly unfolding situation. 'I can't see anything changing until Honecker dies,' my uncle said. On 17th October, Honecker was replaced as General Secretary by Egon

Krenz; three weeks later, the Berlin Wall came down. In 1991 Honecker, wanted by the authorities of a reunited Germany for corruption and the killing of escapees, fled to Chile, where he died of cancer in 1994.

There is a sadly ironic postscript to this history. Just weeks after I crossed this unguarded border, Austria mobilised 2,200 soldiers to patrol it. For months, men, women and children fleeing the civil war in Syria had been crossing the Aegean from Turkey to Greece in flimsy boats, many drowning in the process. From Greece, they made their way through Serbia to Hungary, from where they travelled through Austria to their ultimate goal, Germany. In July, Hungary, ruled by Viktor Orbán's conservative Fidesz party since 2010, began to erect a razor-wire fence along its border with Serbia.

Despite such measures, the crisis continued to escalate, and in August, the Burgenland police made the shocking discovery of the bodies of seventy-one Syrians in an abandoned lorry on the hard shoulder of the motorway between Neusiedl and Parndorf. Four people-traffickers were subsequently arrested. On 1st September, Hungarian police sealed off the main railway station in Budapest, leaving many hundreds of refugees in the square outside; a large group set out to walk along the motorway to Vienna. Germany's Chancellor, Angela Merkel, stood alone in maintaining that her country would place no limit on the number of refugees it would take: '*Wir schaffen das*' ('We will cope'), she insisted. But after European ministers meeting in Brussels failed to agree on a plan to redistribute the refugees among the member states, Germany 'temporarily' suspended its obligations under the Schengen agreement and introduced emergency controls on its Austrian frontier. The next day, Austria closed its border with Hungary.

As I stood on the site of the Pan European Picnic, however, there was as yet no sign of the impending restrictions. Not far beyond the border, the red tiled roofs, spires and cupolas of Sopron came into view on the crest of a hill. The town stands on a peninsula of Hungarian territory that juts deep into Burgenland, almost cutting the region in two. In August 1921, when Austrian police and customs officials attempted to take control of 'German West Hungary' in accordance with the Treaty of Saint-Germain, they met fierce resistance from a local militia called the Ragged Guards who, supported by the Hungarian army, established their own administration in the region they called Lajtabánság. Following diplomatic intervention, both sides agreed to a plebiscite. While the mostly German-speaking inhabitants of the rural areas voted overwhelmingly to become part of Austria, the predominantly Magyar population of the capital Sopron (then known as Ödenburg) opted to join Hungary.

On arrival in this 'most loyal city', I located my pension on the southern edge of town, just outside the traffic-choked boulevards that ringed the historic centre, which was enclosed by impressively preserved Roman walls and bastions. Behind the 19th-century Town Hall were the excavated foundations of Roman Scarbantia, including a paved stretch of the Amber Road itself. The southern side of the main square was defined by the soaring Gothic Church of the Blessed Virgin. Down Új utca, I came upon the medieval synagogue, a plain, steep-roofed Gothic hall built around 1300. Jews were first recorded in Sopron in the 13th century. In 1526, the townspeople, with the connivance of the city authorities, drove them out, looting their homes and wrecking the synagogue, which was only restored in 1967. Jews were readmitted in the 18th century, and in the 19th, Orthodox and Reform synagogues were built in the suburbs. A plaque on the side of the building commemorated the 1,640 Sopron Jews murdered by Hungarian fascists during the Second World War.

The city museum was located in the Fabricius House, a fine merchant's dwelling built on Roman foundations in the 14th

century, with traceried Gothic windows and an arcaded staircase around the courtyard. The displays focused on the Amber
Route and the history of the city. The earliest remains, from
the Bronze-Age urnfield culture, consisted of several large urns
used for cremation burials, 140 of which had been excavated
at the Jerevan housing estate in the northwest of town. There
were also spearheads, axeheads, torcs and other jewellery, and
a strange, crown-like object found in 1913 at Hasfalva (now
Haschendorf in Austria), ten kilometres south of Sopron.
Dating from the late Bronze or early Iron Age (1000–800 BC),
it was about two feet across, pierced with circular openings,
and had ten wheels at the bottom. It is believed to be a cult
object associated with sun worship, and is almost identical to
one found at Balkåkra in southern Sweden, which may have
been traded for amber. Both were made of an alloy containing
tin, which is found at the foot of the Alps, and were probably
manufactured in this region.

In the middle of the 1st millennium BC, the existing population was driven out or subjugated by a warlike group of Celts
usually identified with the La Tène culture. Their dominance
came to an end with the arrival of the Romans. The town,
which Pliny the Elder refers to as Oppidum Scarbantia Iulia,
was established during the reign of Tiberius, half way between
Carnuntum and Savaria, where an ancient east-west route
crossed the Amber Road. It appears to have begun as a settlement for veterans of the 15th legion, which was headquartered
at Carnuntum, and received the status of a municipium around
AD 89. Several large villas have been found in the surrounding
countryside.

The vaulted cellars of the Fabricius House were filled with
Roman sculpture: three large early 2nd-century statues representing the Capitoline Triad of Jupiter, Minerva and Juno,
many gravestones, including that of Cotonius Campanus,
games-master at the amphitheatre, and a shrine to Mithras

from Fertőrákos. Upstairs, over two floors, was an exhibition entitled 'Three Thousand Years on the Amber Road'. The display cabinets were filled with finely carved pieces of amber found in female graves along the road leading out of Scarbantia in 1895, 1956 and 1989: a swan with a cygnet on its back, a bearded male face, and several rings, beads and other items of jewellery. Their workmanship and style indicated that they were made at Aquileia, evidence that the amber trade went in both directions, with the raw material going south and worked pieces travelling back north.

At night, from the hotel window, I watched sheet lightning flickering in the distance, casting a church spire into sharp silhouette. On a nearby hill stood a tall, sail-less windmill, like an upturned shuttlecock. Built in 1841, it was surrounded by granaries and storerooms, now converted into apartments. In communist times, it was topped by an illuminated red star that could be seen from Austria.

The Roman road, knowing nothing of 20th-century geopolitics, continued straight through the Sopron salient back into Austria, through the wine-growing villages of southern Burgenland, and then back into Hungary again. The next morning, less than 10 kilometres south of Sopron, I came to the border at Kópháza. The Hungarian checkpoint was now converted to a service station; the Austrian one straddled the road on a gantry, labelled ZOLLAMT DEUTSCHKREUTZ. A few minutes later I was in Deutschkreutz itself, a quiet market town where I stopped to buy provisions at a Spar.

I was struck by the utter Austrian-ness of the place, despite its proximity to a border that people had been free to cross for a quarter of a century, despite the bilingual signs, and despite the fact that, just a century ago, this was part of Hungary. People do not generally move from one country to another unless forced to by economic necessity or political violence. The ethnic Germans who remained in Sopron after the 1921 plebiscite, and continued to make up 39 per cent of its population, were forcibly expelled in 1946.

Werner Herzog made a short film, *The Unprecedented Defence of the Fortress Deutschkreutz*, here in 1968, a satire on the absurdity of war in which four men dress in old army uniforms to defend the castle from a non-existent enemy. Built in the Italian Renaissance style around an arcaded courtyard, the Schloss stands on a wooded rise to the east of the town. Its most notorious resident was Countess Elizabeth Báthory. Reputed to be a vampire, she supposedly bathed in the blood of virgins to preserve her youthful looks, inspiring countless low-budget horror films. The exact number of her victims is not known, but it is believed to have run into the hundreds, making her the most prolific female serial killer on record. When her crimes came to light in 1610, the servants who abetted her were executed, but to avoid antagonising her powerful family, it was suggested that the 'Blood Countess' be sent to a nunnery, until someone realised that this wasn't the cleverest of ideas. Instead, she was placed under house arrest at another of her castles. There, deprived of her rejuvenation therapy, she died four years later.

The next village I came to was Horitschon, where a road sign announced that I was on the 'Römische Bernsteinstraße' – the Roman Amber Road cycle route. I followed it through neat fields of vines, past wayside shrines, until it crested a small hill, from which I could see mountains away to the south. From here, the road descended into the village of Raiding, birthplace of Franz Liszt. The village green was long, with a tree-lined brook running down the middle of it. On it stood an oversized model of a Bösendorfer grand. 'My piano is to me like a frigate is to a mariner,' Liszt wrote in 1837, 'his horse to an Arab, or even more, for my piano has been my own self, my language, my life.' Nearby, under a rose-covered pergola, was a red plastic cube about a metre square. I pressed a button, and it played a recording of Liszt's *Liebestraum No. 3*.

A little way outside town, I found a tiled information board set up to mark the course of the Roman road. The route continued through a series of villages, none more than a few kilometres apart: Großwarasdorf, Nebersdorf, and Kroatisch Geresdorf. The name referred to the settlement here of Croats driven from their homes by the Turks in the 16th century and given refuge in Burgenland by the Austrian monarchy. An estimated 50,000 of their descendants still live in the region, and have preserved their language and culture; the village is called Geristof in Croatian, and the street signs are bilingual.

Just outside Großmutschen, on the edge of a wood of oak, ash and maple, I found another information board near a simple wayside shrine. Beside it were replicas of a Roman gravestone and milestone; I had seen the originals in the museum at Eisenstadt. A green path led through the woods, and I followed it until it crossed another track, where a sign announced that I was now on one of the best-preserved stretches of the Roman Amber Road – a national monument since 1931. I followed it through the forest, between dog violets and wild garlic. A cool breeze rustled the leaves. The woods were alive with birdsong – a blackbird trilled, and somewhere off to one side a cuckoo was calling. The Roman road surface was not visible beneath the leaf mould, but its raised track, with ditches either side, was clearly discernible. I followed it for about half an hour until it disappeared between fields of oilseed rape. My mind was cast back eight weeks and 800 kilometres to the forest track at Stegna, beside the Baltic; despite the contrast between that dark Nordic pine forest and this temperate woodland, I was standing on the same road.

Beyond the Sopron salient, the countryside became hillier, and by the time the bus dropped me at the crossroads in Bernstein, the village was deserted, with just a few lights on in the upstairs windows. The little market town (Borostyánkő in Hungarian) stood at an altitude of 619 metres at the foot

of the Bernstein mountain range. A fingerpost directed me up
a long drive beneath an arcade of chestnut trees to the castle,
Burg Bernstein, high on its rock above the village.

From an irregular oval enclosing wall, part rendered, part
rough stonework patched with brick, rose a square tower with
a red-tiled Baroque cupola. The sky was dark, with just a band
of greenish light below heavy clouds in the east. The tarmac
drive turned to a rutted track, and as I rounded a bend the
gatehouse appeared before me. Under a swinging lantern,
a marble plaque announced that this was the home of the
Hungarian aviator László Almásy, the protagonist of Michael
Ondaatje's novel *The English Patient* and the film of the same
name. In the courtyard, the air was tangy with woodsmoke,
and the great rock on which the castle was built surged up
through the flagstones.

My hosts Alex and Andrea Berger-Almásy greeted me
warmly: 'We were expecting you. Dinner will be ready soon.'
He was tall and elegant in a dark suit and open-necked shirt,
she more casually dressed in a fawn pullover and slacks. Andrea
showed me across the courtyard, through a heavy wooden door
and along a corridor lined with sabres, hunting trophies and
ancestral portraits, and lit by Moorish lanterns of coloured
glass, to my suite.

The vaulted rooms were hung with portraits of Habsburg-era
ladies and bewhiskered gentlemen, including the Emperor
Franz Joseph. In one corner, a glass-fronted cabinet was filled
with Meissen porcelain; in another stood a large white-tiled
stove. Two comfortable armchairs and a sofa surrounded
a solid, plain wooden table with heavy, splayed legs; on it
stood a vase of nightshade and daisies. Against the wall was a
writing desk with a selection of books, an ancient typewriter
and a table lamp. The windows had heavy wooden shutters,
and were uncurtained. One, approached by four steps, had
been converted into a door giving on to a curious belvedere

that looked out over wooded hills to distant mountains. To one side, an iron door led out on to the battlements; when I stepped out on to the ramparts, I looked down on to treetops a hundred feet below.

To the side of the writing desk, a door led through to the bedroom. This was almost as large, but more nearly square, with a tiled stove and, beside it, a small altar with a brass crucifix. Above the bed hung a very dark Mannerist Deposition; on the other walls, two small portraits of young women, who could have been sisters, in the costume of the late 16th century. There was a huge double bed with a carved headboard, and a chaise longue placed across the foot. On the nightstands on either side of the bed were a copy of László Almásy's *Schwimmer in der Wüste* and a Gideon's New Testament.

After a bath, I made my way back through the castle for dinner, almost getting lost in the labyrinthine corridors. As I crossed the courtyard, Alex Almásy ushered me into the Rittersaal, a large hall, lit only by candlelight, with an ornate Baroque ceiling. There were only two other diners, an elderly Austrian couple to whom Alex Almásy explained the history of the castle. He was a relaxed, genial and erudite host. Over an excellent dinner of local produce cooked on the castle's wood-burning range, he explained that the ceiling was installed by Count Adam Batthyány, who bought the lordship in 1644, and depicted scenes from Ovid's *Metamorphoses*. No fewer than three of the eight panels were devoted to Phaeton, the chariot joyrider whose sisters' tears turned to amber. Both the village and the castle got their name from a side road of the Amber Route which passed through here in the Middle Ages.

The next morning I took a tour of the castle, grounds and ramparts, from which I could see out across the wooded hills into Hungary, Croatia and Slovenia. Alex, more casually dressed in an old suede jacket, showed me around the garden before I headed down to the village. On the square were a couple of shops selling jewellery made of the serpentine mined in the area. The larger had its own museum, down a flight of stairs in a series of underground galleries. An archaeological section exhibited finds from nearby burial mounds: fibulae, toggles, jewellery fragments, Roman bronze coins of the 4th century, *terra sigillata*, a small stone altar, and some hexagonal terracotta floor tiles. The fibulae and other Roman goods were cited as evidence of the amber trade.

The front galleries, lined with artificial rock, were clearly a mock-up, but as I passed through a dank wooden passageway, the temperature dropped, and a sharp mineral smell caught my nostrils. This was the real thing: the walls and roof were tunnelled into the living stone, and a spring bubbling from a fissure in the rock. A few rusty mining trucks stood on a short stretch of rail. Mining had been carried out here since the 12th century, initially for iron, but in 1860, chrysolith serpentine was discovered here. The raw material is almost black, but once polished takes on a greenish glint, and is greatly prized for making jewellery. Although this working was now disused, the stone was still being mined a kilometre up the road.

Herr Potsch, who ran the place and made jewellery and ornaments from the serpentine, also worked in amber, as had his father. Above the shop was an exhibition on amber in all its forms. A reproduction of a woodcut from Johann von Cube's herbarium *Hortus Sanitatis* (Mainz, 1491) showed the Bernsteinbaum (the Amber Tree) weeping resin into a river or sea. There were pieces of amber with the usual inclusions – flies, spiders, plant fragments – under magnifying glasses, and displays on the manufacture of rosaries. There was a reconstruction of a Vienna amber shop circa 1900, and a good selection of antique objects, including amber and meerschaum cigar holders and pipes, beads, earrings, and cabouchon brooches, all with the lovely soft lustre of older amber jewellery.

Back in my room, I examined the cosmopolitan collection

of books ranged along the back of the writing table. There was a scattering of contemporary fiction: a German translation of Philip Roth's *Exit Ghost*, Orhan Pamuk's *Red* (again in translation), and Alessandro Baricco's *Questa Storia*. Among the older works were *Jenseits von Eden* by John Steinbeck; Dürrenmatt's *Besuch der alten Dame*; and Maria von Thurn und Taxis's memoir of Rilke. Between the pages of the last was a postcard of a Christ-child doll, with a Christmas greeting on the back dated Vienna, 19th December 1955.

Over supper that night, the conversation came around to Alex's grandfather, the subject of Ondaatje's novel. He was relaxed about the scant resemblance between this work of fiction and the real story. 'There are many ways of telling the truth,' he said, 'and one is as good as another.'

CHAPTER 12

OLD GODS

The next morning, Alex drove me to the bus stop in his big old Mercedes, and I boarded the 7.57 bus. At Kőszeg, three border guards – the first I had seen since leaving Russia – in high-visibility jackets watched the traffic drive past. I was back in Hungary. Some 20 kilometres beyond the border, I came to Szombathely. Bigger than Sopron, it was the oldest city in Hungary, founded during the reign of the Emperor Claudius around AD 50 as Colonia Claudia Savariensum, or Savaria. Its Magyar name meant 'Saturday Place', referring to its role as a market town.

The main square, Fő tér, was triangular, pedestrianised and flanked by 19th-century buildings. At the narrow southern end, a couple of brutalist concrete edifices recalled the Soviet era. Halfway along one side, I was surprised by a life-sized statue of James Joyce stepping cheekily on to the pavement from the wall of a house. In *Ulysses*, Szombathely is named as the birthplace of Leopold Bloom's father, Rudolf Virág, and the city has celebrated Bloomsday each year since 1994. The civic authorities discovered that, in the 19th century, this house belonged to a Jewish family called Blum – a connection as fictitious as the character himself.

After checking into my hotel just off Fő tér, I rushed to the Savaria Museum before it closed, but found that because of a temporary exhibition devoted, by a strange irony, to the Silk

Road, the Roman galleries were shut. The curator – a stocky, bullet-headed man wearing a German Bundeswehr T-shirt – spoke reasonable English, and after I explained that I was following the Amber Route, it turned out that his forbidding appearance belied a kindly nature. 'In that case,' he said, 'I'll let you have a private view.'

Taking a key from behind the desk, he led me to the basement and unlocked the lapidarium, switched on the lights, and told me I was free to take photos with my mobile phone. There were many impressive pieces of stonework, including statuary, inscriptions, votive altars and gravestones, including one of Marcus Aurelius Romanus, a veteran of the 10th Legion. As at Sopron, three colossal torsos remained of a sculpture of the Capitoline Triad.

As I got back to the hotel, the heavens opened, confining me there for the evening. The next morning was windy and overcast, but the rain had stopped. A few doors down, I found a stretch of the Amber Route, paved with large slabs of basalt, visible through a Plexiglass floor in the main hall of a bank. One column had been reconstructed, rising up between the tellers' counters and topped by an original Corinthian capital.

From the north-west corner of Fő tér, Széchenyi Street led to the twin-towered cathedral, built in 1791 after the city had been promoted to diocesan status; the derelict castle was demolished to make way for it. Behind the church, in the gardens of the Bishop's Palace, were visible remains of Roman Savaria. Capital of the Roman province of Pannonia Superior and a major staging post on the Amber Route, the town was also the birthplace of St Martin of Tours in 315 or 316. The son of a pagan officer in the Imperial Guard, he followed his father into the army. Baptised while stationed in Gaul, he acquired a reputation for humility and sanctity, eventually becoming Bishop of Tours.

I was greeted by a custodian who introduced himself as Peter, a handsome fellow of about forty who also played bass guitar in a jazz band. He explained that this was the highest point of the city, and thus always the centre of power. The medieval fortress was built directly on the remains of the late-Roman imperial palace. Alongside another stretch of basalt-slabbed road stood the foundations of a sanctuary dedicated to Mercury, dating from the time of Vespasian, and a bath-house erected in the reign of Domitian and supplied by an aqueduct that ran all the way from Kőszeg. Most impressive, however, were the remains of the basilica, now covered by a modern shelter. This imperial audience chamber was paved with geometric mosaics.

The building may have been constructed for the ill-omened visit of Valentinian in 375. Ammianus records that while the emperor was staying in Savaria on his way to negotiate with the Quadi, an owl perched on the roof of the imperial bath and could not be brought down by arrows and stones. That night, he dreamt he saw his wife dressed in mourning, with dishevelled hair. When he met the Quadi at Brigetio (now Szőny), they sued for peace and even offered to send detachments to fight on behalf of the Romans, but Valentinian, whose anger management issues were notorious, flew into such a rage that he burst a blood vessel and died.

On the other side of town, opposite a magnificent 19th-century Moorish-style synagogue, stood the Iseum, or Temple of Isis. Excavated between 1955 and 1961, the temple had recently been reconstructed, and the gleaming white six-columned portico, flanked by modern galleries, appeared startlingly new. We are accustomed to temples of this kind being weathered by the centuries, but they must have been new once, and maybe this was how the Iseum looked when it was built during the reign of the emperor Hadrian. The temple appears to have fallen into disuse after Constantine's adoption of Christianity, and was gradually dismantled for building material.

While the cult of Mithras was popular with all ranks in the Roman army, the followers of the Egyptian goddess were mostly senior officers or high-ranking civilian officials. I crossed a reconstructed section of the Amber Road, ascended the imposing steps and entered the temple through wooden double doors. Despite the grandeur of the facade, the interior, dominated by a large statue of Isis, was intimate, even claustrophobic, as befitted a secretive cult. Within, the reconstruction was acknowledged by leaving visible the steel framework around which it had been built. In the same spirit, the carvings on the frieze outside were fragmentary – only what had been found was reproduced. The original fragments were displayed in the adjoining museum: a frieze of grapes on the vine, a carving of the goddess Victoria, and panel of Isis riding on the back of the dog Sothis. There were also votive altars, fragments of wall painting, floor mosaics, a ring of pink amber adorned with the bust of a woman, and coins, from worn denarii of Augustus to well preserved bronzes of the 4th century.

It was time to move on. The railway station lay to the east of the town centre, on a long square beyond the river. Just inside the entrance was a small bronze plaque, in Hebrew and Hungarian, commemorating the 4,228 Szombathely Jews deported to Auschwitz from here. I made my way through the underpass and boarded the train to Körmend, the next post on the Roman road. The line passed through fields of blue-green wheat, maize, carpets of flowering lavender, conifer plantations, and small woods of oak, maple and robinia. This tree, with its small, yellowish leaves that move restlessly in the slightest breeze, grows everywhere in Hungary. Also known as false acacia, the species was introduced from North America in the 18th century to replace woodland felled during the wars with the Ottomans, and now makes up almost a quarter of the country's tree cover.

The train arrived in Körmend around two in the afternoon.

I emerged from the station opposite a cement works and made my way through the quiet streets. Rakóczi utca, the town's main drag, was flanked by Communist-era housing schemes and lined with lime trees. As the sky darkened and a group of hooded crows flapped lugubriously overhead, I had a moment of self-doubt. What was I doing on these streets where I had no business, and where I spoke barely a dozen words of the language – a language more remote from English than Russian or Sanskrit? Would I find anything relating to the Amber Route, which crossed the River Rába here?

The *panzió* was a cheap and cheerful roadside pub with a restaurant and beer garden, and clearly a favourite with locals. After leaving my luggage, I walked back into town and located the main square, a broad expanse flanked on one side by 19th-century mansard houses flying the Hungarian tricolor and, on the other, by the castle. Originally an irregular polygon with four stout towers at its corners, it had been given a more urbane aspect in the 18th century by the Batthyány family, who also owned Burg Bernstein. The entrance was flanked by two dilapidated neoclassical lodges, each with a Doric portico. Hundreds of ladybirds clustered at the base of the columns. Despite a restoration in the 1960s, the main palace was only slightly better maintained, its stucco falling away to reveal successive architectural alterations. A team of builders was busily replacing the render on a wing facing the main square; the other buildings would be spruced up as funding became available. This was no doubt essential to prevent them from falling into ruin, but I found their dilapidation both more eloquent and more revealing.

I walked back through the castle woods, a birdsong-filled forest of maple, lime and hornbeam, punctuated by huge oaks. In a clearing of long grass, a tall obelisk topped with a sculpture of a swan commemorated the Batthyánys. The path, fringed with the yellow starbursts of wood avens and white spikes of enchanter's nightshade, ran alongside a small stream called the Szemcse, over which clouds of midges hovered. Beside this stream, just east of the woods, a cross-section of the Roman road was excavated in 2001. As at Purbach, I was sleeping immediately beside the Amber Route. After supper I retired to my room and looked out of the window across the orchards and gardens. A dog barked in the distance, a blackbird was singing, and Venus blazed low on the horizon.

The next morning was bright and sunny. A parade of cadets from the police academy up the road was marching, three deep in dark blue uniforms, behind a military band, flanked by two motorcycle outriders. Bringing up the rear, four riders in Ruritanian uniforms with plumed shakos lent a touch of Austro-Hungarian pomp. It was the graduates' passing out, culminating in the main square with rousing speeches and the Hungarian national anthem. I wondered how many of them had been present at a recent oath-taking ceremony in Budapest, when the Hungarian Prime Minister Viktor Orbán told police cadets: 'We Hungarians don't want global mass migration to change our country. We have to defend Hungary and Europe, the borders of the country and our way of life, our culture and sovereignty.'

I walked to the station and boarded a bus, which doubled back through town, only to be held up as the parade made its way back to the academy. After the last of the cadets had passed, we turned on to Highway 86, which for much of its length was built on top of, or alongside, the Roman road. In Hungary, as elsewhere, Roman roads were often paved only where they passed through towns; in rural areas, a layer of gravel was laid directly on the topsoil and covered with mortar. After the fall of the empire, the roads ceased to be repaired and the mortar gradually disintegrated, but the gravel surface continued to be used by travellers throughout the Middle Ages and the early modern period. Only in the later 19th century were they abandoned, and began to be destroyed by ploughing. Even today, aerial photographs reveal a line of scattered gravel running through the fields.

Past the village of Nádasd, the bus departed from the straight Roman highway and wound its way between hedgerows and fields, small vineyards and orchards, pasture where brown and white cows grazed, and spinneys of robinia. Chickens scratched by the roadside, and a pale orange cat lifted its leg against a fence. A few old Ladas could be seen in the villages; these derided cars were still going 25 years after they stopped being manufactured. Just beyond Felsőjanofska, we passed from Vas into Zala county, and the landscape became more wooded and undulating. After passing a modern reservoir named Boryzstan (Amber) Lake, the bus deposited me in the centre of Zalalövő.

This small market town stood on the north bank of the River Zal. There were two or three bars, a pizzeria, a stationery shop, a car parts dealer, and two small supermarkets. Highway 86 passed through the centre and continued south, via a level crossing, over the Zal, at this point a sluggish brown stream some five metres wide. This was where the Amber Route crossed the river. On the green beside the bus station was a memorial to both the townspeople killed in the Second World War and its Jewish citizens murdered by the Nazis and their sympathisers. A smaller, carved wooden memorial was set up in 1996 to mark the 40th anniversary of the Hungarian Uprising. Fresh orange irises had been placed in a stone vase in front of it.

I followed the map to the *panzió* I had booked, up the busy 86 as it climbed through densely wooded hills, with no pavement to put a distance between me and the constant stream of trucks. A sign showed the distance to Ljubljana, where I was headed, as 250 kilometres. After three kilometres I arrived, sweating and rainsoaked, to find the *panzió* deserted. By the time a woman drove up and let me in, I had been standing in the rain for 15 minutes and was not in the best of moods. In German, I explained as politely as I could that the place was too far from town to see what I wanted to see. She put me on the phone to her granddaughter, who spoke some English, and assured me that there was nowhere to stay in Zalalövő itself, and no taxi service. The landlady then offered to drive me into town so I could visit the museum, so I bowed to the inevitable. The *panzió* was pleasant, and set in a beautiful hilltop location with views stretching far away to the Austrian Alps.

The landlady dropped me outside the Roman museum, a single-storey 19th-century building next to the Post Office, promising to return within the hour. That proved more than enough time to view the three small rooms of exhibits, including a votive altar to Hercules erected under Marcus Aurelius, a family gravestone with a touching relief of a couple with their child between them, and a typical assembly of red and black burnished pottery, fibulae, oil lamps and amphorae. A dark, narrow room at the back piled with fragments of carved masonry led to a garden where the excavated ruins of the Roman town of Salla could be seen. After a legionary camp was established on the banks of the Zal, a civilian settlement grew up alongside it, and was granted city status by Hadrian in AD 124, under the name Municipium Aelium Salla. The remains, preserved to a height of about a metre, were little different from those found everywhere throughout the former empire. The Romans had no qualms about respecting the local vernacular; they stamped their mark on the places they conquered with an architecture as uniform as that of the Soviets.

When I embarked on this journey, I did not expect to find myself writing so much about architecture, but travelling through a region that has seen so much war, so much destruction and so many boundary changes, it was perhaps inevitable. When we build, we make – and remake – our environment in accordance with our world-view. When an 18th-century aristocrat refashioned his rugged ancestral stronghold as a Baroque palazzo, he was announcing that he was no hairy-arsed warlord like his forebears, but a sophisticated man of the Enlightenment. When a victorious power dynamites every vestige of a city that has survived the fighting, its aim is to obliterate all evidence of prior ownership. When conservators repair a ruin, they preserve those features that represent the historical period they consider most authentic, or reinforce a sense of national identity, and remove or obscure those that do not.

The next day was fine. I headed back down the road to the railway station. The single-storey, white-brick building was deserted, but gradually a few passengers assembled to board the Budapest train, and the stationmaster emerged.

'*Hol kapok jegyet?*' I asked him.

'*A vonaton,*' he replied.

'*Köszönöm.*'

I was travelling in the opposite direction, to Slovenia. The train, a tiny orange single-carriage affair, chugged through the villages of Felsőjanofska and Nagyrakos before slipping across the border at Hodoš. The customs post was unstaffed, the ticket office closed, and there was no bureau de change or even a cash machine. I boarded the 4.10pm to Ljubljana along with two young Scottish backpackers travelling from Budapest. The train – scarcely larger than the one I had left – took us though the high, rolling pastures and Alpine-looking villages of Slovenia's easternmost region, the Prekmurje (the name means 'beyond the Mura'). Some 20 minutes later, at Murska Sobota, we were told to change to another, more substantial train.

Tiny, mountainous Slovenia is the most northwesterly of the former Yugoslav republics. Bordering Austria and Italy, it was always the most western-oriented, the first to extricate itself from the Federation, the first to join the EU and, to date, the only one in the passport-free Schengen area. With a land area of just over 20,000 square kilometres, it is slightly smaller than Wales, and its population of two million is less than that of Brussels or Hamburg. The Amber Road traversed it from east to west, following the valleys of the rivers Drava and Sava through the Julian Alps. Along its route stand the cities of Ptuj, Celje and the capital Ljubljana, all rich in Roman remains.

From Ljutomer, a town famous since Yugoslav days for its Riesling, the railway followed the valley of the River Pavlovski, between wooded and vine-terraced slopes, to its junction with the Drava at Ormož, on the border with Croatia. Beside the railway, a long queue of lorries waited at the checkpoint. A few weeks after I passed through here, several thousand refugees, prevented from entering Hungary, sought an alternative route to Austria through Slovenia. The Slovenian authorities restricted the flow to 2,500 a day, temporarily suspended railway traffic, and put up their own razor-wire fence, sparking protests from the Croatian government.

Crossing the River Pesnica, the train pulled into Ptuj station, and I walked the kilometre or so into town. The compact historic centre was as beautiful as any Tuscan hill town, a harmonious mixture of medieval and Renaissance buildings that spilled down to the river from the castle rock. There was evidence of settlement as early as the Neolithic, and a Celtic oppidum occupied the mound where the castle now stood. The original Roman settlement was established in the 1st century BC on the south bank of the river, where the Amber Road ran, later expanding to the north of the castle. In AD 103, under Trajan, the town was given self-governing status as Colonia Ulpia Traiana Poetovio. Sacked by the Huns in 450, it was subsequently occupied by Avars, Franks, Slavs and Magyars. In the 10th century it became part of the Archbishopric of Salzburg, and in 1555 it was absorbed into the Habsburg Empire.

The main square, Mestni Trg, was dominated by a 16th-century watchtower topped by an onion cupola. In front of it stood a large Roman memorial slab known as the Orpheus Monument, set up there in the 16th century as a pillory. The carving on its lower half had been worn away by the victims' chains, though enough remained to identify it as the tombstone of Marcus Valerius Verus, a mayor of Poetovio in the 2nd century AD. I made my way along Prešernova Ulica, a winding street of Renaissance houses with elaborately carved doorways and a relaxed pavement café scene, to the Park Hotel, an elegant old house at the foot of the castle rock. In the square opposite, the EU flag flew proudly alongside the Slovenian tricolor, something I rarely saw in the UK, at least not at a municipal level; in former Eastern bloc countries, EU membership was not seen as a threat to national identity but as a validation of it, a symbol of a freedom still too recent to be taken for granted.

The next morning I set out to visit the archaeological museum, supposedly located in the former Dominican abbey opposite the hotel. After the monastery was suppressed in 1786 – one of many shut down by the Emperor Joseph II in an attempt to limit the power of the Catholic Church – the buildings were used as a barracks. Purchased by the municipality in 1926, they then became a museum. I entered a cool Gothic cloister. The church itself, painted an austere white, was in the Mannerist style of the late 16th century. The various stages of the building's use and abuse had been left visible, with patches of stucco missing to reveal earlier features, fragments of fresco, and even graffiti. The interior had been converted into an auditorium with a stage and tiered seating. The modern fixtures were black and minimalist, designed to sit within but not touch the historic fabric. Beneath the seats, the crypt was exposed, a jumble of stonework of different eras. But the upper storey was closed for renovation, and the archaeological collection nowhere to be seen. The young woman on the front desk didn't know where it was, or even that it had ever been there – it was her first day in the job, she told me.

Fortunately, Roman remains were scattered throughout Ptuj: on the castle rock; around the base of the watchtower, in passageways off Prešernova; and at the temples of Mithras on the other side of the river. Climbing the steep, cobbled path to the castle put me in mind of similar ascents at Kłodzko and Mikulov, several weeks and hundreds of kilometres behind me. The terrace at the top afforded a sweeping panorama of the meandering Drava and the Haloze hills, and the red rooftops and onion-bulbed cupolas of the town. The oldest parts of the castle dated back to the 10th or 11th centuries, but it owed its present form, a tall white-rendered building with steep red roofs, to a 16th-century renovation. A grandiose Renaissance gateway led into the castle courtyard, enclosed on three sides by elegant arcaded galleries.

The ground-floor rooms were decorated with 17th-century Brussels tapestries, faded 18th-century frescoes, and 19th-century furniture, including a magnificent dragon chandelier with a three-pointed tongue. A musical instrument museum contained a small collection of Roman artefacts, including oil lamps of the 1st and 2nd centuries AD depicting musicians, a pair of pipes made of bone and bronze, and an amber ring with a carving of Cupid playing panpipes. A room devoted to later instruments – harpsichords, lutes, violins, a viola da gamba, made in Vienna and Prague as well as by local craftsmen – demonstrated how fully Ptuj was part of the world of Central European music-making in the 18th and 19th centuries.

The most extraordinary sight was a large reception hall lined with eye-catching if slightly clumsy 17th-century paintings, called *turqueries*, of the Ottoman court in Constantinople: Sultan Mehmet IV himself, janissaries, eunuchs, and women of the harem. They were commissioned to commemorate a diplomatic mission to the Sublime Porte by Walter Leslie, a Scottish mercenary who was made a count of the Holy Roman Empire for his part in the assassination of Albrecht von Wallenstein in 1634, and who bought the castle in 1656. Other portraits stressed the kinship of the Leslie family – who owned the castle until 1802 – to both the Stuarts and the Habsburgs.

From the attendant, an older man with a grey moustache, I got an explanation of what had happened to the archaeological museum: it had closed three years previously, the exhibits were in storage, and 'we are still waiting to hear when and where it will reopen.' By way of compensation, this helpful, well-informed gentleman directed me to a number of pieces of Roman sculpture scattered around the town, where they had been incorporated in the walls of medieval and Renaissance buildings.

Returning back down the steep path, I stopped for a beer at a music café before crossing the river to visit one of the Mithraea. No fewer than five of these temples had been discovered around the town. Mithraism was never part of the Roman state religion, but a sect that flourished among the legions, leaving shrines all over the empire until it was supplanted by another Eastern cult: Christianity. The religion appears to have derived from Zoroastrianism, but many of its features had no equivalent in the Persian faith. Because it was shrouded in secrecy, its beliefs and rituals remain obscure, but we know from the sculptural evidence that a saviour-figure called Mithras – the name has the same Sanskrit root as the Buddhist Maitreya – was born from a rock, and went on to slaughter a bull, an act on which the survival of the world depended. After this, he feasted with the sun god Apollo before ascending to heaven.

The south bank of the river afforded a fine view of the town, with the castle towering above it. I headed west along a busy suburban road lined with bungalows, car dealerships and an

Aldi supermarket. Eventually the buildings gave way to open fields, and at the hamlet of Spodnja Hajdina, a side road led to the Mithraeum III (the sites were numbered in the order of their discovery). The largest and best preserved of the temples, it was enclosed within a Roman-style protective building after its discovery in 1913.

A young woman archaeologist from the university at Ormož arrived to give me a personal tour. Within the shelter, the walls survived to a height of three or four feet, along with a wealth of sculpture: a bench with a pair of lion supports, several votive altars, and reliefs showing Mithras slaying the bull. She shared the man in the castle's frustration with the protracted closure of the museum. Apparently the civic authorities wanted to develop the monastery as a conference centre, despite the profusion of such facilities up the road at Maribor, Slovenia's second city. Ptuj is one of the richest Roman sites on the Amber Route, yet many of its treasures were in storage, to the embarrassment of the archaeological community. She told me that she had been visited by curators from Vienna and Szombathely, who were baffled that the city was not making more of its Roman heritage.

To avoid the main road, I tramped back along dusty farm tracks through fields of wheat, maize and yellow-flowered squash under the hot afternoon sun. In Ptuj, I tracked down a few more fragments of Roman sculpture embedded in the walls of houses; they had generally been used as building material and rediscovered when the houses were repaired. Probably inspired by the Orpheus Monument, a 19th-century curate had collected Roman statues and tombstones from around Ptuj and set them up around the walls of the tower in a kind of open-air museum. The staff at the appropriately named Hotel Mitra obligingly showed me another sculpture of Mithras slaying the bull in the courtyard of their establishment.

The next morning was overcast; a heavy, blue-black cloud

obscured the summit of Ptuj Mountain. I made my way along Prešernova to view a temporary exhibition, Archaeology of the Lower Drava, at the Salon Umetnosti – the Salon of the Arts – in a Renaissance house with a black-painted mask on its façade. The chronological displays ranged from stone axes and Iron-Age pottery to Roman oil lamps, along with the stone moulds in which they were made. Here too was evidence of the Amber Route: seven fat amber rings dating from the 1st to 2nd centuries, one with a carving of Amor and Psyche, another with the bust of a woman, and amber spindles, symbols of femininity throughout the ancient world. Like the objects I had seen in Sopron, they were of Aquileian workmanship.

I returned to the hotel under a thin drizzle and ordered a taxi to the station. At Pragersko, the train overshot the platform and then reversed back into the station. Amid general confusion, passengers for Celje were herded on to a replacement bus. As it sped along the motorway, the ground became hillier. Villages clung to the steep pasture, sheep grazed on the hillsides, and cattle lower down. The road tunnelled through the hills before emerging into the suburbs of Celje.

Slovenia's third city is surrounded by wooded hills, which were shrouded in mist as the bus deposited me beside the railway station in the rain. Across the road, the exterior of the Hotel Evropa exuded old-world Central European grandeur; when I checked in, it became apparent that the imposing façade fronted a luxurious but bland modern business hotel. With an umbrella borrowed from reception, I set out along Prešernova – like every town in Slovenia, Celje had a street named after the Romantic poet France Prešeren. At its junction with Savinska, two parallel rows of brass studs marked the course of the main Roman road through the town, the Cardo Maximus, excavated in 1997. I continued past the Church of the Annunciation, where some fragments of Roman carvings were embedded in the wall. On Trg Celjski Knezov stood the Princely Palace, the former residence of the Counts of Celje, which now housed the Regional Museum. A clangorous metal staircase led down into a city beneath the city: Roman Celeia. Here were the foundations of temples, public buildings and private houses, and a well preserved stretch of road paved with large, irregular stone slabs, six metres wide between its drainage ditches and steeply cambered. This was the Decumanus Maximus, which crossed the Cardo Maximus at right angles at the centre of town.

Just up the road was the Old Counts' Mansion, a galleried Renaissance house that contained the Celje Ceiling, a dizzying *trompe l'oeil* painted around 1600 and rediscovered in the 1920s behind a false ceiling. In the basement, Roman stone carvings were exhibited. Dominating one end of the gallery were a head, and fragments of an arm and knee, from a colossal Apollo. There were a Mithraic altar, a mesmeric head of Medusa, and an altar set up on 13th December 215 invoking Jupiter Arubianus – a typically Roman conflation of a local Celtic god and their own supreme deity – for the health of the emperor Caracalla. The energy and plasticity of the figures, and the elegance of the inscriptions, testified that Celeia was no rude outpost, but a sophisticated Roman city with a high level of material culture.

I set out by taxi for the Roman cemetery at Šempeter, 12 kilometres to the west, through a valley flanked by pyramid-shaped hills wreathed in mist, past fields of hops, their tendrils snaking upward on wires strung between tall wooden poles. Šempeter was an attractive village with a yellow Baroque church immediately opposite the Roman necropolis. The ticket booth shared a cabin with a kebab shop, but was closed; an apologetic sign instructed visitors to ask at the nearby tourist office. As I approached, a cheerful woman grabbed her umbrella and dashed over to the kiosk to get the keys and let me into the small park that housed the monuments. She looked relieved when I said I didn't need a guided tour.

The cemetery was discovered in 1952, after a statue was unearthed by chance in an orchard. Here as elsewhere the Romans buried their dead along the road leading out of town, in this case, the Amber Road from Celeia to Emona – modern Ljubljana – as it ran along the northern bank of the Savinja. The tombs owed their survival to a flood that swept them into the river around AD 270, where they were preserved by the silt; had they remained standing they would have almost certainly have been pillaged for building material.

The plot contained numerous carved fragments and smaller tombstones, but was dominated by four substantial mausoleums. The oldest was that of the Vindonius family. The plinth stood on a simple base that once contained the ashes of the deceased. On the upper part, an inscription declared that the tomb was set up by Gaius Vindonius Successus, an aedile (administrator of public buildings) of Celeia, in memory of himself and his wife Julia, who died at the age of fifty; the text described her as 'an extremely faithful wife'. The reliefs on the sides represented a manservant and maidservant.

The largest, that of the Spectatii, stood more than eight metres high, and was graced by superb reliefs of Iphigenia and Castor and Pollux, in addition to busts of the dedicatees, now sadly headless. An inscription above the lintel declared that Gaius Spectatius Finitus set up the tomb for himself and his son Gaius Spectatius Prisciaiius, both of whom served as duoviri (mayors) of Celeia in the 2nd century. At the apex of the pediment, the snake-tressed head of Medusa, whose gaze turned anyone she looked on to stone, guarded the tomb.

The magnificent canopied tomb of the Ennii was set up by Quintus Ennius Liberalis and his wife Ennia Oppidana in memory of themselves and their seventeen-year-old daughter Kalendina. Beneath the busts of her parents, Kalendina stood between two genii, their torches quenched to signify her early death. Her hairstyle resembled that of the Empress Faustina, wife of Antoninus Pius, suggesting that the tomb dated from his reign (AD 138–161).

The latest of the monuments was that of the Secundinii, from the middle of the 3rd century, one of the last to be set up before the flood destroyed the cemetery. Smaller and simpler than the others, it was built during the lifetime of Gaius Spectatius Secundinus, in memory of himself, his wife Tutoria Avita, their son Spectatius Cervius, his nephew Rusticius Tutorius, and *his* son, Rusticius Albinus.

All four tombs were embellished with reliefs of exceptional beauty, depicting scenes from classical mythology: naked, muscle-bound Hercules leaning on his knotty club as he led Alcestis from the underworld; Europa carried off on the back of Jupiter, who had transformed himself into a bull; the boy Ganymede undergoing the same fate at the hands of the lustful deity, now disguised as an eagle. Eloquent in their silence, the figures spoke of a vanished world. In this village in the Balkan hills, under the soft, unremitting rain, the old gods were alive.

A leaflet bearing an endearingly hand-drawn sketch map guided me along a path through the churchyard to the eastern necropolis, where a section of the actual road was found in 1962. The surface had been eroded by ploughing, and was now covered with modern gravel, but the ditches on either side were clearly visible for a length of about 150 metres, running parallel with the newer road. Of the graves that lined its northern side, only the foundations survived; because this stretch had not been washed away by the flood, the stones were later removed for use as building material.

I caught a bus back to Celje and took refuge from the rain in the hotel bar. The downpour continued into the night, streaming down the roofs and gutters. The next morning, some blue sky showed between the clouds. I walked over to the station, where I boarded a dilapidated train covered with exuberant graffiti. Travelling west, the railway followed the turbid brown Savinja through steep, wooded gorges and rocky outcrops, past villages of neat Alpine chalets clinging to the slopes. At Zidany Most, where a quarry cut deep into hillside, the Savinja joined the Sava, so that instead of travelling downstream, we were now running against the current as it tumbled over jagged rocks, flowing eastward through Croatia and Serbia to join the Danube at distant Belgrade.

CHAPTER 13

BY THE
DRAGON BRIDGE

The train pulled in to Ljubljana between gleaming new office buildings. The area around the station had an air of confident modernity, yet there were still many archetypal Balkan faces to be seen, especially on the older men, their long noses curving over ragged, bandit moustaches. I walked up Resteva Cesta under a thin drizzle, past dilapidated Habsburg-era villas, an old-fashioned tailor's, a bakery and a shop selling religious paraphernalia, until I came to the river. My father must have passed the same way nearly eighty years earlier when, fleeing Italy with his brother Andreas, he arrived in Ljubljana by train. I recall, at his seventieth birthday dinner, him asking Andy whether he remembered how they found lodgings in the city, and would sleep all day to save money on food.

Nestling in the lee of the castle, the Old Town was a graceful assembly of Renaissance and Baroque buildings curving round the banks of the Ljubljanica River, which was spanned by a series of elegant bridges. The city had gone by several names in the course of its history: Emona in Roman times, Laibach during the long centuries of Habsburg rule and, since Yugoslav independence in 1918, by the Slovenian Ljubljana. As at Ptuj, the pre-Roman settlement was on the castle rock, whereas the Roman *urbs quadrata* was founded on the other side of the river. Emona was destroyed by the Huns in 452, and in the following century the area was settled by the Slavic ancestors of the present population. After several centuries during which the region was contested by the Franks, the Magyars and the Kingdom of Bohemia, it fell to the Holy Roman Emperor Rudolf I of Habsburg in 1278.

My hostel was located in a row of old houses that lined the northern embankment. The room, up two flights of wooden stairs backing on to a semi-derelict, pigeon-infested tenement, was small, spartan but spotlessly clean. From here, it was a short walk to the Dragon Bridge, with its four green bronze monsters, their spiked tails curling round the plinths. The bridge took me across the river to a large square lined by a curving colonnade, one of the many works of the Slovenian architect Jože Plečnik that adorn the city. A busy street food market was taking place, with cuisines from around the world – Indian, Argentinian, Italian, Middle Eastern. I continued past Prešernov trg, a grand square dominated by the pink Baroque facade of the Church of the Annunciation, whose bells set up an insistent clangour. From the square, the Triple Bridge arched over the river, and the embankment curved south, lined with cafés and restaurants.

One block back from the river ran Stari trg – the name means old square, but it was actually a long, curving cobbled street lined with boutiques, jewellers and secondhand bookshops. In the window of an antique shop, I saw a large amber brooch and a meerschaum pipe with an amber mouthpiece. A tray of militaria reflected the nation's history: Austro-Hungarian medals, an Iron Cross, a blue Mutterkreuz with a swastika at its centre, a Luftwaffe cap badge, and an array of red stars and Yugoslav medals.

At a waterfront bar, I ordered a beer and sat beneath an umbrella watching the knots of pedestrians: young people in animated conversation, older couples making their way with difficulty and on sticks. A few German and English voices could be heard amid the gentle, mostly Slovenian hubbub. Across the river, a tall pilastered house, its beige stucco flaking benath a subsiding roof, resembled a scene from a 17th-century Flemish painting. From across the water came the insistent thump of rock music and the occasional gust of laughter. Between the lime trees, bats skittered, first one, then two, then many. Plump-bodied, translucent-winged, they swooped and dived, feasting on the midges that hung over the sluggish green water.

The next morning, I set out to locate the remains of Roman Emona. Outside the City Museum, people in medieval costume demonstrated a variety of ancient crafts: book binding, calligraphy, archery and coin minting. The museum was housed in the Auersperg Mansion, the oldest parts of which dated back to the 15th century. The basement had been excavated, and beneath its vaults, the ground level of Emona could be seen, including a stretch of the Amber Road, eight metres wide and made of layers of flattened riverside gravel mixed with sand and lime mortar.

The Roman town lay to the west of the river, where grandiose 19th-century administrative buildings tailed off into suburbs of Jugendstil villas and allotment gardens. In a small park, I came across a stretch of the city walls. Reconstructed in the 20th century on the original foundations, the ensemble owed less to the Romans than to Plečnik, who erected a bizarre pyramid incorporating fragments of Roman masonry at the centre. Nearby, behind some old villas, were the foundations of a Roman house dating from the 4th or 5th centuries, complete with hypocaust and a fragment of geometric mosaic.

At the eastern end of Congress Square, an oblong public space densely planted with plane trees, the stone parapet of a Roman well was visible. At the western end, Emona's northern cemetery was marked by a pillar surmounted by a replica of a gilded bronze statue of an Emonan citizen. Excavated here in 1836, the original was now in the National Museum. Nearby stood a Roman sarcophagus. In the southwest corner, opposite the Church of the Holy Trinity, part of the northern gate was visible in a bleak underpass where homeless men took shelter.

Further west, I came to Republic Square, a wide plaza framed by the modernist architecture of Tito's Yugoslavia – sleek, elegant buildings that owed more to Le Corbusier than to the Socialist Realism of the country's Soviet-dominated neighbours. At the northern end stood the parliament, designed by Vinko Glanz in 1960, its portal surrounded by heroic bronze nudes by Zdenko Kalin and Karel Putrih. In front of this building, on 25th June 1991, Slovenia's first president, Milan Kučan, declared the country's independence from Yugoslavia. The next day, the Yugoslav People's Army invaded Slovenia, beginning what is known as the Ten-Day War. After fierce resistance by the Slovenian Territorial Defence force, a ceasefire was declared; 44 Yugoslav soldiers were dead, and 19 Slovenes. Many YPA troops of Slovenian origin simply changed sides. Now, the square was deserted except for a few young skateboarders who were not even born at the time of that conflict.

Ljubljana is a city of bookshops, many of which stay open well into the evening, housing readings and talks. Slovenia's literary tradition goes back to the 16th century, when the Protestant reformer Primož Trubar published the first book in the native tongue. Its two most outstanding figures were the 19th-century Romantic poet France Prešeren and the early 20th-century modernist Ivan Cankar, both of whom, in their use of the Slovene language and assertion of national identity, did much to foster demands for independence. Ljubljana has a lively literary culture today, and is home to a number of globally recognised writers including the philosopher Slavoj Žižek, the novelists Drago Jančar and Brina Svit, and the poets Svetlana Makarovič and Aleš Šteger.

I had encountered Šteger a few years earlier at a European

Literature Week at Spitz an der Donau in Austria's Wachau region. Discussing literature and nationalism in the former Yugoslavia, he made reference to the suggestion in Plato's *Republic* that poets should be expelled from the state as fomentors of discontent (I once heard Iris Murdoch lecture on the same subject in Oxford). He went on to take issue with Žižek's book *Living in the End Times*, which blames romantic poetry for sowing the seeds of the aggressive nationalism that led to genocide in Yugoslavia.

Through the offices of a mutual friend, I had arranged to meet one of Slovenia's most celebrated authors, Evald Flisar, at the jazz club behind the Slovenian Writers' Association on Tomšičeva, opposite the National Museum. Flisar had written 15 plays and more than a dozen novels, of which *The Sorcerer's Apprentice* sold more than 45,000 copies, making it by far the most successful Slovenian novel since the Second World War. He was president of the Slovenian Writers' Association from 1995 to 2002, and since 1998 had been the editor-in-chief of the oldest Slovenian literary journal, *Sodobnost* (Contemporary Review). At the time of our meeting, he was president of Slovenian PEN.

A man of seventy with a fringe of grey hair and a dark, neatly trimmed goatee, Flisar suggested we go up to the PEN restaurant, a sunny first-floor room hung with modern paintings. His genial manner belied the dark and disturbing nature of his most recently translated novel, *My Father's Dreams,* but he questioned me watchfully about the purpose of my visit and the book I was writing. We discussed the travelogue: he had written three, but now felt that, despite the work of writers such as Paul Theroux, whom he admired, the genre 'has gone out of fashion somehow'. This he attributed in part to the cultural homogeneity of the modern world: 'That's why I don't travel any more.'

He told me that his Hungarian-Austrian father was born in

one country, married in another and died in a third, without ever moving from his home town. He himself spent 20 years away from his homeland, driving underground trains in Sydney before going to London to work in publishing. Yugoslavia, he said, was never an isolated Eastern bloc country, attributing the idea to 'ignorance and lazy journalistic thinking'. He pointed out that as early as 1952 the Third Conference of Yugoslav Writers, here in Ljubljana, made a decisive break with Socialist Realism, opening the door to modernism and contemporary literary ventures, and that the PEN Writers for Peace Conference had been held in Bled since 1984.

Expanding on the Western identity of his country, he observed that the old border between the Eastern and Western Roman Empires ran through what became Yugoslavia. While the West was Catholic and used the Latin alphabet, the East was shaped by Byzantium, the Orthodox religion and the Cyrillic script. Slovenia's proximity to this ancient fault-line made it vulnerable. 'Almost anyone who wanted to march somewhere had to march through Slovenia, conscripting young men to fight on both sides,' Flisar said, citing the Isonzo battles during the First World War, in which a million died just across the border in Italy, and which formed the setting for Hemingway's *A Farewell to Arms*.

'We feel protected as a member of NATO,' he added, 'having a European identity and European culture. For 700 years we were part of Austria. Unlike our neighbours to the east, we have been through all the great movements: the Reformation, the Renaissance, the Enlightenment. Culturally speaking we are part of the West, though of course,' he added, 'much is wrong with the Brussels bureaucracy.'

Our discussion turned to the refugee crisis. 'People here are sympathetic,' he said. 'We know what it means to run away from war – there are 30,000 Slovenians in the United States. Little old ladies offer food and water. Yet despite the welcome, they are afraid of what to do if they come in droves. We are a very small country, though most want to get to Germany. We are not blessed with the best of neighbours,' he added wryly, referring to the recent influx of migrants through Slovenia's southern border, 'where the so-called Balkans begins.' Reception centres had been established around the country. A Jordanian flight had recently brought 40 children from Gaza to be treated at the government's expense, and since 2011, Ljubljana had been part of the International Cities of Refuge Network (ICORN), funding residencies for writers persecuted in their own countries.

Flisar then apologised that he had to break off, explaining that he had a meeting upstairs to discuss the forthcoming PEN Congress in Québec, which he would be attending. Shaking hands, he warmly wished me all the best for my travels and my writing. As I made my way across the road to the National Museum, I was relieved to find myself a little early for my next appointment, as our meeting had given me much food for thought.

In the park in front of the museum stood a large bronze statue of a burly, long-haired man in the swashbuckling costume of the mid 17th century. On the stone plinth, the single word VALVASOR reflected the subject's importance to the nation's identity. Janez Vajkard Valvasor (1641–93) – Johann Weikhard von Valvasor in German – was an Austro-Slovenian nobleman and polymath whose *Glory of the Duchy of Carniola,* published in German in 1689, recorded the natural history, folklore, industry and agriculture of what is now Slovenia. It also included the first detailed survey of the region's unique limestone topography, its caves, sinkholes and subterranean rivers, which he identified by the Slovenian name *kars*. In its German form *karst*, the word has entered the terminology of international geology. In recognition of his achievements, Valvasor was elected to the Royal Society in London on the recommendation of Edmond Halley.

Off the grand neo-Renaissance lobby was a small, wood-panelled reception area. The receptionist put a call through to Peter Turk, who came downstairs to meet me. A slim, dark-haired man in his forties, Dr Turk was a prehistorian, and keen to emphasise that the amber trade in Slovenia pre-dated the Romans by several centuries. Raw amber, he explained, was imported and made into products in this region as early as the 8th century BC, in the Hallstatt era of the Iron Age. Thousands of amber artefacts had been found here, including necklaces, a fibula with four amber beads, and a multi-headed bronze pin with six beads on the end – an object local to Pannonia and northern Italy, and not found in the Baltic. At Novo Mesto, in southern Carniola, amber beads had been discovered in both male and female graves, along with bronze situlae – libation vessels, often decorated with elaborate friezes – dating from the 6th to 5th centuries BC. Chemical analysis showed the amber to be of Baltic origin.

Much of our knowledge of the early Iron Age in Slovenia is owed to an Austrian noblewoman, Marie, Duchess of Mecklenburg-Schwerin (born Princess Marie of Windisch-Graetz), who excavated several important sites along the Amber Route between 1905 and 1914, including the cemeteries at Magdalenska Gora and Stična in the vicinity of Ljubljana. A stout lady given to wearing a broad-brimmed hat on digs, she investigated hundreds of graves, recovering helmets, armour, swords and spearheads, along with situlae and bronze and amber jewellery. Assisted by her secretary Gustav Goldberg and a crew of local labourers, she conducted excavations that were, by the standards of the day, meticulously scientific. 'The Duchess's archaeological work is truly admirable,' wrote the French prehistorian Josef Déchelette. 'One rarely employs such care in the conducting of the work in order that neither objects nor valuable observations are lost.'

The First World War brought the Duchess's excavations to

an end. After her death in 1929, the National Museum was able to retain a few of the finds, but the majority were auctioned by her heirs. As the fledgling state of Yugoslavia couldn't afford to buy the material, most went to Harvard and the Ashmolean in Oxford. One breastplate was in Berlin, a gift to her husband's cousin Kaiser Wilhelm II, who part-financed the digs.

With the transition to the La Tène culture in the 5th century BC, a change in burial practice made it harder to establish the presence of amber in the region. Inhumation was replaced by cremation, and the ashes were buried in urns, with few grave goods. The Roman period, however, was abundantly represented in the museum. Here was the original statue of the Emonan citizen, a replica of which I had seen on Congress Square. Amid the pottery and metalwork were an amber ring and a beautifully carved figurine of a lion.

One of the museum's prize exhibits was an inscribed stone recording the foundation of the COLONIA IVLIA EMONA in the year Augustus held tribunician power for the 38th time, AD 14, the year of his death. His stepson Tiberius was already named as joint ruler. A stone inscribed MVRVM TVRRISQ DEDERVNT recorded the construction of the city walls, and was found at the eastern entrance to the Roman city. In AD 6 to 9 there had been an uprising in Pannonia, hence the need for defensive walls. Another, found just south of Ljubljana in 2011, marked the border between the territories of Aquileia and Emona. Inscribed FINIS on the top, AQVILEIENSIVM on one side and EMONENSIVM on the other, it dated from the early 1st century. Dr Turk pointed out that, since such boundary stones were only set up within provinces, it indicated that Emona was part of Italy, not of neighbouring Pannonia.

Afterwards, I walked a few blocks to Metelkova Mesta, an artists' colony near the station, where a collection of ramshackle, brightly spray-painted buildings housed various clubs and bars. Sheltering from the rain under a bandstand,

I met a couple of backpackers, a bearded Argentinian and a young Australian woman. We were soon joined by a Frenchman then living in Ukraine. They were discussing the refugee crisis when I arrived. The girl had had to fly here from Croatia because the border was closed. The Argentinian had been working with Syrian refugees in Belgrade. All had experienced travel difficulties as a result of the crisis; journeys that would have been easy a few weeks earlier were now problematic. As we sat under the bandstand, our conversation was punctuated by the deafening crashes of apples falling on the tin roof, like shells exploding.

That evening, I went to a wine tasting at a small shop on Trubarjeva, just around the corner from my hotel. The owner was Spanish. While his Slovenian wife was a lawyer undertaking conveyancing work for British expats in Murcia, Andrés ran the business in Ljubljana, distributing olive oil from his family estates – they owned 70 hectares in Jaén – along with wine from Spain, Italy and Slovenia. Two smart, forty-something women from Sarajevo came in and looked around the shop.

'Sarajevo,' Andrés remarked after they had left. 'So many things started there . . .'

That night, my last in Ljubljana, I sat in a bar by the Dragon Bridge drinking a glass of wine far inferior to those in Andrés' shop. I was lost in thought, ignoring the background music, when Suzanne Vega's 'Marlene on the Wall' came on, and I was transported back to Olomouc and my meeting with Fernando Saunders. I thought back over all the other evenings in towns along the length of the Amber Route. In the Casa Havana in snowy Tallinn. In the Hawelka in Vienna. On a night of thunderstorms in Sopron . . .

All that lay behind me; ahead, the Amber Route followed the Ljubljanica River through the lower reaches of the Julian Alps, which the Greek geographer Strabo called the Mons Ocra.

While the valleys and passes facilitated the transport of amber and the building of the road, they were also one of the weakest points in the defences of the Roman Empire, affording invaders a direct highway into the heart of Italy. It was here, therefore, that the Romans constructed one of their largest and most elaborate fortifications, a series of three walls studded with castles, watchtowers and gatehouses, referred to by Ammianus Marcellinus as the *Claustra Alpium Iuliarum* (Barrier of the Julian Alps).

The easternmost wall snaked for some 80 kilometres from the coastal city of Tarsatica (now Rijeka in Croatia) to the Austrian Alps, passing through the Slovenian town of Vrhnika; the second ran through Logatec, while the westernmost followed the higher outcrops through the Hrušica pass. The barrier may have been built in response to the invasion of northern Italy by the Alemanni in AD 271, but it could also have reflected the growing rivalry between the eastern and western halves of the empire. Whatever the motive for building the wall, it failed: for the rest of my journey, I would be following in the footsteps not only of amber traders and Roman legionaries, but of Attila the Hun.

I set off the next morning by bus. Once clear of the petrol stations, car dealerships and supermarkets on the outskirts of Ljubljana, the road ran between wooded hills, their tops wreathed with cloud. In one village, I noticed a street called Rimska Cesta – Roman Road. As we approached Vrhnika, the hills began to look more like mountains. I found the old town off to one side of the main road, clustered around a small white church and dominated by a large Mercator supermarket. The tourist office did not open until 1:30, and the museum shown on my map had disappeared. I had a coffee and consulted my maps and notes. The remains of Roman Nauportus lay to the south of the present centre, where the road curved west around the cemetery. I followed it, and turned right past a new cultural centre and a faded housing estate, across a burbling stream to where the tall, cream-coloured church of St Pavel stood on a rise amid orchards and fields of maize.

By the entrance to the well-tended modern cemetery, I came across the foundations of a circular Roman watchtower, half covered in ivy. I continued uphill past a stone monument to the Yugoslav partisans of the Second World War, to the hamlet of Hrib, where I was rewarded with spectacular views of distant mountains. To the right, a road led between neat modern villas, past a BMW service centre, before ascending a series of hairpin bends through a forest of birch and hazel. Somewhere around here was another Roman watchtower, but it was proving a devil to find. I poked up private driveways, setting guard dogs barking, an unkempt interloper in this prosperous village.

Eventually, I came across an elderly man hosing down his car, and asked in halting Slovenian for the *Rimski Turm*. He led me round the side of his house and pointed the way through an orchard. Up a steep bank overgrown with nettles and brambles, I found it: the stout, square lower storey of a Roman watchtower, standing almost two metres high at one corner. Beside it was a child's tree house and inside, to my surprise, neat rows of brightly painted wooden beehives, each a different colour. The rarely visited ruin had been quietly absorbed into the communal area behind the gardens. Over the mist-capped mountains, a buzzard wheeled lazily.

A 15-minute bus journey took me to Logatec. A ribbon development strung out along the main road, with a few old buildings and two Baroque churches, it was little more than a staging post on the highway, and probably had been since the Romans founded Longaticum here. More by luck than judgement, I had disembarked at a bus stop close to the Villa Tollazzi where I had booked a room for the night.

My landlady was a middle-aged lady called Rossana, who explained that her Italian great-grandfather made a fortune as a carrier on what was then the main road from Vienna to Trieste, and built this imposing house with its overhanging roof. An enlargement of a 19th-century postcard of the building hung over the reception desk. The Communist government confiscated the property, but after Slovenian independence it was returned to the family. Having worked as an au pair in Notting Hill in the 1980s, Rossana bought out her relatives, and set up a hotel in the building. I asked whether it had needed restoration. 'If I had known how much work it would take,' she said, 'I don't think I would have started.'

After a shower and change of clothes, I set out to explore the town before it got dark. There was a tang of woodsmoke on the damp night air. Passing a couple of kavarnas, I ended up at a blue-collar pizzeria by the railway station, where I dined alone to a soundtrack of vintage Country and Western, from Patti Page's lovely 'Tennessee Waltz' to Willie Nelson's 'Whiskey River' – 'Feeling the amber river flowing from my mind...' – punctuated by the clanks and whistles of freight trains in the sidings.

A short walk the next morning revealed, in addition to a handful of bakeries and kebab shops, two opticians and two shops selling petfood and supplies. Opposite the church was a small modern shrine to St Martin of Tours. The St Martin's Way, which coincided with the Amber Route in these parts, ran through here. There was nothing, however, about the Amber Route, and few locals had heard of it. The current mayor, Rossana told me, was not much interested in promoting tourism, despite the region's cultural riches and karst caves. To her outrage, he was proposing to demolish a couple of old buildings next to the hotel to make way for a shopping centre.

From Logatec, there was no way of reaching the next places on my itinerary – the Roman forts at Lanišče and Hrušica – by public transport; the bus took a more northerly road. I asked Rossana to arrange a taxi, and a friendly local man arrived in a people-carrier promptly at 1pm. We passed through the village of Kalce, where a fine old farm building was falling into ruin by the roadside. Beyond, the land rose, and the road wound through dark pine forest with piles of logs stacked by the verge. The driver turned up a narrow, rutted track, and waited while I inspected the remains. The square tower had been reconstructed to a considerable height, and contained a most un-Roman looking embrasure.

Beyond the fort, the woodlands became more mixed, the maples beginning to be touched by autumn gold while the hazels and birch were still in their summer greenery. The road continued to rise, and by 1.30 we were at Hrušica, the highest pass on the route at some 900 metres above sea level. The fort here was much larger than the one at Lanišče, and its walls extended on either side of the road. Within its confines was a small guesthouse, the Stara Pošta (Old Post House). There were two other houses nearby, and that was it. Around this wind-blasted summit, hills and mountains stretched in all directions.

The modern road followed the course of the Via Gemina through the fortress. This stretch was built during the reign of Augustus; though steep and winding, it shortened the journey from Emona to Aquilea by a day compared to the alternative route through the flatlands to the south. The fort was 16 kilometres from Longaticum – half a day's ride by horse in Roman times, a whole day with a loaded cart. The road presumably ran past a pear tree, whose white blossoms stood out against the green of the surrounding forest in spring when the pass reopened to traffic, since the Romans called the station Ad Pirum – 'At the Pear Tree'. This tradition survived in its modern name, derived from *Hruska,* the Slovenian for pear tree, and in the old German *Birnbaumer Wald*.

The Post House had been part of the Austrian mail system since the 16th century. Valvasor described it as standing alone in the middle of a 'horrible wilderness, in which one must have displeasure, annoyance, tedium, fear, danger and inconvenience as travelling companions'. The building still retained the proportions and the Baroque doorway shown in the print that illustrated his 1689 survey. In the 19th century it was used as a hunting lodge; after falling into disrepair in the 20th, it was restored as an inn in the 1990s. The middle-aged couple who had run the place for 20 years were welcoming, but spoke little English, although their son, a young man in his twenties, had a good command of the language. I was the only guest, though the house served as a pub for a handful of local farmers. There was little to do except explore the ruins and walk the surrounding hills during the day, and write and plan my onward trip in the evening.

Attached to the guesthouse was a small but sophisticated exhibition put together by a team from the National Museum in Ljubljana. Information boards displayed the layout and history of the fort, and juxtaposed modern maps of the road with the Peutinger Table, on which Hrušica was named In Alpe Iulia. A number of artefacts found in and around the fortress were on display: a key, a drill, a plane, a knife with a bone handle, an awl, fragments of pottery, a 4th-century fibula, a bone hairpin and part of a glass bracelet. Among the weaponry were iron projectile heads, bronze armour scales of the 3rd century, and a piece of sheet armour engraved with a beautiful head of Minerva. A sequence of nine well-preserved Roman coins spanned the century when the site was fully garrisoned, from an antoninianus minted under Diocletian in the late 3rd century to a centenionalis of Theodosius from around 395, after which the fort was abandoned.

On the guesthouse side of the road the walls, still standing to the height of about a metre, rose to a steep bluff, which was crowned by a polygonal defensive tower. The gatehouse spanned the road to control traffic, and its footings could still be seen on either side; there was even a circular depression into which the lower hinge of one of the doors once fitted. Just inside the gate were the foundations of the tiny medieval church of St Gertrude, patron saint of travellers. It was still standing in Valvasor's engraving; I have been unable to discover when or why it disappeared.

On the other side of the road the fort rose sharply uphill, divided by an internal wall with semicircular defensive bastion. The upper part was normally used for grazing livestock, but if an attacker took control of the lower fort, the garrison could withdraw to this enclosure and continue the fight, raining missiles on their enemies below. At the top was a narrow exit so the defenders could escape if the second line of defence was also breached.

The fort was besieged on several occasions. In 351 Constantius II captured it in the course of his war against his rival Magnentius. The Emperor Theodosius, a fanatical Christian determined to exterminate all trace of the old gods, marched through in 394 on his way to do battle with the usurper Eugenius, who wished to restore the pagan religion. By the time Attila arrived in 451, however, the defences had been abandoned and he encountered no resistance.

The views from the top were exhilarating, across fold after fold of hills, over the town of Postonja and away to the distant mountains, clouds moving like a skein of smoke along a wooded valley hundreds of feet below. Once again, I was standing on one of the great watersheds of Europe: a raindrop falling to my left would find its way into the Ljubljanica and then, via the Sava, into the Danube and the Black Sea; one falling to my right would become part of the Vipava and the Isonzo before draining into the Adriatic.

The next morning, the young man kindly drove me the 10 kilometres to Ajdovščina, along a precipitous road through wooded hills. The countryside reminded me of Mid-Wales.

As we rounded a bend at the village of Col, the hills parted to reveal an enormous vista along the valley of the Vipava to distant mountains: the gateway to Italy. At the edge of the village, a small castle stood derelict.

'No people,' the young man said, gesturing around him. 'We live with ghosts.' As in many rural areas of Europe, there was little work here, and young people moved to the cities. His girlfriend was studying geology in Ljubljana.

The road dropped steeply into Ajdovščina, where he dropped me in the town centre. By now the sun had burnt off the mist and the sky was clear. I found a café built up against a Roman tower and had a coffee, before setting out to explore the little town. Awarded to Italy by the Treaty of Rapallo in 1920, Ajdovščina (Aidussina in Italian) only became part of Yugoslavia after the Second World War, and its pantiled houses looked Italianate. The town sits beneath looming grey mountains on the right bank of the river Hubelj, a bubbling tributary of the Vipava. Known to the Romans as Flumen Frigidus (icy river), it was the scene of a ferocious battle in 394, in which Theodosius crushed his pagan rival Eugenius. The poet Claudian reported that a fierce north wind known as the Burja contributed to Eugenius's defeat by blowing his archers' arrows back on to his own troops. Probably more decisive was the fact that Theodosius was supported by a force of 20,000 Goths under the leadership of Alaric. The victory made Theodosius the last ruler of both the eastern and western halves of the empire, but a year later he was dead, his domains divided between his feeble sons Arcadius and Honorius. In 410 Alaric, tired of the Romans' broken promises, led a Visigothic army into Rome itself.

Ajdovščina's main square, once the forum of the Roman town Castrum ad Fluvio Frigido, bore witness to a more recent ideological conflict. It was now called Lavričev after the 19th-century liberal politician Karel Lavrič, but above the modern sign, an older one named it after Marshal Tito. A pattern in the cobbles mapped the foundations of a Roman house excavated here in 1960s. Just to the south were the remains of a bath-house. From here I followed the circuit of the Roman walls. At intervals, some of the 14 original towers survived to various heights. Some were shattered remnants incorporated in private gardens, or visible only in the curved wall of a later building constructed on their foundations. Rounding the north of the circuit, I came to the best preserved section beyond some vegetable gardens, with one tall, castellated turret, its upper levels reinforced in the Middle Ages, an arcaded stretch of wall, and another bastion, of which only the lower portion survived. Framed by the mountains, these fortifications made an impressive sight.

There was little to do of an evening, so after supper at the seedy Casino Hotel I headed back to the apartment I had rented. In the night, a fierce wind blew up, shaking the rafters. The next morning, it was even stronger, bending trees double and scouring the narrow streets. I now realised why the pantiles on many of the houses were weighed down with large stones.

'So this is the famous Burja, then?' I asked the receptionist.

'Yes,' she replied. 'It can get a lot worse than this.'

I took refuge in the small City Museum. The upper floor was devoted to the Roman settlement. The smaller artefacts, mostly grave goods from outside the walls, included pottery fragments, a couple of oil lamps, a glass flask, a crossbow fibula and a thick, carved amber ring, dark with age, of the type manufactured in Aquileia. There was a small, beautiful bronze figurine of a goddess, cosmetic tweezers, some arrowheads and iron nails. Among the carved masonry were a couple of tombstones, and fragments of the architrave, pediment and a column base from a temple that once stood just inside the town walls.

I still had several hours to kill before the next bus to Nova

Gorica. Practically everywhere was closed, and the wind was so strong I could hardly stand except in the lee of a wall, so I made my way back to the café from which the apartment was managed and asked the young woman if she could call a taxi. There was no cab firm in town, but a few calls produced a local man willing to drive me for €25.

'Super wind,' the stocky, grey-moustached fellow remarked cheerfully as we bowled along a dual carriageway in the lee of the mountains. 'No wind, no life. Better than mist and rain.'

By the time we had covered the 20 kilometres to Nova Gorica, the Burja had dwindled to a stiff breeze. Ahead, on the summit of a sheer rock, we could see the castle of Gorizia, across the border in Italy. We passed through a tunnel in the hillside, and emerged in Nova Gorica, an orderly modern town built to house the Slovene population of Gorizia after it was annexed by Italy in 1947. My driver dropped me beside a shopping centre, and I walked down a long avenue lined with cedars and marble plinths bearing busts of Yugoslav partisan heroes. Finding a bar open, I stopped for a last beer in Slovenia. I was less than a hundred metres from the frontier. Opposite was a shabby-looking nightclub called Monaliza; this model socialist town now did a brisk trade in low-rent casinos and nightclubs catering to Italians from across the border. I finished my beer and walked over a level crossing into Italy.

CHAPTER 14

A HAVEN BLESSED

There was nothing to stop me: no checkpoint, no guards, no passport control. I just walked down an urban street past a sign with the EU flag and the word ITALIJA, yet the atmosphere changed instantly. Not only the language, but people's clothes – or the way they wore them – and their gestures. The way the drivers sounded their horns continually, the women walking dogs the size of gerbils, the green-shuttered villas with umbrella pines in their gardens, the black-bordered death notices pasted on the walls *(Giuseppina Marini, Anni 97)* were all typically Italian. Though there was nothing whatever to prevent people passing freely from one country to the other, the culture changed visibly right there at the border.

I made my way uphill to the main square, a long isosceles triangle under the castle rock, dominated by the orange Palazzo del Governo and the huge Baroque church of St Ignatius Loyola. Like many other buildings here, it was largely reconstructed after the First World War, when the city was repeatedly shelled during the long, grim struggle on the Isonzo. I continued past the Questura into the smaller Piazza Cavour, and down the Via Cappuccini, past a statue of St Francis of Assisi, to the hotel I had booked. It stood on an unremarkable suburban street, and the restaurant and bar were permanently closed; a notice in the window gave a phone number. As I sat on the metal stairs at the side of the building and keyed the number into my phone, it began to rain. A woman answered, and ten minutes later arrived and let me in. The reception area was fusty and cluttered with dark, heavy furniture. On the wall was a family tree of the Habsburgs, on the shelves a Bible, illustrated books on art and archaeology, and a row of VHS videos (*Chocolat, Highlander, Harry, Li Presenta Sally . . .*) After photocopying my passport, she showed me to a cheerless apartment on the first floor with cooking facilities in a chipboard cupboard.

Ravenous, I walked back into town in search of supper. Down a side street, a green neon sign reading TRATTORIA beckoned invitingly. Did I have a reservation? '*Mi spiace . . .*' I tried three others with the same result. It was Saturday night. Eventually, up a narrow alley, I found a small *osteria*, a relaxed, welcoming place with a bohemian crowd of all ages spilling on to the pavement. Although I could have done with a cooked meal, I settled for bruschetta and polpetti washed down with red wine. On the counter was a copy of the regional newspaper, *Il Piccolo*. My eye fell on a report that the National Alliance – a far-right party that once numbered Alessandra Mussolini, the dictator's grand-daughter, among its ranks – had attacked the government of Friuli-Venezia Giulia for allowing the region to become 'the Lampedusa of the North'. It alleged that the former barracks at Cavarzerani and Monti that now housed some 2,700 refugees would become 'ghettos, unmanageable sources of lawlessness', and demanded that Italy close its borders 'as France has done at Ventimiglia'.

The bus to Aquileia did not leave until after lunch the next day, so I headed into town and enjoyed a scaldingly hot, bitter espresso in the main square before setting off on the long walk to the railway station, where I would pick it up. On Via Roma, a fascist-era statue of the Emperor Augustus, 'Father of the Country', gestured away from an Agip petrol station. A poster advertising an anti-immigration rally in Milan screamed, 'Defend our borders! Resist the Invasion!' Someone had ripped it across. Opposite the station a sombre memorial made of rusted iron chains commemorated, in Italian and Hebrew, the citizens of Gorizia deported from here to Auschwitz, Mauthausen and the other death factories of the Third Reich.

On the way out of town, the bus crossed the broad, green Isonzo. Between 1915 and 1917, this wide, fertile river valley was the scene of fighting as intense as any on the Western Front. It was here, just 45 years after Italian unification, that the young nation was forged, as a million men who had previously thought of themselves as Calabrian, Umbrian or Piedmontese fought and died side by side. It was here that the iron entered the soul of the nation and the ideas of Mussolini took shape.

The road followed the course of its Roman predecessor through Mainizza – Roman *Pons Soneto* – and Gradisca (*Ad Undecimum*). Away to the west rose the long, jagged silhouette of the Dolomites. At Fumicello, a young man in a leather jacket, with a Lincoln beard and long blond hair, got on. He sat down next to an equally blond young woman, and they embraced affectionately. A golden couple: stylish, relaxed, confident and utterly self-absorbed. She pulled a book, still in its wrapping, from her shoulder bag and excitedly showed it to her friend: Bruce Chatwin's *In Patagonia*. Across the flat estuarine marshland, the campanile of Aquileia appeared in the distance.

At a T-junction, the bus lurched to the left past a long row of reassembled columns that marked the Roman forum. I got out in the town centre, walked back through the piazza in front of the huge basilica, and called at a café for a beer. Summer's lease had not yet expired in Aquileia. The honeyed stone was warmed by the afternoon sun; butterflies flapped between lime trees still unyellowed by autumn, and roses bloomed on the pergolas.

With a population of just 3,500, the pretty modern town was far smaller than its Roman predecessor. According to the poet Ausonius in *The Order of Famous Cities,* Aquileia was the fourth largest city in Italy (after Rome, Milan and Capua) and the ninth largest in the empire. Its cosmopolitan population, which may have numbered as many as 50,000, included not only Romans and Greeks but Syrians, Egyptians, Jews and Celts. 'Blessed Aquileia,' wrote Martial around the end of the 1st century, 'You of mine age will be the haven blessed/ If I may choose at last my place of rest.' In the event, though, the poet retired to his native Spain.

The remains of the Roman city were strewn around the streets and surrounding fields. Besides the forum was a stretch of paved road; part of an amphitheatre; the foundations of various houses; and a large tomb, which was mostly a 20th-century reconstruction but incorporated fragments of original carving, including two stone lions and an exquisite relief of a bull.

The basilica was an impressive Romanesque church with a tall, free-standing campanile and an octagonal baptistry connected to it by an arcade. It would be the highlight of many an Italian town, but the austere beauty of its columned nave and frescoed apse were eclipsed by what lay beneath my feet. In the early 20th century, excavators lifted the floor to reveal a mosaic that carpeted the first basilica on the site, built by the archbishop Theodore soon after Constantine legalised Christian worship in 313. I could see the footings of the original columns, on top of which the later ones had been set. The church was rebuilt several times: in the late 4th century, when the floor was raised and the mosaic covered up; in the 10th, when the frescoes in the apse were painted; and again after an earthquake in the 14th, when the upper part was restored, giving the nave its lancet arches.

Nothing could have prepared me for the size, the artistic quality, or the astonishing preservation of the mosaic. It was enormous – some 760 square metres. Within its intricate geometrical framework were the figures of James and John fishing in the Sea of Galilee; Jonah and the Whale; portraits of Roman men and women; fishes; birds; a fight between a hen and a tortoise; hares; stags; a goat; a lobster. A circular shield proclaimed the church to be the work of Bishop Theodore. I was surprised that the mosaic was not better known beyond Aquileia; it must be one of the earliest surviving examples of Christian iconography on this grand, public scale. Permeated by lively pagan imagery, including Nereids riding fantastic creatures and Neptune in his chariot drawn by sea-horses, it gave the lie to the idea that the Christians of the early 4th century were an austere, joyless cult: the mosaic was full of energy, humour and joie de vivre.

Just 70 years after its creation, this glorious work of art was covered in a metre of earth when Theodore's successor Chromatius ordered a new basilica to be built on the site. Was this a constructional necessity, or did it reflect a new climate of intolerance? For much of the 4th century, several variant interpretations of Christianity had coexisted with paganism, Judaism and the many other creeds of the Roman Empire. In 381, however, St Ambrose organised a church council in Aquileia that denounced as heretics the followers of Bishop Arius, who maintained that Christ was the Son of God, but not God – a belief that attracted many followers, including the emperor Valens, and found widespread favour among the Goths. Valens's fiercely orthodox successor Theodosius banned pagan sacrifice, closed cult centres and suppressed the Olympic Games. While he did not go as far as to order the destruction of synagogues and pagan temples, he acceded to Ambrose's demand that the Christian mobs that perpetrated such acts should go unpunished.

A steep external stair led up to the first floor of the 73-metre campanile, built in 1030 using stones from the Roman amphitheatre. Some 130 worn spiral steps wound their way to the octagonal belfry, with its three great bronze bells in their wooden cage; a notice advised visitors not to climb the tower when the bells were ringing. Away to the north rose the snow-capped Alps; to the south spread a watery maze of lagoons and mudflats, through which the road from Aquileia extended, ruler-straight, across a causeway to the port of Grado on its sandbar. Beyond it shimmered the Adriatic, my first glimpse of open water since leaving the Baltic many months before. To the east, the Isonzo emptied into the Gulf of Trieste; to the west spread the Venetian lagoon. By a strange symmetry, the lagoons that ringed the littoral where the amber arrived at the end of its long journey mirrored the two that curved around the Baltic coast where it was found, a thousand kilometres to the north.

Behind the basilica was a sad First World War graveyard of metal crosses under the deep shade of cypress trees. Each memorial carried the inscription, rendered forever bitter by Wilfred Owen's poem, *'Dulce et Decorum Est Pro Patria Mori'*, while a more recent monument bore the words of Pope John XXIII: *'Madri e padri detestano la guerra'*. Beyond the cemetery, a tranquil walk ran between fields that spread toward the distant mountains. From this angle, it became clear that the campanile was slightly skewed. The path continued along the bank of the Natissa to the Roman port. Though still a glorious afternoon, it was past 4 o'clock, when the archaeological park closed, but a fallen tree had brought down the fence at one point, and I slipped though. Beneath an avenue of cypresses, substantial docks with carved stone mooring rings lined the water's edge, though the river had long since dwindled to a stream that would scarcely float a canoe.

On top of the wharves, a defensive wall had been built. When the city was founded in 181 BC, it had walls, like many Republican-era towns, but as it grew and prospered, they were allowed to decay and were built over. By the time Rome reached the zenith of its power in the 1st and 2nd centuries AD, the idea that its cities might require defensive fortifications had become unthinkable; but in the 3rd century, the empire was torn apart by internecine power struggles. In 238, Maximinus the Thracian, commander of the legions on the Danube, advanced on Aquileia. He was one of the most brutal of the warlords to seize the throne in that bloody era – his coin portraits, with buzz-cropped hair, broken nose and protruding chin, make him look like an old-school East End gangster. His reputation had clearly gone before him, for the townspeople hurriedly threw up a defensive wall. The extent of their panic is evident from the number of fine monuments they tore down to use as building rubble. In 1936, after they were excavated by Giovanni Brusin, then director of the National Archaeological Museum of Aquileia, they were set up along the avenue leading to the dock: column bases, altars, tombstones, inscriptions. However hasty its construction, the wall appears to have done the trick: when Maximinus failed to capture the city, his troops mutinied and killed him.

This was but the first of many sieges suffered by the city during the protracted death-throes of the Roman Empire. In 340, Constantine II was killed beneath its walls while attempting to capture it from his brother Constans. Twenty years later Constantius II, by then the sole surviving son of Constantine the Great, seized Aquileia, which was then besieged by troops loyal to his rival Julian the Apostate. Alaric, marching down from Hrušica, attacked the city in 401, and in 452 it was sacked by Attila. Jordanes, in his *Origins and Deeds of the Goths*, tells that the leader of the Huns, contemplating the strength of its defences, seriously considered bypassing the city until he saw the storks carrying their young away from its walls, which he took as an omen that they were destined to fall. (The scene is depicted in a charming woodcut in Sebastian Münster's *Cosmographia* of 1544.) The inhabitants fled to the lagoons, where they founded Grado and Torcello. In the 6th century, Aquileia was captured by the Byzantines and became a frontier post in their war against the Goths who now ruled much of Italy; they built a zig-zag wall across the middle of the town and abandoned the northern half, including the forum.

Overall responsibility for the archaeological sites rested with the Fondazione Aquileia, an EU-financed organisation set up to promote cultural tourism, raise funding and carry out research, conservation and restoration work. I found its offices, where I had arranged to meet its director, Cristiano Tiussi, in a dark-red 19th-century palazzo just opposite the basilica. The receptionist showed me to a stainless-steel lift, which whisked me to the top floor, where the modern office furniture and shelves of ring binders were relieved by the old beams of the sloping wooden roof.

Seated at his desk, Tiussi, a relaxed and affable man with a neat goatee, outlined the prehistory of the settlement. The Timavo, an underground karstic stream that bursts to the surface at San Giovanni di Duino, some 20 kilometres to the east, and flows into the Gulf of Trieste, once marked the border between the Veneti, and later the Romans, and the Istrians. Long before the Roman settlement, it was the point where the Amber Route reached the sea. Livy called the estuary the Lacus Timavi, and Virgil mentioned the river in the *Aeneid*, while according to Strabo, a temple to Diomede stood on its banks. Many prehistoric remains had been found in the area during excavations the previous year, including amphorae and other pottery.

I asked Tiussi when the amber trade gave rise to an industry making finished objects in Aquileia. 'The oldest objects date from the 1st century BC,' he told me, 'and there appears to have been a boom in production in the last years of the 1st century AD – maybe as a result of the travels of the Neronian knight.' I was curious to know whether it could be associated with any particular quarter of the city, but no evidence for this had been found. 'In the 19th century, raw amber was found in a house at Aquileia. It may have been a workshop, but we don't know for sure.'

Much of what we know about the Aquileian amber industry is based on grave goods: rings, beads, amulets and other personal adornments buried with the dead. Some, excavated in the 18th and 19th centuries, found their way into private collections; many were in the National Archaeological Museum, which I had arranged to visit the next day. The latest seemed to date from the beginning of the 3rd century; for whatever reason, the city's amber-working industry appears to have come to an end around this time. This accords with a passage in the *Augustan Histories* (admittedly not the most reliable of sources), which states that the eccentric Emperor Elagabalus, who reigned from 218 to 222, 'would strew gold and silver dust about a portico and then lament that he could not strew the dust of amber also', suggesting that there may have been some decline in supply. The most recent grave containing amber dated from the last years of the 4th century but, Tiussi warned, these objects may not have been new at the time of burial, but heirlooms. Lombard-era graves had also been found containing grains of amber, but again these may have been handed down for generations.

Much of Aquileia lay unexcavated beneath the fields, making it one of the greatest archaeological reserves of its kind. Recent excavations had been carried out by the universities of Trieste, Padua, Venice and Udino, and were still in progress around the circus in the western part of the city. Not long before 300, a new imperial quarter was constructed there, enclosed by its own wall. 'This was an important moment for Aquileia,' Tiussi told me, 'when it became an imperial residence like Milan. Almost all the emperors came here – it was the gate between the eastern and western halves of the empire.'

A panegyric written by an anonymous Gallic orator to

celebrate the marriage of Constantine to Fausta, daughter
of his co-emperor Maximian, in 307 mentions the palace at
Aquileia (*aquileiense palatium*), and describes a painting in
its banqueting room that showed the young bride offering her
husband a bejewelled gold helmet crested with 'the plumes
of a beautiful bird'. The palace probably connected directly
with the emperor's box in the hippodrome, as in other imperial centres. This city within a city would have housed a range
of administrative offices, including those of the provincial
governor and his officials. A mint was established at Aquileia
in 294 as part of Diocletian's currency reform, which devolved
the production of coins to regional centres around the empire.
'We think the mint was located here, in the imperial quarter
near the round end of the circus, for security,' Tiussi said,
though he warned that the evidence was far from conclusive.
'There are some traces – not the structures, but we have found
a coin hoard, and silver ingots were found in this area back in
the 18th century. We think it was the place, but there is still a
lot of work to be done.'

 After our meeting, I explored the centre of the present-day
town, which lay to the west of the basilica around the Piazza
Garibaldi, a small square dominated by the Municipio, with
one café, and bounded on the other side by the river. On a
road out of town, I found the Sepulcreto, an excavated section
of graveyard. Restoration was still in progress, with fragments
of original carving reassembled using modern stone and
cement to replace missing sections. While the reconstruction
was inevitably conjectural, the strict conventions of Roman
architectural ornament allowed a fair degree of plausibility.

 I awoke the next day to rain, a steady, horizontal downpour
that blurred the outlines of everything and dispelled my happy
notion that Aquileia basked in an eternal summer. I was due
to visit the National Museum, where I had an appointment to
meet Elena Braidotti, its Director of Education. While waiting

for her to arrive, I examined a chronologically arranged collection of portrait busts. The uncanny realism of the Republican and early Imperial portraits brought these long-dead inhabitants of the town to life: men, women and children, including a very old man with thin lips and hollow cheeks. During the 3rd century, a new style came into vogue, with flattened noses, square jaws and buzz-cut hair represented by sharp chisel strokes; the civil strife of the period found expression in both the economy of labour and the gritty machismo of the male faces. The busts of the 4th century, following the model set by Constantine, were bland, idealised stereotypes, eyes turned heavenwards.

In the next gallery stood two large marble statues of Augustus and Claudius, discovered in 1879 near the forum, and a headless statue of a woman who may have been Antonia, the mother of Claudius. Two busts represented Augustus's grandsons Gaius and Lucius, the heirs he hoped would inherit the throne, but who died before him. Another was thought to depict Messalina, the notorious wife of Claudius, her braided hair pinned back from a quite ordinary and slightly vacuous face. In another gallery was a gilt bronze head of an unidentified emperor of the turbulent 3rd century, ripped from a statue and flung down a well, toppled like the monuments to Nicolae Ceausescu, Enver Hoxha or Saddam Hussein.

Dottoressa Braidotti arrived in a red waterproof, umbrella dripping, and took me straight to the display of amber on the second floor. Filling several cabinets, it was the most impressive collection of ancient worked amber I had seen, although she told me it was just a selection of the many hundred such items in the museum's storerooms. There were statuettes, ornamental boxes, beads, amulets, dice, reproductions in amber of animal bones thought to have magical properties, scarabs, squirrels, sleeping dogs, acorns, pomegranates, and three delicate amber leaves inscribed with a New Year greeting. Most were recovered from graves, though the exact provenance of all the items was not known; many were found in the 18th and 19th centuries when record-keeping was sketchy. They were mostly associated with female burials.

'Women loved amber because of its colour and perfume,' the dottoressa told me. In his *Interpretation of Dreams*, Artemidorus, writing in the 2nd century when many of these items were made, asserted that 'rings of amber, ivory, and such like, are good only for women.'

There were many such rings on display, some plain, others engraved with spiral grooves, and several with detailed figures carved on the bezels. A popular type featured a female head, possibly modelled on coin portraits of empresses, which may account for the fact that they were more convincing in profile than full-face. The hairstyles helped to date them. One, combed backwards and gathered in a bun at the nape of the neck, seemed to follow the Egyptian fashion brought to Rome by Cleopatra. Another appeared to be modelled on Livia, the wife of Augustus. Some copied the fashion of the imperial women of the Flavian era, with a high crown of curls around the forehead, while others sported the elaborate hairstyle, piled on top of the head with the support of a metal circlet, seen on coins of Hadrian's wife Sabina. The latest hairstyles were the corn-rows favoured by the women of the Severan dynasty of the early 3rd century, when the industry appears to have come to an end.

Other rings were ornamented with sculptures of Venus and Cupid, or animal figures such as the tiny Maltese dogs that Roman women loved. 'Little Ladies dogs,' wrote Artemidorus, 'signifie delight and pastime.' Amber rings made in Aquileia were exported all over the empire: I had seen them in Sopron and Ptuj, and one, bearing the head of Minerva, was found as far afield as Carlisle. Their thickness, their fragility, and the fact that few showed any sign of wear, suggested that they were made to adorn the dead as a propitiatory offering to the gods.

There were also numerous 'bastoncelli', spindles of the type I had seen in Ptuj and Ljubljana. Dr Braidotti suggested that, like the rings, they were probably votive items that symbolised femininity. This was plausible. A spindle depends on gravity to twist the wool, so most spindle whorls intended for actual use were made of lead or stone; amber is too light for this to work. The same was true of the model oil lamps; amber is inflammable, so they could never have been used except to light the dead on their journey to the underworld.

Elena Braidotti confirmed what Cristiano Tiussi had told me, that no amber working quarter had yet been identified. 'We don't know where the town's glass workshops were either.' There was, however, a magnificent array of Roman glassware – dishes, bottles and scent phials – in delicate blues, greens and orange, some with swirling patterns in white: miraculous, fragile survivors rendered iridescent by long burial. All were excavated, and many actually made, in Aquileia. Most everyday items were mould-blown, allowing their patterns to be replicated many times, and some manufacturers signed their moulds. Among them was Sentia Secunda, who worked around the end of the 1st century AD, and was one of only two women glassmakers we know of from the ancient world. Many glassmakers were Jewish; St Jerome, who lived in Aquileia at the end of the 4th century, complained in his treatise *Romano Occupato* that glassmaking was one of the trades 'by which the Semites had captured the Roman world'. After Attila sacked the city, the glassworkers fled to the Venetian lagoon, where they still practise their craft on Murano.

A magnificent display of jewellery – fibulae in silver and gilt bronze, cameos, intaglio signets in carnelian and other semi-precious stones – testified to the wealth of the city, and the standard of living enjoyed by its better-off inhabitants. The existence of a body of skilled intaglio carvers in Aquileia may have encouraged Diocletian to locate a mint here; the engraving of coin dies, which must also be done in mirror-image, is a closely related craft. A superb numismatic display explained the denominations and development of the Roman coinage from the Republican era to the fall of the Western Empire, before focusing on the mint of Aquileia. Its signature, AQ, can be seen on the reverse of the coins struck here, often followed by the letters P, S or the Greek Γ to indicate which of the mint's three *officinae* (workshops) was responsible. As with most Roman mints, the coins it produced circulated mostly in the surrounding provinces, but some found their way as far afield as Britain and North Africa.

The mint ceased production during the catastrophic reign of Honorius (395–423), but re-opened briefly in 425 in curious circumstances. The usurper Ioannes, having been captured at Ravenna, was executed at Aquileia after being paraded through the city on an ass. Galla Placidia, regent for her infant son Valentinian III and effective ruler of the Western Empire, took up residence in the city, and ordered coins to be struck in her name and his. The daughter of Theodosius and half-sister of Arcadius and Honorius, Placidia was clearly gifted with more intelligence, courage and statecraft than her hapless brothers put together. Taken hostage by Alaric when he sacked Rome in 410, she married his successor Ataulf to cement a peace treaty between the Romans and the Goths. When Ataulf died the following year, she returned to Rome and was persuaded by Honorius to marry his *magister militum* Constantius. In 421, Constantius was appointed co-emperor by the childless Honorius, only to die shortly afterwards. Placidia was now empress and mother to the heir to the throne.

I made my way through a covered arcade that surrounded the dripping gardens, lined with yet more statuary, column capitals and gravestones, including those of legionaries who died in their twenties and thirties, and some mosaics from the baths, including a fine portrait of an athlete. It was the amber that stayed in my mind, however. The frolicking nymphs, cupids, dryads, fauns and satyrs evoked a world in which every spring and grove was alive with mischievous pagan demigods; a world that was soon to come to an end. The Greek historian Plutarch, attempting to explain the silence of oracles in his day, told of a sailor who, passing the island of Paxi, heard a mysterious voice that ordered him, on reaching land, to proclaim: 'The great god Pan is dead.'

CHAPTER 15

WATERLOGGED

The headlights of the Trieste–Venice train appeared through the rain and mist, and a couple of minutes later it was carrying me through the waterlogged fields of Friuli. A few seats away, a bearded young man was studiously annotating a copy of Charles Jencks's *Storia del post-modernismo: Cinque decenni di ironico, iconico e critico in architettura*. Across the aisle, a man in a sharp black suit and a week's grey-flecked stubble scanned a folder. At Portogruaro, a group of students got on. Two girls sat absorbed in their mobile phones. The more demure-looking was dutifully calling her mother. Her friend appeared more street-wise: whippet thin, clad in bomber jacket and jeans, she had the androgynous features of a youth in a painting by Caravaggio. Racked by a cough, she gave off a strong smell of tobacco. The unlikely pair got off at S. Donà di Piave with several of their classmates.

The train pulled in to Quarto d'Altino, a small town of red-pantiled houses. During the dry summer of 2007, crop marks in the surrounding fields revealed the ground plan of the Roman city of Altinum, whose inhabitants took refuge in the islands of the lagoon after the place was sacked by Attila. The railway skirted the shore, through a landscape criss-crossed by drainage canals. A white egret stalked the puddled clay of a construction site. After stopping at Mestre for 15 minutes, we continued past smokestacks and dockyard cranes, and out along the long, low bridge that ran just a few feet above the lagoon. The 222 arches were built by Venice's Austrian rulers between 1842 and 1846. Ruskin saw it being constructed while working on *The Stones of Venice*. Characteristically, he loathed it, feeling that it made Venice resemble 'the suburbs of an English manufacturing town'.

Between flat, shrub-covered islands, boats edged their way along channels marked by the wooden tripods known as *bricoles*. A cormorant flapped low over the water. In the distance, the domes and campaniles of the city rose from the lagoon. As the island drew near, the brakes were applied and the train squealed into Santa Lucia station. I had not been in Venice for years, and was disappointed to find the grand Art Deco concourse now cluttered with the retail outlets that disfigure stations everywhere. Whatever the purpose of our journey, our first duty as citizens is to consume. On the station steps, patient African men were selling beautiful fabrics. I walked over to the vaporetto station, bought a ticket for the Rialto, and squeezed on to the river bus between Belgians and Koreans wheeling suitcases the size of refrigerators.

From the Rialto, I cut through narrow lanes and across a bridge over the Rio de la Fava into the *sestiere* of Castello. Immediately the streets were quieter, almost empty. The hotel was tucked away in an alley behind the church of Santa Maria della Consolazione. The surly middle-aged receptionist demanded payment in advance. When I saw the room, I understood why: many guests would have walked out on the spot. Distemper flaked from the walls, the wood-effect Formica bedhead was furrowed with post-coital cigarette burns, and the window gave on to a malodorous alleyway strewn with litter and lined with rat-bait boxes. At €100 a night, it lacked even the excuse of being cheap.

Yet despite the hotel's shortcomings, the location was good: midway between the Rialto and the Piazza San Marco, but in a quiet pocket bypassed by the crowds. The shops catered for everyday needs: a greengrocer, an ironmonger's, a Co-op and an electrical store. The voices on the street were Italian. Just a hundred yards away on the Sottoportego Perini, the stores sold designer goods and the accents were American and German.

It is hard to walk purposefully in Venice. The city's topography defeats it: the canals, the dead ends, the alleys too narrow to pass a person carrying an umbrella. I made my way slowly south to San Marco through a fine drizzle. As I approached the square, the atmosphere became more brashly touristic. Yet despite the crowds, despite the many millions of times it has been photographed, 'the finest drawing room in Europe', as Napoleon called it, still had the power to awe: the barbaric glitter of St Mark's, the four gilt horses looted from Constantinople during the Fourth Crusade, the cool Moorish rhythms of the Doges' Palace, and the towering campanile – a fake, of course, since the original telescoped in on itself in a cloud of brick dust in 1902.

Venice is said to have been founded by citizens of Aquileia and Altinum fleeing the invading Huns and Lombards. The story was propagated by the Venetian chronicler Giovanni Diacono in the 11th century, and subsequent histories elevated it to the status of a founding myth, conferring on the mercantile republic the authority of ancient Rome. Like many such narratives, it is only partially accurate. The archaeological evidence shows that the islands of the lagoon were inhabited centuries before the invasions of the 5th century, prompted by the silting up of the ports on the mainland. What remains true, though, is that Venice took over the role of Aquileia as a point of contact between Northern Europe and the Mediterranean. With the revival of trade after the Migration Era, Venice became the southern terminus of the Amber Route, and the point where it met the Silk Road from China.

In Dorsoduro, across the water from the Doges' Palace,

shimmered the white dome of the Salute. The original monastery was given to the Teutonic Knights as a reward for their help in the War of St Sabas against Genoa in 1256. After the loss of Acre in 1291, the Knights transferred their headquarters to Dorsoduro, where it remained until 1309. When the Order's lands were transformed into a Lutheran duchy in 1525, the complex was returned to the patriarchate of Venice; the great Baroque church that now occupies the site dates from the 17th century. The Knights' base in the city facilitated the transport of amber from their Baltic domains, and the merchants of Venice then exported it throughout the Mediterranean, to North Africa and Asia Minor. By the 16th century, Venetian luthiers were using amber in a varnish for musical instruments. A manuscript (now in the British Library) by Theodore de Mayerne, a Swiss doctor working at the Stuart court in England, records that:

> Gentileschi, excellent Florentine painter, adds on his palette a single drop of amber varnish coming from Venice, with which they varnish lutes, chiefly to the flesh areas, and this is to spread the white and soften it easily, and to make it dry sooner. By this means, he works when he wishes, without waiting for the colours to dry entirely. The varnish, although red, does not spoil the white.

De Mayerne mentions that his informant received the recipe, which involved dissolving the amber in walnut oil, directly from Orazio Gentileschi's daughter and fellow painter Artemisia.

After an uncomfortable night on a knackered mattress at The Dump, I set off for the Archaeological Museum in the Palazzo Correr on St Mark's Square. As I approached, the streets became increasingly waterlogged. At a pavement café, I phoned to book alternative accommodation. While I drank my double espresso, the water rose visibly. The staff busied themselves fitting a metal baffle across the bottom of the doorway. Throngs of tourists shuffled back up the street to escape the malodorous tide, only to find themselves trapped in a cul-de-sac. An air of quiet panic spread through the crowd, while the Venetians remained phlegmatic, smoking in groups of two or three as the water gurgled at their doorsteps.

Eventually, I made my zig-zag way to the museum. By then, St Mark's Square was under three feet of water. Following the raised pathways under the arcades, I ascended the monumental staircase of the Palazzo Correr. The grand enfilade was created for Napoleon after his conquest of the city, and dominated by larger-than-life white marble busts of the emperor and his second wife, Marie-Louise of Austria. The suite of rooms that followed documented the history and social life of the republic that Napoleon snuffed out. Portraits of doges, senators and other civic dignitaries looked down from the walls in their archaic finery. Models of galleys, paintings of naval battles, globes, an armillary sphere, solar horologues and other nauticalia bore witness to the city's maritime history. A *Wunderkammer* was stuffed with gold and silver reliquaries, cameos and other gems, while a long sequence of Venetian coins – including enormous gold 12 zecchini pieces – expired with the Republic at the end of the 18th century.

One of the most impressive exhibits was Jacopo de Barbari's stunning panorama of Venice. Printed on six sheets of paper, the thing was huge – 1.3 by almost 3 metres – and the detail of the buildings, many still recognisable, astonishing. Laid out on a table beneath it were the woodblocks from which it was printed. Engraved in 1500, it was the first such aerial view of a city, and inspired many others, including Braun and Hogenberg's famous series. Created centuries before any human being could have seen the city from this viewpoint, it was an astounding achievement, requiring both a powerful imagination and a sophisticated understanding of the laws of perspective.

The archaeological section conveyed little about the ancient history of the Veneto, but a great deal about the way the city's rulers appropriated the mantle of ancient Rome. The exhibits, assembled from all over Italy, included marble busts of Pompey, Octavian, Tiberius, Vespasian, Trajan, Hadrian, Lucius Verus, and a young Caracalla. Two coin hoards gave evidence of the Roman presence on the Venetian mainland, while a long series of Byzantine coins emphasised Venice's trading links with the Eastern Empire.

I approached Venice with some trepidation. The city had inspired so much fine writing, from Henry James to Jan Morris – and a mass of regurgitated cliches. While I had no expectation of approaching the former, I had no desire to add to the latter. Reading the dog-eared copy of Joseph Brodsky's *Watermark* I had bought in St Petersburg at the start of my journey (the price sticker, 491 rubles, was still on the back cover), I noticed how the Russian poet elegantly sidestepped the dilemma by concentrating on his memories and personal experiences. There were no set-piece descriptions; like St Petersburg, his Venice was all artifice, glimpsed fleetingly, by night ... At the end of my journey, I had come full circle to a phantasmal city of canals, mists and mirrors.

Though just around the corner from The Dump, my new lodgings could not have provided a greater contrast: a comfortable two-room apartment on the second floor of a converted palazzo, with antique furniture and 18th-century prints on the walls. They even provided Wellington boots for guests in the event of an *acqua alta*, and a tide table to evaluate the risk. It was becoming easier to move about; as the tide receded, streets that had been impassable opened up, and I gained a clearer view of my surroundings.

One route I found myself taking repeatedly led through the Campo San Bartolomeo, with its statue of the playwright

Goldoni, and into the *sestiere* of Cannaregio. Here, the Calle Dolfin took a dogleg through an arcade and over the bridge into the Campo Apostolico, with its balconied houses and German Lutheran church. From the Strada Nova – a street so broad and straight that it seemed less Venetian and more like any other Italian city – I continued through Santa Fosca to the Fondamente del Ormesini, and crossed the iron bridge into the Campo di Ghetto Nuovo. The broad square enclosed a few trees, an ancient stone wellhead and a fountain, and was ringed by tall houses, some seven storeys high, a sign of how overcrowded the Ghetto had once been. On some of the doorposts, I could make out the diagonal notch that held the mezuzah. Around the quiet square stood the Jewish Museum, a handful of pavement cafés and a kosher restaurant.

The Venice Ghetto is the oldest in the world, and the origin of a word that has become a synonym for segregation and prejudice. In 1516 the Council of Ten ordered all the Jews of Venice to live together on this island. The name is said to derive from the *getto*, or cannon foundry, that formerly stood here; the soft Italian g became a hard *gh* in the mouths of Ashkenazi Jews. The area was enclosed by two gates that were opened in the morning on the striking of Marangona, the great bell of San Marco, and closed at midnight. Two boats of the Council of Ten would patrol the canals around the island 'to ensure security'. The inhabitants could not own property, enter politics, the professions, schools or universities, while providing the trading relations and financial services that the mercantile city needed.

A narrow bridge took me across the Rio di Ghetto Nuovo into the Ghetto Vecchio. Paradoxically, this 'old ghetto', which extended southwards to the Cannaregio Canal, was the newer of the two, incorporated in 1541 to accommodate arrivals from Romania and the Levant. In its main square, the Campiello delle

Scuole, stood Venice's two functioning synagogues. The two-storey yellow stone Levantine Synagogue, which served Jews of Middle Eastern descent, was a relatively modest 16th-century building, though in the half-light within, I could glimpse rich wooden panelling, twisted columns, sparkling chandeliers and plush red hangings.

Far more imposing was the Spanish Synagogue *(Scola Spagnola)* opposite, a four-storey stone edifice built in 1550 and remodelled a century later in the Baroque style. Its congregation were Marranos, Sephardic Jews forced to convert to Catholicism in Spain, who were able to return to their original faith in Venice. The wealthiest community in the ghetto, they were said to retain the haughtiness of Spanish hidalgos towards its other inhabitants. In the ornate interior, three large chandeliers and a dozen smaller ones hung from an ornately carved wooden ceiling.

Visiting the Ghetto in 1608, the English traveller Thomas Coryat commented on the variety of clothing worn by the Jews here:

> Some of them doe weare hats and those redde, onely those Jewes that are borne in the Westerne parts of the world, as in Italy, &c. but the easterne Jewes being otherwise called the Levantine Jewes, which are borne in Hierusalem, Alexandria, Constantinople, &c. weare Turbents upon their heads as the Turkes do: but the difference is this: the Turkes weare white, the Jewes yellow.

When he met a 'learned Jewish Rabbin that spake good Latin', Coryat thought it appropriate to ask him why he did not recognise Christ as the Messiah. The rabbi courteously replied that he acknowledged Jesus as a great prophet, but not as the Son of God. After they had exchanged 'many vehement speeches', Coryat reported,

> some forty or fifty Jewes flocked about me, and some of
> them beganne very insolently to swagger with me, because
> I durst reprehend their religion: Whereupon fearing least
> they would have offered me some violence, I withdrew my
> selfe by little and little towards the bridge at the entrance
> into the Ghetto, with an intent to flie from them . . .

Fortunately for Coryat, Sir Henry Wotton, the English ambassador in Venice, happened to be passing under the bridge in his gondola, and sent one of his men to rescue him.

For some of the Ghetto's Jews, however, the Messiah was closer at hand. In this maze of *sottoportegi*, secret passages, sagging roofs, crooked floors and dusty attics, religious disputation was rife and strange ideas took hold. In 1648, a twenty-two-year-old Jew from Smyrna, Sabbatai Zevi, declared himself to be the Messiah who would lead the Ten Lost Tribes back to the Holy Land. He sent his disciple Nathan of Gaza to Venice, where he spread the word. The Ashkenazi communities of Central Europe, reeling from the pogroms instigated by the Ukrainian Cossack Bohdan Khmelnytsky, were also receptive to Zevi's message. Among them was my ancestor Josef Goldschmidt. His daughter-in-law Glückel records that left his home in Hameln for Hildesheim to await the coming of the Messiah.

> He sent on to us in Hameln two enormous casks packed
> with linen and with peas, beans, dried meats, shredded
> prunes and the like stuff, every manner of food that would
> keep. For the old man expected to sail at any moment to
> the Holy Land.

The casks stood in Glückel's house for three years while Josef waited for the sign to depart. In 1666, however, Zevi was imprisoned by the Ottomans and converted to Islam, after which most of his followers became disillusioned and fell away.

Standing in these silent streets, it was hard to imagine the alleyways packed with traders, the yeshivas resounding with passionate theological debate, the women's galleries of the synagogues peopled by ladies 'so gorgeous in their apparel', Coryat reported, 'that some of our English Countesses do scarce exceede them'. The Ghetto was now largely empty except for a few Americans, some wearing yarmulkes, visiting the museum and synagogues. When Napoleon took Venice in 1797, he burned down the gates and declared the emancipation of the Jews. The inhabitants moved to other neighbourhoods, and many assimilated. Some 1,200 were living in the city when the Nazis invaded in September 1943. On the 16th of that month, the President of the Jewish Community, Professor Giuseppe Jona, committed suicide rather than hand the Nazis a list of its members. A memorial on the Campo Ghetto Nuovo recorded the names of the 246 Venetian Jews deported to extermination camps over the following year, including the Chief Rabbi, Adolfo Ottolenghi. Today Venice has a Jewish population of about 500, only thirty of whom live in the former Ghetto.

Beyond the Ghetto, on the Campo San Geremia, I found a jeweller's shop with an impressive display of Baltic amber, including necklaces of big, chunky beads. It was the first amber I'd seen in the city. Since 2007, the European Commission had designated the Amber Route from St Petersburg to Venice as a 'touristic corridor', subsidising the creation of cycle routes and awarding grants to museums from Kaliningrad to Ljubljana. I saw no evidence of this project in Venice, but then the city had no need to promote tourism; it had been utterly dependent on it for two hundred years, with industry located on the mainland at Mestre and Marghera. Since the 1980s, the island's permanent population had fallen from 120,000 to 55,000, and young people could no longer afford to live there. Such dependency can curdle into resentment, and while many Venetians are gracious hosts, it goes some way to explaining the behaviour of the staff at The Dump.

The situation had been aggravated in recent years by the docking of grotesquely large cruise ships, floating skyscrapers that dwarfed the city and whose displacement aggravated the *aqua alta*. Their passengers, who eat and sleep on board, troop through the city taking photographs, leaving a mountain of litter and contributing little to the local economy. The situation had led to calls to regulate tourism, diversify the economy, and introduce a rent cap, and a pressure group called No Big Ships was active.

To find some amber, I had to catch a train to Bassano del Grappa on the mainland, where a Lithuanian woman had established a shop called La Via dell'Ambra – the Amber Way – selling the products of her homeland. The town was famed for the spirit grappa, distilled from the residues left after grapes are pressed to make wine, a process supposedly invented here by a Roman soldier in the 1st century AD. I walked through the Piazza della Liberta, past the 15th-century Palazzo del Comune with its frescoed façade and astronomical clock, and down through the arcaded streets towards the river. The wide expanse of the Brenta was spanned by a covered wooden bridge, the Ponte degli Alpini, designed by Palladio in 1569; from the middle, I had a spectacular view of the river and the snow-capped Dolomites that ringed the town.

I found the shop nearby, on Via Ferracina. As I entered, there was my journey painted on the wall: a map of the Amber Route from Lithuania to northern Italy. A tall, handsome young woman with clean-cut, Baltic good looks, wearing jeans and a brightly coloured Lithuanian smock, rose to greet me. Ramunė Kupšytė had lived in Italy for eight years after marrying an Italian. 'I made the Amber Road myself,' she told me. 'My father comes from a small town by the sea.'

She had opened the shop two years previously after being made redundant. 'I was travelling to the Far East selling paper and plastic for recycling. The company folded with 30 days' notice. Then' – she clicked her fingers – 'I decided to open an amber shop. I always loved amber and wanted to deal with something beautiful after the scrap.'

Ramunė's interest in amber went back to her Lithuanian childhood. 'In the USSR everybody had amber – a necklace. It was associated with something old and unfashionable. In the 1950s people burnt it for fuel. Now natural things are becoming fashionable again. I opened the shop here where the amber was worked, between Aquileia and Rovigo.

'Coming from Lithuania, you think everybody knows about amber. Here it's not so easy to find. Italians have the idea that amber costs a lot, like diamonds – they cannot imagine the raw amber. Amber has only become popular here in the past 20 years, since the borders were opened. The Chinese are now buying up to 90 per cent of the world's amber; it has increased five times in value in the past three years.'

Ramunė was the first person involved in the trade to admit what I had long suspected – 'All the amber actually comes from Kaliningrad now' – and the trade embargo on Russia had created problem with sourcing. 'People are collecting amber from the coast in Lithuania, but it is artisanal – you don't know how much you will find. But all the jewellery here is made in Lithuania by Lithuanian craftspeople.

'I work with about ten jewellery makers, but I am very strict – I don't want intermediaries, I want to see how they're working it. A lot of suppliers also make pressed amber, and if it's done well, you can't tell. So, if I see pressing machines, I don't buy.

'I'm not a specialist in working silver or gold,' she explained. 'I don't want to seem too much like a jewellery shop, so we only use small, necessary fastenings for earrings and other things.'

I looked at the items displayed around the shop. Most were

necklaces or pendants, the individual pieces of amber left in their original shape and polished to a soft finish rather than the high gloss of more industrial products. A few had plant or animal inclusions. One of her suppliers used pieces of leather to support the amber in a manner that reminded me of the pieces crafted by the women in Kaliningrad.

'I am the only shop that specialises in amber,' Ramunė said. 'Not just jewellery but also beauty and therapy products.' Around the shop were a range of amber-based cosmetics, soaps and creams. Succinic acid, she told me, purifies and regenerates the skin. Pointing to a bowl filled with small chips of amber, she told me to take a handful. 'Rub your hands,' she said. 'Don't worry about dropping any – there are little bits of amber all over this shop. Now smell.' I inhaled the rich, resiny scent. 'That's the smell of pine trees from 40 million years ago.'

The next morning, I parcelled up the many books and pamphlets I'd collected on my travels, took them to the post office and mailed them to myself in London, reducing the weight of my backpack by several pounds. I cut through the little squares and alleys of Cannaregio, and there, suddenly, was open water, the sound of gulls and the view across to the cemetery island of San Michele. At the Fondamente Nuove I boarded a vaporetto and was soon out on the lagoon. With its tall, dark cypresses, the Cimiterio recalled Böcklin's painting *The Isle of the Dead*. Brodsky was buried here, as were Ezra Pound, Stravinsky and Diaghilev. As the city's dead now outnumbered the living, they were extending the island on the side facing away from the city, where a crane was at work on a new red wall that formed a brash contrast to the mellow brick of the old.

As I looked back towards Venice, the glinting reflections off the water created a subtle play of light and shadow on the stone façades and terracotta roofs. My wife and I had recently visited Lamb House in Rye, Henry James's home in his later years, and

I thought of him hiring a gondola and being rowed out to the deepest part of the lagoon, where he attempted to submerge the dresses of his friend Constance Fenimore Woolson, who had thrown herself from the balcony of her Venetian house.

The vaporetto made for Murano and its white stone lighthouse, where the boat docked. The glassblowers of Venice were relocated here in 1291 because of the danger of fire, and still constituted the island's main industry. Although their products included high quality, artistic vessels, the island is perhaps best known for the twirly glass figurines of harlequins and little dogs that gather dust on mantelpieces from Manchester to Milwaukee.

Beyond Murano, the boat moved out into the wider expanse of the lagoon. To the right lay the wooded shores of Sant'Erasmo, a long, narrow island separating the lagoon from the Adriatic. As we neared the more northerly archipelago, the red-tiled roofs and leaning campanile of Burano came into view. We entered the canal that divided the long, green island of Mazzorbo, before docking at its boat-lined quay. Red, blue and ochre houses lined the wharf, one with ogive windows straight out of Ruskin; behind them rose the island church's short, stocky campanile. Emerging on the northern side of the island, the boat turned to starboard and made for the densely built-up harbour of Burano, where most of the passengers disembarked.

There were perhaps half a dozen of us left as the boat made the short final stretch to Torcello. After we had docked at the tiny ferry port, I walked up the redbrick canal path through fields and gardens. A handful of red-painted houses appeared, and the tall campanile of the cathedral came into view. Groups of daytrippers trooped up and down the towpath; there can't have been more than a few score of them, but the track was narrow enough for them to form a throng. I continued across the Santa Maria bridge, an ancient, miniature version of the bridges that arch every canal in Venice, to the main square, if this village green could be so described. On one side stood the huge, austere cathedral of Santa Maria Assunta, and the smaller octagonal basilica of Santa Fosca. On the crumbling brick wall that closed the far end of the square, several ancient relief sculptures had been fixed; between them, lizards darted in and out of the cracks. Beyond the cathedral were fields and vineyards bordered by canals lined with willows and reedbeds. Few visitors ventured this far, and the silence was profound. I sat on a bank watching the sky and the water, the wading birds and the butterflies.

This sleepy island, its cathedral beached like a great ship on the mudflats, was all that remained of what was once a vital trading hub between east and west, its docks bristling with masts, its canals lined with warehouses, workshops, taverns and brothels, its skies pierced by the towers of seven churches. Tradition has it that Torcello was founded by refugees from Altinum fleeing the Huns. 'After the manner of water-fowl have you fixed your home,' Cassiodorus wrote to the islanders in 537. By the 8th century, some 3,000 people lived on Torcello; Paris and London were then no larger. In his *De Administrando Imperio*, written circa 850, the Byzantine emperor Constantine VII Porphyrogenitus referred to Torcello as an *emporion mega* – a great port. Around AD 1000, however, the channels around the island silted up, and the inhabitants moved to Rivoalto – the Rialto – which became Venice. Malaria set in, and by the end of the Middle Ages Torcello was a backwater occupied only by monasteries and convents, vineyards and fish farms.

The apartment I had booked was located in a tall red house beside the Ponte del Diavolo, above a charming little shop selling Burano lace. Next door was an open-air bar and grill serving seafood. By five the church and museum had shut, and the four restaurants had closed their doors. Only the grill was still serving food, and it too appeared to be getting ready to shut, so I grabbed a quick supper of rubbery *fritto misto di mare* and washed it down with a beer. By 6.30pm the last daytrippers had left. The island fell silent, and a crescent moon rose above the canal.

At about 8.30 I ventured out for a nocturnal walk. The only lights were the old-fashioned lanterns that lined the canal path and the odd glimmer from a farmhouse across the fields. The sole sign of life came from the Locanda Cipriani, a low yellow house with a long verandah and its own private mooring. Having concealed itself from the day-trippers all afternoon, it had now, after everywhere else had closed, discreetly opened its doors to those staying on the island or possessed of a boat. I entered a large room furnished with square tables. The heavy ceiling beams hung with ship's lanterns, the inglenook, and the dark oak dresser stacked with floral plates gave it the appearance of an old-fashioned inn in an English fishing village. Three middle-aged Australians were talking quietly at the middle table. Three of the four corner tables were occupied: one by me, the one diagonally opposite by another solitary man, and the third by a French woman writing intently in a notebook. From the adjoining dining room came the gentle murmur of conversation and the clatter of cutlery. Old photos adorned the walls, including several of Ernest Hemingway, who wrote part of *Across the River and into the Trees* while staying at the locanda and shooting duck in the marshes.

The following morning, I set off early on the short walk to the centre before the daytrippers arrived. The museum occupied two ancient buildings, set at right angles, that once housed the civic authorities of Torcello. The larger of the two, the Palazzo del Consiglio, was purchased in 1870 by Luigi Torelli, prefect of Venice, to display archaeological finds from the island and the nearby mainland. The smaller, with its elegant ground-floor arcade and triple lancet window, was the Palazzo dell'Archivo, bought in 1887 by the museum's director, Cesare

Augusto Levi, to house its expanding collection. Many of the ancient Egyptian, Greek and Roman artefacts were not local finds, but had been bought and donated by Levi, although a fine collection of Bronze- and Iron-Age fibulae, torcs and necklaces, including a string of ten chunky amber beads, came from Altinum, as did a series of tiny, beautiful bronze animal figurines: birds, a mouse, a bear and a goat. A fine Roman marble portrait bust was found on Torcello itself.

The collection continued chronologically in the Palazzo del Consiglio. Marble capitals, plinths and friezes carved in the Byzantine style, along with Byzantine coins and ceramics from the 7th to the 11th centuries, made clear the greater proximity – geographically, culturally and politically – of Torcello to the Eastern Empire than to the Italian mainland, occupied successively by Goths and Lombards. A 7th-century bracelet of large beads of silvered bronze, onyx, adamant and amber was found on Torcello; the amber may have been recycled from older artefacts, but its presence testified to the continued demand for the material in the region after the fall of the Western Empire.

The highlights were some fragments of Byzantine mosaic removed from the basilica during a 19th-century restoration, including a fine head of John the Baptist, and a sequence of 15th-century silver-gilt plaques depicting the Virgin Mary flanked by archangels, prophets and saints. There were originally 41 of them hanging above the high altar in the cathedral; after 29 were stolen in 1806, the rest were moved to a storeroom before being rediscovered and put on display in the museum.

The upper floor was devoted to Renaissance paintings salvaged from the island's disbanded monasteries, including a late 16th-century canvas by one of the less gifted followers of Veronese depicting the Flagellation of St Christina. Whatever prelate commissioned this scene of a naked young woman tied to a pillar and flogged by a couple of heavies, I suspected his interest was not entirely devotional.

The two palazzi that housed the museum were dwarfed by the western façade of the cathedral, a sheer brick cliff relieved only by blind arcading. The massive stone shutters on the aisle windows gave the impression of a place of refuge rather than of worship or civic pride. It was as if one of the great churches of Venice had been arrested at an early stage of its development, before the city's swelling coffers smothered it in Gothic and Renaissance embellishments. First built in the 7th century, the church was enlarged in the 11th, but the interior still preserved the appearance of an early Christian basilica, its robust columns capped with acanthus-leaf capitals. Its austere dignity won high praise from Ruskin, who remarked that 'the actual condition of the exiles who built the cathedral of Torcello is exactly typical of the spiritual condition which every Christian ought to recognize in himself, a state of home-lessness on earth.'

The most astounding feature of the interior, however, was its mosaics. Rising tall and slender into the semidome of the apse stood a blue-clad Madonna, serene against a gold backdrop, impassive but for a single tear falling down her cheek as she contemplated the terrifying Last Judgement on the west wall.

Adjoining the basilica was the smaller, octagonal church of Santa Fosca. Built in the 11th and 12th centuries on a Greek cross plan, with an elegant colonnaded narthex and central dome, it was typical of Byzantine churches of the period, and would not have looked out of place in Thessaloniki or Istanbul. More used for religious services than the cathedral, it was a popular wedding venue; Santa Fosca, to whom it was dedicated, was a local patron saint of newlyweds. I was mildly alarmed to find her cadaver in a glass coffin beneath the altar, mercifully shrouded in drapery.

Then I climbed the 11th-century campanile. Brick ramps,

rather than the more usual stairs, took the visitor up to the 50-metre high belfry. I could see the steel braces inserted during a recent restoration; I was fortunate that the external scaffolding had been taken down not long before I visited. On one side, the brickwork was a slightly different colour, the result of earlier repairs undertaken in the 17th century after the tower was hit by lightning. From the top, the climb was rewarded by astonishing views across the lagoon – a maze of channels, islets and mudflats – to Burano, Mazzorbo and, in the distance, Venice itself.

Returning to the grill by the apartment, I asked Anna, the barmaid, how many people actually lived on the island. She told me there were just six; she herself travelled in from Mestre, a two-hour journey, every day. As it was getting towards evening, I checked the map to see if there were any footpaths I had not yet explored. Not far from where I was sitting, I saw that a track ran towards the Casa Museo Andrich, so I decided to investigate. A sign announced that the house was dedicated to the Venetian artist Lucio Andrich, and was open to visitors every hour from 10.30am–5.30pm. I was just in time for the last visit of the day. I walked up the long track between market gardens and untended plots choked with brambles to an iron gate where a sign read *'Suonare il campanello'*. There was indeed a brass bell hung in a metal cage above the gate. I tugged the cord, and a wiry middle-aged man with a neatly trimmed, greying beard crossed the lawn and let me in.

'My last guests have not quite finished,' he said. 'Do you mind waiting for five minutes?' He was accompanied by a large, friendly mastiff, who bounded across the lawn with us. The dog and I waited outside the house, a modern, one-storey affair of white concrete and glass, until the previous visitors, two women, departed, laughing happily.

My host introduced himself as Paolo Andrich, and informed me that he had inherited the house from his uncle, the artist and ceramicist Lucio Andrich, the last professor of mosaics at the University of Venice, who died in 2003. First, however, he led me through the garden, proudly showing me the small, spiny, bluiesh artichokes he grew on his land. He gestured across the maze of brackish water and low islands of purple vegetation known as the Rose Lagoon.

'On a clear day,' he said, pointing at the cloudy horizon, 'I can see the Dolomites, 140 kilometres away.' I recalled that Ruskin had seen their snow-capped peaks from the top of the campanile, but this day the weather was too overcast. Paolo described how the River Piave brought down silt from the mountains to form islands and sandbars in the lagoon. He pointed out the site of the Roman port of Altinum on the mainland, 'just where you see the white and red houses.'

The river-borne sediment created *velme*, tidal shallows that lay just above the water at low tide. When further sediment-ation raised the velme above the average sea level, they were colonised by salt-tolerant vegetation and turned into mudflats known as *barene*. Paolo bent down and picked up a sprig of the greenish-violet plant growing beneath our feet.

'*Salicornia veneta*,' he said. 'It's what gives the Rose Lagoon its name.' It was a kind of samphire, and he invited me to bite into a piece; it tasted of salt and iodine.

Paolo pointed to a white cottage some distance away across the saltmarsh. 'The clavecin player Egida Sartori lived there. She had no telephone, so when she wanted to invite my uncle to dinner, she would light a lantern in the courtyard.' Sartori died in 1999, and the house now stood empty, like many on the island.

Back at the house, some of Lucio Andrich's experiments with glass were set out on a table on the terrace: boldly coloured discs, cubes with gold pearls inside them, and white opalescent glass which, Paolo explained, was no longer made because of its high lead content. There were two beautiful, almost translucent boxes carved from horn. On the walls hung oils and aquarelles, and a tapestry entitled *Save the Lagoon*. The elder Andrich was also a book illustrator; his nephew handed me a beautifully bound edition of E. T. A. Hoffmann's *Princess Brambilla* he had illustrated. Ezra Pound had asked him to illustrate one of his books, but, as Paolo remarked tactfully, 'he was not well' and the project got no further than a couple of lithographs that hung on the wall.

In summer, Paolo told me, he could see flamingos from his window. We got to discussing the state of the island. He believed there were just nine permanent residents; the owner of the Cipriani didn't live there, though some of his staff stayed overnight. A few fishermen still worked Torcello's waters, but most lived on Burano. I had seen them in the morning, standing in the stern of their narrow wooden boats, one hand on the outboard motor, the other holding a cigarette, as they navigated the canal beneath my window, the deck splashed with silver shards of whitebait.

Paolo accompanied me to the gate, between the gnarled trunks of 150-year-old olive trees. On the way he asked if I would like to see the ruins of the monastery of San Giovanni. Bats flitted above the Devil's Bridge as we crossed it and continued along the path until we reached a gate in a high hedge. Beyond this point was private property, but Paolo knew the owners; they were away, he said, and wouldn't mind his showing me around. He pushed open the gate on to a neat lawn, at one end of which stood a large 16th-century villa with typical Venetian-Moorish windows. Beyond a yew hedge, we emerged on to another lawn flanked by funereal cypresses. Beside the incongruous blue of a swimming pool, the foundations of a church were visible in the dusk. I could make out the groundplan: the walls, the rows of column bases marking the nave, the semi-circle of the apse at the east end. An 18th-century print showed it as a typical Venetian church of the Renaissance with a porticoed façade, surrounded by outlying monastic buildings. Sometimes marked as San Zuane – Venetian dialect for Giovanni – on old maps, the monastery was demolished in 1810 on the orders of Napoleon. The remains were excavated in the 1960s and now stood as a kind of folly in the grounds of the villa.

I returned to the apartment for the last time. With its tongue-and-groove panelled walls and beamed roof, it felt like a cabin in the wilderness. I wondered how many other people would be spending the night on the island. Whose estimate, Anna's or Paolo's, was correct? Even allowing for guests at the Cipriani, there couldn't have been many more than twenty souls on Torcello at this hour of night. Biskupin, Carnuntum, Aquileia, Torcello . . . There is something sobering about these abandoned cities. They offer us a *Sinnbild der Vergänglichkeiten,* a symbol of transience, of the fragility of our way of life. 'Mother and daughter,' observed Ruskin, looking across at Venice from Torcello: 'Behold them both in their widowhood.'

The Amber Route stretched behind me, like a string of beads across the continent. Another traveller might have followed a different route or, while keeping to the same itinerary, spent longer in places where I had stopped just briefly, and sped through others where my interests prompted me to linger. But it was done. I had travelled through a gazetteer of countries that no longer existed: the Roman Empire, Imperial Russia, Austria-Hungary, Prussia, the Soviet Union, Czechoslovakia, Yugoslavia. I had visited places where my ancestors, just a few generations back, had lived and loved, struggled and prospered – and been forced to flee.

I am a refugee's son. Had Britain been a less welcoming place in 1939, I would not exist. I was glad to live in a world where a Spaniard can run an import business in Ljubljana, while his Slovenian wife practises law in Spain; where a Syrian doctor may save my life in a London hospital; where I can freely travel the length of Europe without hostile scrutiny. All that now seemed in peril. As I embarked on the Amber Route, the Eurozone crisis was already threatening the survival of the common currency that eased my passage from one country to the next. In the Baltic Republics and Poland, the growing friction between Russia and the EU over oil and gas was palpable. After I left the territory of the Federation, Russia invaded eastern Ukraine and annexed the Crimean peninsula, intensifying a growing mood of nationalism throughout the region, while nativist movements such as Viktor Orbán's Fidesz party in Hungary, Poland's Law and Justice party, and the Northern League here in the Veneto, were on the rise.

During the final stages of my journey, thousands of migrants, many of them refugees from the civil war in Syria, crossed the Aegean from Turkey to Greece, to make their way through the Balkans to Germany. Just weeks after I had passed in and out of Austria and Hungary with no more formality than on a winding road on the English-Welsh marches, razor-wire fences went up. As the Serbian Prime Minister, Aleksandar Vučić, remarked in September 2015 as my journey drew to a close, 'Instead of a Europe without borders, we have an Iron Curtain again.'

Earlier that evening, Paolo Andrich played me a video of his uncle's works installed around the island. The footage was accompanied by an overture by Baldassare Galuppi, a younger contemporary of Vivaldi who collaborated with Goldoni on a number of operas. The composer, Paolo told me, was born on the neighbouring island of Burano. Did this fisherman's son from the fringe of the archipelago view the follies of the Serenissima with an outsider's cynicism? Robert Browning thought so. His poem 'A Toccata of Galuppi's', written around the same time as Ruskin's *Stones of Venice*, sees in the Baroque virtuoso's 'cold music' an ironic commentary on the luxury and frivolity of the Venetian republic in its declining years:

> As for Venice and her people, merely born to
>   bloom and drop,
> Here on earth they bore their fruitage, mirth
>   and folly were the crop:
> What of soul was left, I wonder, when the kissing
>   had to stop?

I opened the shutters and looked out over the island. The only sounds were the call of a peewit, the croaking of frogs, and the buzz of an outboard motor as a water taxi nosed along the canal, taking the last diners home from the Cipriani. Egida Sartori recorded several of Galuppi's keyboard pieces; I thought of Browning's poem, and imagined her fingers moving across the keys of the harpsichord in her lonely house, 'those lesser thirds so plaintive' floating out across the lagoon.

ACKNOWLEDGEMENTS

This book has been years in the making, and the list of people to whom I owe thanks for help in its creation is correspondingly long. I have relied on many friends and colleagues for practical assistance, introductions and advice, even if I have not always heeded the latter, and though the opinions expressed in these pages may not necessarily concur with theirs.

First, thanks to my wife, Geraldine Beattie, for her literary insight and unstinting encouragement. I am indebted to my cousin Irene Newhouse, on whose researches into our family history significant parts of this book are based; to my agent, Tom Cull, for his energy, persistence and belief in the project; to Robert Davidson, my editor at Sandstone Press, and the whole Sandstone team; and to Helen Stirling, for the superb maps that grace its pages.

I would particularly like to thank the writers Sara Wheeler, Ian Thomson and Rachel Lichtenstein for taking the time and trouble to read earlier drafts of the manuscript and give me the benefit of their advice. The late Michael Jacobs – 'el vagabundo literario' – was also enormously generous with his support and encouragement.

Thanks are also due to Georgia de Chamberet, Mary Dejevsky, Mark Ellingham, Henrietta Foster, Katya Galitzine, Mary Novakovich, Deborah Orr, Christina Patterson, Simon Rigge, Nigel Rodgers, Miranda Seymour, Sunny Singh,

Professor Fritz Stern, Marcus Tanner, Boyd Tonkin, Melissa Ulfane, and Meike Ziervogel, all of whom provided help, advice or encouragement in one form or another. My thanks also go to all those along the Amber Route who shared their time, their knowledge and their experience with me, and who are named in these pages.

Finally, I wish to record my gratitude to the Society of Authors and the Royal Literary Fund for the generous grant of a John Heygate Award to assist in the completion of this book, and to the unfailingly helpful and erudite staff of the London Library, of the Bodleian and Sackler libraries in Oxford, and of the State Archives (Archiwum Panstwowe w Gdansku) in Gdańsk.

BIBLIOGRAPHY

The greatest part of a writer's time is spent in reading, in order to write: a man will turn over half a library to make one book.

Samuel Johnson

Allan, Charles, 'Amber Route'. In Northrup, Cynthia (ed.), *World Trade: A Historical Encyclopedia of Economics, Politics, Society and Culture*, Vol. 1. Armonk, NY: Sharpe Reference, 2005.

Ammianus Marcellinus, *The Later Roman Empire (A.D. 354–378)*, trans. Walter Hamilton. London: Penguin, 1986.

Andrée, Karl, *Bernstein und seine Bedeutung*. Königsberg: Gräfe und Unzer, 1937.

Barnavi, Eli, (ed.), *A Historical Atlas of the Jewish People*. London: Kuperard, 1994.

Bastéa, Eleni (ed.), *Memory and Architecture*. Albuquerque: University of New Mexico Press, 2004.

Beck, Curt W., Bouzek, Jan & Dreslerova, Dagmar, *Amber in Archaeology: Proceedings of the Second International Conference: Liblice 1990*. Prague: Institute of Archaeology, 1993.

Bliujien, Audron, *Northern Gold: Amber in Lithuania*. Leiden: Brill, 2011.

Borchers, Roland, *Berent: Ein Landkreis in Westpreußen*. Hude: Schadrau Verlag, [1998].

Calvi, Maria Carina, *Aquileia: Le Ambre Romane*. Aquileia: Associazione Nazionale per Aquileia, 2005.

Cassiodorus, Magnus Aurelius, *Letters*, trans. Thomas Hodgkin. London: Henry Frowde, 1886.

Čižmářová, Jana, 'Bernstein auf dem keltischen Oppidum Staré Hradisko in Mähren'. *Arheolški vestnik* 47, 1996.

Clark, Christopher M., *Iron Kingdom: The Rise and Downfall of Prussia, 1600–1945*. London: Allen Lane, 2006.

Clark, Neil, *Amber: Tears of the Gods*. Edinburgh: Dunedin Academic Press, 2010.

Clark, Peter B., *The Death of East Prussia: War and Revenge in Germany's Easternmost Province*. Chevy Chase, MD: Andover Press, 2013.

Cohn, Willy, *No Justice in Germany: The Breslau Diaries, 1933–1941*, ed. Norbert Conrads, trans. Kenneth Kronenberg. Redwood City, CA: Stanford University Press, 2012.

Conwentz, H. W., *Die Moorbrücken im Thal der Sorge auf der Grenze zwischen Westpreußen und Ostpreußen*. Danzig: T. Bertling, 1897.

Coryat, Thomas, *Coryat's Crudities: Hastily Gobled up in Five Moneths Travells*. Glasgow: James MacLehose & Sons, 1905.

Cosmas of Prague, *The Chronicle of the Czechs*, trans. Lucy Wolverton. Washington, DC: Catholic University of America Press, 2009.

Davies, Norman, *God's Playground: A History of Poland*. Oxford: Oxford University Press, 1981.

Davies, Norman & Moorhouse, Roger, *Microcosm: Portrait of a Central European City*. London: Jonathan Cape, 2002.

Diaz-Andreu, Margarita & Champion, Timothy (eds), *Nationalism and Archaeology in Europe*. London: UCL Press, 1996.

Długosz, Jan, *The Annals of Jan Długosz: A History of Eastern Europe from AD 965 to AD 1480*, trans. Maurice Michael. Chichester: IMP Publications, 1997.

Dönhoff, Marion, *Before the Storm: Memories of My Youth in Old Prussia*, trans. Jean Steinberg. New York: Knopf, 1990.

Freely, John, *Celestial Revolutionary: Copernicus, the Man and his Universe*. New York: I.B. Tauris, 2014.

Freeman, Lucy, *The Story of Anna O: The Woman Who Led Freud to Psychoanalysis*. Northvale, NJ: Jason Aronson, 1994.

Freud, Sigmund & Breuer, Joseph, *Studies in Hysteria*, trans. Rachel Bowlby. London: Penguin, 2004.

Glückel of Hameln, *The Memoirs of Glückel of Hameln*, trans. Marvin Lowenthal. New York: Schocken, 1977.

Grabowska, Janina, *Amber in Polish History*. Edinburgh: City of Edinburgh Museums, 1978.

Graetz, Heinrich, *Tagebuch und Briefe*, ed. Michael Reuven. Tübingen: Mohr, 1977.

Grempler, Wilhelm, *Der Fund von Sackrau*. Berlin: Lunitz Verlag, 1887.

Grunfeld, Frederic, *Prophets Without Honour: Freud, Kafka, Einstein, and Their World*. New York: Kodansha, 1996.

Guttman, Melinda Given, *The Enigma of Anna O: A Biography of Bertha Pappenheim*. Wickford, RI: Moyer Bell, 2001.

Haffner, Sebastian, *The Rise and Fall of Prussia,* trans. Ewald Osers. London: Weidenfeld & Nicolson, 1988.

Istenič, Janka, *Roman Stories from the Crossroads.* Ljubljana: Narodni muzej Slovenije, 2015.

Joenniemi, Pertti & Prawitz, Jan (eds.), *Kaliningrad: The European Amber Region.* Aldershot: Ashgate, 1998.

Kershaw, Ian, *To Hell and Back: Europe 1914–1949.* London: Allen Lane, 2015.

Kieser, Egbert, *Danziger Bucht 1945: Dokumentation einer Katastrophe.* Esslingen am Neckar: Bechtle, 1978.

King, Rachel, 'Whose Amber? Changing Notions of Amber's Geographical Origin'. in Haug, H., Bushart, M. & Lipińska, A. (eds.), Gemeine Artefakte. Zur gemeinschaftsbildenden Funktion von Kunstwerken in den vormodernen Kulturräumen Ostmitteleuropas. *Ostblick 2.* 2014

Kronberger, Michaela (ed.), *Vindobona; Roman Vienna.* Vienna: Wien Museum, 2009.

Laar, Mart, *War in the Woods: Estonia's Struggle for Survival, 1944–1956,* trans. Tina Ets. Washington, DC: Howells House, 1992.

Łagiewski, Maciej, *An Old Jewish Cemetery in Wrocław.* Wrocław: [nd].

Lehndorff, Hans von, *Ostpreußisches Tagebuch.* Munich: DTV, 1997.

Michaels, Anne, *Fugitive Pieces.* London: Bloomsbury, 1996.

Musil, Robert, *Young Törless,* trans. Eithne Wilkins & Ernst Kaiser. St Albans: Granada Publishing, 1979.

——*The Man Without Qualities,* trans. Eithne Wilkins & Ernst Kaiser. (3 vols). London: Pan Books, 1979.

Navarro, J. M. de, 'Prehistoric Routes between Northern Europe and Italy Defined by the Amber Trade.' *Geographical Journal* 66: 481–507. 1925.

Nick, Dagmar, *Jüdisches Wirken in Breslau.* Würzburg: W. G. Korn, 1998.

——*Eingefangene Schatten: Mein judisches Familienbuch.* Munich: C. H. Beck, 2015.

Nicolaus von Jeroschin, *The Chronicle of Prussia,* trans. Mary Fischer. Farnham: Ashgate, 2010.

Pescheck, Christian, *Die Frühwandalische Kultur in Mittelschlesien.* Leipzig: C. Kabitzsch, 1939.

Piotrowska, Danuta, 'Biskupin 1933–1996: Archaeology, Politics and Nationalism.' *Archaeologia Polona* 35–36, 1997/98, 255–285.

Ransome, Arthur, *Racundra's First Cruise.* London: Allen, 1923.

Rice, Patty C., *Amber: The Golden Gem of the Ages.* New York: Van Nostrand Reinhold, 1980.

Richmond, Theo, *Konin: A Quest.* London: Cape, 1995.

Rigby, Elizabeth, *Letters from the Shores of the Baltic.* London: John Murray, 1846.

Riley-Smith, Jonathan (ed.), *The Atlas of the Crusades.* London: Guild Publishing, 1990.

Roemer, Nils, *Jewish Scholarship and Culture in Nineteenth-Century Germany: Between History and Faith.* Madison: University of Wisconsin Press, 2005.

Scheyer, Ernst, *Breslau – so wie es war.* Düsseldorf: Droste Verlag, 1969.

Schreiber, Hermann, *The History of Roads from Amber Route to Motorway,* trans. Stewart Thomson. London: Barrie & Rockliff, 1961.

Scott-Clark, Catherine & Levy, Adrian, *The Amber Room.* London: Atlantic Books, 2004.

Somers Cocks, Anna, 'The Coming Death of Venice'. *New York Review of Books*, 20th June 2013.

Spekke, Arnolds, *The Ancient Amber Routes and the Geographical Discovery of the Eastern Baltic.* Stockholm: Ares, 1957.

Stern, Fritz, *Five Germanys I Have Known.* New York: Farrar, Straus & Giroux, 2006.

Strakauskaitė, Nijolė, *Klaipėda, Curonian Spit, Königsberg: A Guide.* Vilnius: R. Paknio leidykla, 2005.

Teuber, Alfons, *Die Schlesischer Bilderbibel* (4th ed.). Munich: Verlag 'Christ Unterwegs', 1953.

Thum, Gregor, *Die fremde Stadt: Breslau 1945.* Munich: Siedler, 2003.

Tiefenbach, Josef & Fertl, Evelyn (eds), *Die Bernsteinstraße: Evolution einer Handelsroute.* Eisenstadt: Landesmuseum Burgenland, 2008.

Turnbull, Stephen, *Crusader Castles of the Teutonic Knights (1): The Red-Brick Castles of Prussia.* Oxford: Osprey, 2003.

Tweedie, Mrs Alec, *Through Finland in Carts.* London: Adam & Charles Black, 1897.

Weinreich, Max, *Hitler's Professors.* New Haven: Yale University Press, 1999.

Wells, Peter S., 'The Excavations at Stična in Slovenia by the Duchess of Mecklenburg, 1905–1914'. *Journal of Field Archaeology* 5(2) (summer, 1978), pp. 215–226.

Wielowiejski, Jerzy, *Główny szlak bursztynowy w czasach cesarstwa rzymskiego (The main amber route in the time of the Roman Empire)*. Wroclaw: Ossolineum, 1990.

Zweig, Stefan, *The World of Yesterday*, trans. Anthea Bell. London: Pushkin Press, 2009.

INDEX

Note: the entry 'f.' in brackets indicates the former or alternative name(s) of the place indexed.